SUNDAY BEST

Edited by Donald Trelford

SUNDAY BEST

Introduction by Clive James

London
The Observer/Victor Gollancz Ltd
1981

Published by Victor Gollancz Ltd
© The Observer Limited, 1981

ISBN 0 575 03071 2

Victor Gollancz Ltd
14 Henrietta Street
London WC2E 8QJ

Introduction
Clive James

The secret, indispensible ingredient of a great Sunday newspaper is that a good proportion of its copy should be supplied by interlopers. Skilled regular journalists provide its backbone but part of the musculature and much of the flesh come from people who would probably not be journalists at all if the great Sunday newspaper were less great. Instead they would never doff their usual hat, trencher, helmet or gardening cap. They are journalists only by an historical fluke. In my land of origin such people are known as ring-ins. I have been a ring-in on *The Observer* for ten years and would feel hopelessly unqualified to write this introduction if I were not somehow aware that being unqualified is what qualifies me. Like dozens of my fellow contributors, I belong because I don't. Like them, I spend a lot of time being suitably grateful that those on the paper's staff who have to spend the whole week in the building are willing to share the limelight with those of us who put in a corporeal appearance only on Friday mornings or else never show up at all except in the form of a typed manuscript. In even more ethereal cases the byline signifies nothing more substantial than the occasional long telephone call from somewhere else in Europe. At least once a year, at a cocktail party in the boardroom, I will meet some man who looks nothing like his prose.

Having only a dim idea of how the whole vast enterprise is put together, I will go on sticking by what I know and tell you what *The Observer* office is like on Friday mornings. Since it is an open plan office I can see most of it from what I like to call my desk. (Gillian Widdicombe, one of our music correspondents, also likes to call it her desk, but on Fridays she is usually at Glyndebourne, Salzburg or somewhere like that.) From my desk I can gaze out over the filing cabinets at the secretaries in the 'Living' section. Coming from a regular staff-member this would be tantamount to sexual harrassment but for a casual contributor it counts as searching for inspiration. Then I type a few words before the coffee trolley arrives at ten o'clock. It stops first at the Colour Magazine, makes another stop between the features desk and the literary department, and then turns right before beginning a long circumnavigation of the news desk, completing the circuit at the financial section and heading back towards where it came in, which gives everyone between me and the Colour Magazine a much-envied chance for a second cup. During the transit of the coffee trolley it is possible to see Alan Watkins arriving with his completed column and Trog leaving after having delivered his finished cartoon.

Model girls are being auditioned in the fashion section, which is easily visible if I stand up in order to stretch my aching back after typing a few words. Other critics write their stuff at home but I find the atmosphere of a great Sunday newspaper positively inspiring.

Here, however, a caveat must be entered. Tabloid newspapers probably feature the same hustle and bustle but inspiration for my sort of writing would be in much shorter supply. Indeed there would be the active discouragement guaranteed by a set of circumstances in which to care for language would be to whistle in the dark. At *The Observer* the specialist contributor will find himself surrounded by sub-editors who know how to spell and section editors who care about good expression. Even on the news desk it is automatically assumed that a story's content is to some extent dependent on the way it is written down. This general assumption about the importance of literacy is the reason why I find it as possible and necessary to write for *The Observer* as I would find it unnecessary and impossible to write for most of the tabloids. And of course – although there is no of course about it – the readership shares that assumption. Every Sunday a million intelligent people buy *The Observer* and read what is in it. They are the reading public whose disappearance has so often been bewailed in academic circles but who have somehow failed to disappear.

Since you can't have literacy without general interests, the fact that *The Observer* is written rather than thrown together is both the emblem and the essence of the wider fact that it is composed by and for people who have some sort of humanist world view extending beyond their special areas of professional or vocational competence. The possibility of taking a general interest in the world, far from being an anachronism, is at the heart of civilization, which means that *The Observer* is at the centre of what makes Britain a civilized country.

In the United States even the best newspapers are more concerned with current news stories than with literate features, which are taken care of by magazines. By those standards, *The Observer* is both a newspaper and magazine combined. Blending the two impulses would not be an easy thing to achieve if one were starting from scratch. But as with many of the best things about Britain, there is no necessity to start from scratch, since the tradition is so well-founded that everybody has forgotten when it began. If *The Observer* were to be forced out of business tomorrow, it would start up again the day after and probably be contributed to by largely the same people. Hence the comparative equanimity among the staff about changes of ownership, which, while not being taken lightly, are never regarded as catastrophic. The institution is stronger than any pressure which can be brought to bear on it.

The strength comes from spontaneity, as with one of those football games that go on in London parks on a Sunday afternoon, and to which ageing young poets and novelists bring their tattered kit. Some of them die from the exercise but other aspirants replace them. The ball goes on being repaired until it has to be replaced. Wives and children mark the sidelines and folded coats represent the goals. Everything is mutable but nothing really changes. It is a spiritual occurrence as tangible as the earth. *The Observer* is the same kind of Sunday event except it happens in the morning. It is one of the things I came to Britain for, didn't really expect to be part of, am delighted to be identified with and would find it hard to give up.

Editor's Foreword

'The observ'd of all observers' (Hamlet III, i)

This book was conceived during the long takeover of the newspaper. In part it was an attempt to define or assert the paper's character at a time when its identity seemed to be at risk – an ambitious, perhaps impossible, task. But I hope that some coherent sense of style and values can be traced in this collection.

Each Sunday's issue of *The Observer* contains nearly 100,000 words, the same as a full-length novel; over a year that amounts to five million words, or 50 novels. The period covered by this selection is a year and a half, which means that the book contains only a fraction of the published content of the newspaper in that time – less than one article a week. Inevitably, something of a newspaper's flavour is lost in this process. Virtually all passing news, for example, and most arts and book reviews; any story which has been overtaken in the reader's mind by later events. Book serials are naturally excluded, along with material that has been reproduced in any other form.

This still left a formidable bulk from which to choose. The guiding principles of selection were that the article should be a good read, that its appeal should have survived the passage of time, and that the great variety of articles should hold together as a book, a quite different medium. The editor's choice is unashamedly personal; he has also cut and revised the articles where this seemed to be needed.

Thanks are due to my wife, Kate, to Monica Craig and Julia Barker, and to Jeffrey Care and his staff in *The Observer* library for help in preparing the material for publication.

1.
Mrs Thatcher's Britain

The Iron Lady
Adam Raphael

In her moment of triumph Mrs Thatcher stood outside the door of No. 10 Downing Street and quoted St Francis of Assisi.

'Where there is discord,
  may we bring harmony;
Where there is doubt,
  may we bring faith;
Where there is despair,
  may we bring hope.'

It has not turned out quite like that. Nor, given the determined character of Britain's first woman Prime Minister, was it likely to. Mrs Thatcher has had an extraordinary impact: her climb to the top of the greasy pole, as Disraeli called it, marked the arrival of the most forceful and aggressive political leader since Winston Churchill.

Two budgets, three rounds of public expenditure cuts and many Cabinet rows later, her colleagues acknowledge her determination to pursue her 'politics of conviction.' Mrs Thatcher may not be much loved, but even those colleagues who find her difficult, divisive, and at times almost impossible, respect her resolution and phenomenal capacity for work.

'Her initial instincts are almost invariably wrong,' said a senior Minister. 'But if you can get to her before she has time to voice them publicly, there is hope.'

In foreign affairs, the impact of the Thatcher personality has been no less felt. From the triumph of the Commonwealth Conference at Lusaka to the impasse of the European Summit at Dublin, the Iron Lady (a nickname she likes) has engaged in full-blooded personal diplomacy. The other Heads of Government have found it as difficult to adjust to this new phenomenon as the Foreign Office.

The West German Chancellor, Helmut Schmidt, is said to have compared her, in a moment of extreme irritation, to a rhinoceros – a description which Labour's Shadow Chancellor, Denis Healey, seized on in the Commons: 'She has,' he told MPs, 'an impenetrably thick hide, she is liable to mount charges in all directions, and she is always thinking on the trot.'

A characteristic of the rhinoceros which Healey did not mention is that it goes straight for its target. On her way to the Commonwealth Conference, Mrs Thatcher told Lord Carrington, as the RAF VC-10 circled over Lusaka, that she feared the proceedings would be very rough and that the Commonwealth might break up. The Foreign Secretary tried in vain to reassure her.

On the Prime Minister's lap lay a pair of dark glasses with huge lenses. 'You know why I have taken these?' she said quietly. 'I'm afraid I'm going to have acid thrown in my face.'

As the VC-10 touched down, the Prime Minister's party were alarmed to see a vast crowd of gesticulating, chanting black faces surrounding the plane. It was impossible to tell whether they were friendly or hostile. Without a second glance, Mrs Thatcher went down the steps into the crowd, leaving her dark glasses on the seat.

'She has got guts; no one can deny that,' said a colleague.

The Prime Minister's relative lack of experience of major office (she knew almost nothing of foreign affairs, Education being the only department she had run) was matched by an even graver handicap – the divided state of the party she had inherited after ousting Ted Heath. The backbench rebellion that had propelled her to the leadership was not a stable basis for power, nor were the wounds of 1974-75 easily healed.

Arguments in the Shadow Cabinet, so fractious over such a wide range of policy, provoked her famous remark to *The Observer* shortly before the election: 'As Prime Minister, I couldn't waste time having any internal arguments.' But when it came to the formation of her Cabinet, Mrs Thatcher discovered severe limits to her freedom of choice.

She ensured the dominance of her essentially minority right-wing views by creating a Praetorian Guard of economic Ministers. The Treasury team of Sir Geoffrey Howe, John Biffen and Nigel Lawson were supported by Sir Keith Joseph at Industry, John Nott at Trade, and David Howell at Energy. In the key economic posts, only Jim Prior at Employment – an appointment she could hardly avoid – stood well outside this monetarist circle. At the Foreign Office and the Home Office, Lord Carrington and William Whitelaw provided continuity with the previous Heath Government. These appointments were accepted as a shrewd blend of opinion within the Party. But the strains soon began to show.

No Tory Government has ever bared its internal disputes quite so openly as this one. Mrs Thatcher has become more skilful in avoiding confrontations, but the central problem is that on many issues she does not have a natural majority in her own Cabinet. That makes her natural style – leading from the front rather than acting as a neutral chairman – extremely perilous.

'Occasionally,' said one Minister sardonically, 'we're told the conclusions before the opening remarks.' Unlike Mr Callaghan, Mrs Thatcher makes a point of never totting up the votes, which is perhaps just as well. During discussions on one round of public expenditure cuts, it was clear that the Prime Minister, despite the support of her economic Ministers, did not have a majority.

'She just rammed them home without taking a vote,' said one participant.

On economic issues, these strong-arm tactics have tended to work; with less certainty on others. In the early months she suffered a number of humiliating reverses. On MPs' pay, Mrs Thatcher ignored the warnings of the Leader of the House, Mr Norman St John-Stevas, and insisted on rejecting the recommendations in the Boyle report. This led, as she was told it would, to an all-party backbench revolt, leaving her no option but to capitulate.

Her colleagues are understandably chary of talking about her in public but John Nott, one of the more independent spirits in Cabinet, noted recently that the Prime Minister's style of leadership was rather like a First World War subaltern leading troops over the top.

Her lack of a natural Cabinet majority has forced the Prime Minister to seek new methods of control. Her power to rig Cabinet agendas and fix the composition of Cabinet committees is considerable. She has slimmed the number of committees and restricted their membership. She has also taken to convening small ad hoc groups of Ministers to reach a consensus in advance of important Cabinet decisions. She has learnt painfully that she has little to gain from all-out rows.

Apart from economic policy, where the conciliating instincts of the Home Secretary, Willie Whitelaw, have helped, her freedom for manoeuvre is strictly limited. On the key Overseas Policy and Defence Committee (OPD) she found herself in a minority. Apart from Geoffrey Howe and John Nott, there was no one she could rely on. Confronted by a solid line-up of the Foreign Secretary, Lord Carrington, the Lord Privy Seal, Sir Ian Gilmour, and Defence Secretary, Francis Pym, the Prime Minister constantly had to stifle her own instincts.

On the occasions when she has failed to do this, the reversals have been spectacular, notably over the Vietnamese boat people. She first declared that she wasn't prepared for Britain to take a single one, and then found herself bowing to her colleagues and to public opinion. What appeared to settle the argument was an editorial in the *Daily Telegraph* saying that Britain must play its part in the refugee operation. The Prime Minister has a hearty contempt for most newspapers, in particular the *Guardian*, of which she tells colleagues proudly, 'I never read it.' But the *Telegraph*, whose first edition she sees last thing at night, is carefully scrutinised.

The most dramatic example of Mrs Thatcher's ability to change course is Rhodesia. It is often forgotten that she was only just prevented from publicly pledging recognition of the Muzorewa-Smith regime during the election campaign. Soon afterwards, exhausted by the Tokyo economic summit, the Prime Minister let slip that she had no intention of forcing another sanctions vote through the Commons – an admission which threatened to jeopardise the Commonwealth Conference. But by the time of Lusaka, Lord Carrington and Sir Anthony Duff, Deputy Under-Secretary at the Foreign Office, had persuaded her that the only solution was to ditch Smith and convene a peace conference leading to new elections.

The Lancaster House peace conference, attended by all the Rhodesian combatants, has rightly been hailed as a triumph for British diplomacy, but it must also be counted a tribute to Mrs Thatcher's realism. The solution went right against her instincts, and even more against the advice of those to whom she feels closest. Yet she not only listened, but learnt.

'If enough people argue with her for long enough,' said one colleague, 'she'll see the force of the argument even if she doesn't like it.' What makes her such an interesting Prime Minister is that, for all her strong prejudices, she is capable of both listening to advice and profiting by her mistakes. She is much more flexible than many critics give her credit for.

A similar exercise, seeking to dig Mrs Thatcher out of a ditch she dug for herself at Dublin, went on over Britain's contribution to the EEC budget. Phrases such as 'I am not going to be satisfied with half a loaf' and 'It is our money' have now been replaced, in the interests of a budget compromise, by a willingness to reach agreement on lamb, energy and farm prices.

President Giscard and to a lesser extent Chancellor Schmidt found their first meetings with Mrs Thatcher something of a strain. Mrs

Thatcher has a nervous habit, particularly with strangers, of so dominating a conversation that other people find it difficult to get a word in edgeways. The former Irish Prime Minister, Jack Lynch, gave a first-hand description of her negotiating technique at the Dublin summit: 'It was adamant, persistent, and if I may say so, very repetitive.' Statesmen as proud as Giscard d'Estaing are not used to that, nor to being continually interrupted.

The only time Mrs Thatcher has decisively met her match was when Chairman Hua of China came to London. When Mrs Thatcher asked Hua through an interpreter if he would like to give her his views on the world scene, the Chinese leader launched into an interminable *tour d'horizon*. After he had gone on for a very long time, Mrs Thatcher tried politely to intervene. Hua, however, was having none of this, and continued in full flood – whereupon Lord Carrington slipped her a note saying, 'You are talking too much,' which reportedly provoked a rare fit of Prime Ministerial giggles. (Few others in the Cabinet have such a frank and open relationship.)

The extraordinary outbursts of semi-public fighting within the Cabinet stem mainly from deep political divisions, but they have not been helped by Mrs Thatcher's personal style of leadership. Without perhaps realising it, she can be extremely rude in argument. In meetings she interrupts constantly, she browbeats and she hectors.

'She treats her colleagues abominably,' said one observer.

After a particularly bruising encounter at No. 10, one Minister retired in tears to her Department and had to be comforted with a glass of whisky. The sharpest division in Cabinet is not between the Wets and the Hawks, but between those, like Prior, who stand up to the Prime Minister and shout back, and those who allow themselves to be pecked to death.

Mrs Thatcher's abrasiveness is not confined to her colleagues. Her visits to every major department – something no Prime Minister has done before – have sent shockwaves through Whitehall.

'She gives the civil servants hell,' said one observer. 'She writes these brusque, caustic notes accusing them of woolly thinking, and they are absolutely terrified of her.'

Both the generals and the Treasury mandarins have come away shaken from the Prime Minister's dressing downs. During a visit to the Ministry of Defence shortly before Christmas, Mrs Thatcher is said to have torn into the appalled Chiefs of Staff, her most fervent admirers, accusing them of every wasteful sin in the book. At the Department of Employment, she left a trail of bruised feelings.

Those who do best are those who answer back. At the Department of Industry, when Mrs Thatcher launched into her familiar attack, John Lippitt, a deputy secretary, said quietly: 'That's absolute rubbish, if I may say so, Prime Minister.' There was a moment's appalled silence in the serried ranks of deputy and under-secretaries, kowtowers to a man. The Prime Minister, amazed, stopped dead in her tracks, but she made it clear afterwards that she was delighted to be taken on.

When Mrs Thatcher arrived at Downing Street, many predicted she would become as much a prisoner of the Whitehall machine as the man she had ousted, Edward Heath. But after a year in office there is absolutely no sign of that. Nor, as some colleagues had hopefully forecast, has she become a prisoner of her Cabinet. Despite many well-publicised reversals, she is still in the driving seat.

The predictions of an early 'U' turn on economic policy seem less and less credible. Her passionate belief in her mission to rid Britain of State socialism, however painful the short-term consequences, will not be easily or quickly undermined. Her Cabinet may be sceptical, but she has made sure she has a solid Party base from which to operate. If she fails, it will not be by default, nor through a failure of nerve.

As Prime Minister, she conforms to no previous rules. It is not just that she is a woman; that is perhaps the least part of it. She knows she became Leader of her Party by an accident. And she knows she will be given only one chance.

As a politician, she prides herself on her caution, but it is her boldness that commands attention.

'What have you changed?' she was asked shortly after becoming Conservative Leader. 'I have changed everything,' she replied. That boast is far from being fulfilled, but few doubt the strength of her political convictions and her instinct to test them to the limits. Whatever else it is, her period in office will not be dull. *(27.4.80)*

If the Lady's Not for Turning . . .
Editorial

This was to be the Budget that took us round the corner and up the long road to prosperity. Instead Sir Geoffrey Howe's unyielding package, sprung on his colleagues without warning, will (according to the CBI president) 'increase prices, bankruptcies and unemployment.' It leaves Britain in its worst economic crisis for 50 years, bound to a theory which is at best unproven, at worst a catastrophe. Mrs Thatcher

– wheels locked, pedal hard down – is rapidly running out of road.

The Conservative Party now seems embarked on a battle for its own soul that is as fundamental as the one splitting Labour. But, being Conservatives, they conduct the debate in a recondite way by earnest invocation of Disraeli's ghost to confront the twin Svengalis (Hayek and Friedman) bewitching Mrs Thatcher. She, however, has no such inhibitions. Her recent tone, on economic as well as on world affairs, has been distressingly strident.

At the 1979 election Mrs Thatcher caught a public mood. In part, this was a temporary, bitter reaction against the Winter of Discontent, against rotting refuse and unburied bodies. But in part it was more fundamental, a feeling that the entire post-war consensus had broken down, that successive Labour and Conservative administrations had failed, that something new must be tried. Mrs Thatcher offered a new faith and a new face. The fact that she was the first woman Prime Minister, and a person of admirable honesty and courage, appealed to an electorate in desperate search of fresh leadership:

When in danger, or in doubt
Turn the sitting Member out.

So Mrs Thatcher came in on a tidal wave for change. But even her own supporters were not clear what changes to expect. Like the Alderman and Art, they didn't know much about politics but they knew what they liked – and what they didn't like. Specifically, they didn't like their lives disrupted by strikes and they did like the promise of lower taxes. Most of her Cabinet colleagues, though sceptical of the economic doctrine which had captured her imagination, papered over their differences – a problem which is coming home to roost. Never again must any party – Conservative, Labour, Liberal or Social Democrat – be allowed to achieve power with its internal disagreements so inadequately exposed.

Mrs Thatcher and Sir Geoffrey believed they had a mandate for their first Budget, which switched sharply from direct to indirect taxation. But it was an economic disaster from which Britain has not recovered. Ironically, a Prime Minister whose self-proclaimed target is to conquer inflation has so far only succeeded in bringing inflation back to 3 per cent above the level she inherited. The period between was caused by the 1979 VAT increases; renewed inflation may be the result of the higher duties in the present Budget.

The Government can plead in its defence the adverse world conditions: that oil prices have risen and recession has deepened. But higher oil costs are already built into the economic models. As for recession, that brings out the worst in Mrs Thatcher's character: her stubbornness, the obverse of her courage. Unfortunately, that courage has attached itself to an economic dogma of doubtful worth. Those acolytes who remind the Prime Minister how far her servants are falling short of the chosen creed are cherished. Those who tell her that the time has come to change are reviled.

And so, in the deepest world recession since the war, Britain pursues manifestly unattainable monetary targets and public borrowing objectives whose imprecision is rivalled only by their growing irrelevance. The Government has driven interest rates and the pound to levels that, week by week, are destroying manufacturing industry – sound firms as well as shaky ones – and forcing unemployment inexorably up towards three million. Sir Geoffrey's measures to help small business are well-meant but, with demand so flat, they come at the worst time to launch a new enterprise.

When Mrs Thatcher's political opponents assault such a Budget, she must expect it. When the TUC warns of its effects on inflation and on jobs, she must remain unsurprised. But does the Prime Minister feel no concern when the president of the CBI, who has produced his own thoughtful programme, says the Budget is 'at best a brush-off, at worst a kick in the teeth'?

The Prime Minister must be disappointed with the minimal benefits to industry produced by her first, tax-cutting Budget. The temptation is for her to blame industry, to ignore businessmen's alarm about her economic policies. If he had done more for industry, Sir Geoffrey would have got away with his harshness to consumers. Industry is at the sharp end of the recession. For the Chancellor to pay such little heed to its appeals – on sterling, interest rates, National Insurance surcharge ('the tax on jobs'), fuel costs, and public investment to stimulate construction and other private industries – is simply perverse.

Reaction to this perversity has now set in. The Cabinet 'wets' believe that the Prime Minister is pursuing dogma well beyond the limits of duty or common sense. They had hoped that the compromise on public spending last autumn, together with recent decisions on steel, coal and British Leyland, represented a return to flexibility in the face of an economic blizzard. They were shocked now to learn that her instinct to meet recession with deflation remains undented.

The Cabinet is split from top to bottom. The Prime Minister confirmed as much when she rebuked her colleagues like erring schoolboys, at a City luncheon and in the House, for not being prepared to meet the bill for their own public spending. (Mr Foot's role as the purported whipping-boy deceived no one.) It was as if the Budget had been designed to punish them all.

The fight is not over. Another battle on public spending must follow. Worse, any Minister with political prescience must know what else is coming. For Mrs Thatcher, unlike Sir Keith Joseph, is a determined, even ruthless politician, not just a theorist. She is steadily painting herself into a corner. Britain faces the prospect, in 1982 or 1983, of a pre-election Budget which will come too late to save manufacturing industry from grave damage, yet still set off an inflationary boom.

The time to change economic policy is now. Last week's Budget should have begun the rescue of British industry. In the coming review of public spending plans, a bleak look at current expenditure, notably wage and salary rises in the public sector, should be mixed with a more generous approach to public investment in the railways, telephones, drainage and roads. The age when capital spending meant one more superfluous Town Hall extension has passed. What swells public borrowing most uselessly now is the payment of unemployment benefit to more and more people who desperately want to work and produce.

The Cabinet 'wets' have history on their side. In 1945, even under Churchill, the Conservatives suffered resounding defeat because of what happened in the Thirties, when the nation had stigmatised them as the Party of Unemployment. It was to remove this stigma that a group of younger men, under Butler's leadership – Macleod, Maudling, Heath, Boyle and others – abandoned laisser faire economics and revived the politics of One Nation.

The economics and politics of this Budget, albeit clothed in modern intellectual dress, are a reversion to the Thirties. Short-term, it will cause human distress to three million unemployed people and their families. It may damage irretrievably parts of Britain's industrial base. Longer-term, it jeopardises the social cohesion of a nation that is now multiracial.

The Budget was wrong in thrust and often wrong in detail. In his refusal to index income tax allowances even partially, the Chancellor has underscored the question now facing the unskilled: Why work at all? The poverty trap grows wider. It will be a sad memorial to Mrs Thatcher's high aspirations if she inadvertently erodes the will to work among millions of our people. It will be a sad end to two generations of political consensus if a stubborn leader is allowed to divide the nation further – between workers and workless, South and North, the well-off and the deprived.

The 'wets' in Mrs Thatcher's Cabinet now face a choice that comes to politicians only once in a lifetime – if they are fortunate, not at all. It is to save their country – and, incidentally, their own Party – from disaster. The threat from the new Centre alliance is greater to the Tories than to Labour. Unless the Government recovers popularity quickly, Tory citadels in the suburbs and the South will fall like leaves in autumn. The local elections already look like bringing a Conservative disaster.

The choice for those in the Cabinet who share this view is hard, but clear. To demand an earlier voice in a Budget 12 months hence is fiddling while Rome burns. To seek Sir Geoffrey's removal to the Woolsack misses the point. A change of policy is what is needed, and this Prime Minister controls economic policy more rigorously than any predecessor. The inescapable conclusion is that Mrs Thatcher must be persuaded to change course, or she must be removed. The lady must turn – or she must go. *(15.3.81)*

Dreadful Secret at Wooh Corner
Adrian Hamilton

'I've lost it,' said Howie-the-Wooh. 'I thought I had it. But it's gone.'

'Lost what?' said Niglet, who was easily excited.

'Well, that's just it,' said Wooh dolefully, kicking at the leaves and wondering when the people who were supposed to look after the paths would come and sweep them up. 'I'm not quite sure what it is.'

'What what is?' squeaked Niglet, who was getting more and more impatient with Wooh.

'You know,' said Wooh. 'The Money Thingummyjig that She's always going on about and asked me to look after. It's around here somewhere but I just can't seem to put my paw on it. It keeps running away.'

'Oh,' said Niglet, who imagined that it was a dangerous animal like the Rampaging Stagflation or the dreaded State Interventionism-prism, or whatever it was called.

'We must track it down and find it,' he added eagerly.

'Well, the trouble is that it's not exactly like a jungle beast,' answered Wooh, who knew he ought to say something but had difficulty sometimes in putting all his points together in his mind. 'But it does seem to move about an awful lot and it keeps flying away like a bird. Buffin Owl seems to understand it and there's all sorts of clever people in America who've made drawings of it and keep giving it numbers as if it was a road. It's sort of. . . .'

And he hummed to himself a little song he'd been making up while thinking where he would start looking:

There's not enough honey
And far too much money.
But I don't know how to control it.

20. Mrs Thatcher's Britain

I've put on a squeeze
And put up the fees,
But I don't know how to control it.
I've thrown men from work,
Rates have soared with a jerk,
But I don't know how to control it.
Some say it's the inflow;
They all say that they *know;*
But still I cannot control it.

And he gave a little jump to show how pleased he was with it, when his mood was suddenly brought down by Niglet squeaking:

'But you can't have lost it. She told you it was important. It's the Most Important Thing in the Whole World, more important than people.'

Naturally the first thought that then came to the two was to go and see Joseph Eeyorperhaps, who had believed in the Money Thingummyjig before anyone else and who had lots and lots of books about it and seemed quite affectionate towards it.

They found him puzzling over two sticks lying side by side. 'Don't interrupt me,' he snorted without looking up. 'I am considering what is before me.'

'What is that?' asked Niglet, who felt he had been asking the same question all morning.

'That,' said Eeyorperhaps, 'is an equation. Why, I was reading only the other day the question of whether equations were really infinite parallels or parallel infants or whether. . . .'

At which point Wooh, who was afraid that Eeyorperhaps would go on forever like this, which he was apt to do if there seemed to be anything nasty like a Big Decision about, interrupted:

'But we've come to ask you about Money Thing.'

'Oh,' said Eeyorperhaps. 'At the centre, that. Explains all our Problems.'

'But it's not at the centre, wherever that is. The trouble is that it's nowhere. At least it isn't here,' Wooh said – slowly, because he knew he only had a Little Brain and therefore had to go cautiously, step by step, as if he was crossing some stepping stones and couldn't turn round, as he once did, which caused him to fall in the water.

'Oh,' said Eeyorperhaps, putting his head on his feet and desperately rubbing his ears. 'Oh dear, oh dear.'

'It's all very well saying "oh dear" like that,' said Niglet, whom Eeyorperhaps had chosen to ignore, 'but it's serious and I'm getting extremely cold standing here talking about it.'

'Yes,' said Eeyorperhaps apologetically. 'I'm afraid I've cut down all the trees at the edge of the field.'

'Whatever for?' asked Wooh.

'To let in the fresh air. I was afraid that the plants would become weak if they continued being protected like that. So I cut them down to let in the fresh air and make them grow stronger.'

'And have they?' asked Wooh with interest.

'Well, not exactly,' said Eeyorperhaps. 'In fact, I suppose they're not doing well at all. I've lost rather a lot of them to frost and the others are getting rather thin.'

'Perhaps we ought to build up the trees again. Niglet could help,' suggested Wooh, who couldn't help noticing that even the thistles were huddling against the wind and looking Not At All Happy.

'But that could be even worse,' said Eeyorperhaps sniffily. 'They might feel happier. You might feel happier. But I, who am responsible for these things, can see that they would only get fat and round again and not work properly. And all the plants that I don't like will keep growing. Anyway I'm sure that new ones will grow.'

'You don't *sound* very sure,' said Wooh, who was beginning to get doubts himself.

'Oh let's find Buffin Owl,' said Niglet impatiently.

So off they went, avoiding the parts of the field where the wind had laid bare the earth. And they hadn't gone very far, or at least it didn't seem so very far, when they were both bowled over, to Wooh's great indignity and Niglet's great annoyance, by a big rushing, pushing, blond, hairy beast.

'Oh, it's you,' said Wooh, getting up carefully and checking that nothing was broken.

'Who?' said Niglet.

'No, Wooh is you,' replied the blond beast, who turned out to be Hazelhead Hugger, as he bounced around.

'Oh Hugger,' said Wooh. 'Don't you ever look where you're going?' he asked, without really meaning it to be a question.

'No time,' said Hugger. 'It's the rates you see. I've got this simply terrific idea. Nobody's thought of it. But I have. You jump in and you jump about and then you say you've done the Bravest Thing that Anyone Has Ever Done.'

'Oh,' said Wooh doubtfully. 'But how does all this jumping help?'

'Well,' replied Hugger enthusiastically, 'you tell everyone that they can't have what they want and you're not going to give it to them.'

'But what good does that do?' asked Wooh, feeling more and more that his Brain was Not Big Enough.

'Well,' said Hugger, 'when you've jumped into them, they jump about and say that you're causing them to stop doing all sorts of things that people want, and they try and ask for more money – only you don't give them it because you've got a new formula or whatever it is and

22. Mrs Thatcher's Britain

everyone feels better for being shaken up.'

'But what has this to do with Money Thingummyjig?' interrupted Niglet, who thought he understood something called interest rates but didn't understand what rates Hugger was talking about.

'Nothing at all,' replied Hugger cheerfully as he bounded off. 'What you two need is not a Money Thingummyjig but an Industrial Policy.'

At this point Wooh and Niglet froze. Hugger was always doing terrible things – but to mention *that!* She had said never to mention it and Eeyorperhaps would certainly not approve of it.

'He's too big for his own boots,' said Niglet, really meaning that he was too big for Niglet's boot.

And, as if he were thinking the very same thing, along came Nott A. Rabbit out of the bushes.

He was called Nott A. Rabbit by Christopher, because when they had first met, Christopher had said, as seemed right and polite, 'Hello, rabbit.' But Nott A. Rabbit had replied: 'I'm not a rabbit.'

'Well, what's the matter?' asked Nott A. Rabbit with an air of importance.

'It's our Money Thingummyjig,' said Wooh. 'We've lost it, or at least it's escaped.'

'Ah, that's bad,' said Nott A. Rabbit, who liked to seem wise although he could never quite make others believe it, not even Her, whom he tried so hard to please.

'Yes,' said Wooh, anxious not to be made even smaller than he was already feeling.

'But perhaps it's a question of Definition,' he added more brightly, remembering something Owl had said once. 'Maybe we should sort of describe it better.'

'Quite, quite,' said Nott A. Rabbit, not wishing to be caught out by this new word. 'Absolutely right.' And anxious to seem already ahead of Wooh, he added quickly: 'But I don't have time for that. You will have heard about my Great Programme. I'm freeing everything and selling everything. I'm a most radical rabbit.'

Wooh hadn't heard about the Great Programme at all, but didn't like to say anything in case he hurt Nott A. Rabbit's feelings. Anyway he didn't like radishes. Meanwhile, Niglet couldn't resist saying: 'The only thing you seem to have freed, Wooh, is the Money Thingummy-jig.'

Wooh wondered sometimes about Niglet's friendship. But he decided that wondering only got a Bear of Little Brain into trouble. So he said instead, in a firm voice: 'We must go and see Owl, then.'

They found Buffin Owl sitting in his tree looking distinctly sad in an owlish sort of way.

'Oh Owl,' said Wooh, looking upwards, 'do help us. We've lost our

Money Thingummyjig.'

'Where did the "we" come from?' muttered Niglet, but he was ignored, particularly by Owl, who always felt so old when Niglet was around.

'You have, have you?' he said in an understanding and wise tone. And he looked across the fields.

'From where I'm sitting,' he said, 'I can't see it. Indeed, I've been wondering,' he said in a tone that always frightened his friends (because they never knew what he would come out with next), 'whether it's really worth hunting at all.'

'What?' said a genuinely astonished Wooh. 'You can't say that. It's Very Very Important. She's told us so.'

'Maybe,' said Owl with an air of unfathomable understanding. 'But from where I sit I can only see the plants dying in Eeyorperhaps's field. Maybe it isn't worth all this suffering,' he said, remembering the phrase from the day he flew into a church in pursuit of a mouse.

'But that's terrible,' said Wooh, in a voice so alarmed that Owl felt he had to say something to calm him.

So he said, with an air of great authority: 'But then,' – and he paused for a moment – 'There Is No Alternative.'

Wooh brightened and immediately a hum came into his head.

Whatever they say, tiddely pom,
There's no other way, tiddely pom,
There's no other way, tiddely pom,
To start growing.

And Wooh was feeling much better when along came Christopher Carrying-on.

'I thought I'd find you here,' said Christopher pleasantly. 'What have you been up to?'

'Well Niglet and I have been chasing the Money Thingummyjig,' said Wooh, feeling a bit let down about having to go through it all again. 'Eeyorperhaps, Nott A. Rabbit and Owl all say it's frightfully important but they can't tell us where it's flown to.'

'Oh, I wouldn't worry about that,' said Christopher, who had just been travelling to America and before that to Europe and was rather enjoying himself.

'But we have to,' Wooh went on. 'She says its Very Important and She'll never forgive us when she finds that we haven't got it trapped and in a cage.'

'Well,' continued Christopher, 'I've just come from Nanny and she says that all this Money Thingummyjig doesn't matter any more. Indeed, it may never have existed.'

For the first time in his life, Wooh could think of nothing to say, nothing at all. He just sat down.

24. Mrs Thatcher's Britain

'Yes,' said Christopher with the air of a man who had seen many comings and goings and would see more yet. 'She says that the main thing was never the Money Thingummyjig. It was whether the sweet shop was charging too much and whether the valet knew his place, and the parlourmaid curtseyed to the nanny and the nurserymaid was tidy and the butler served the wine without asking for more wages. And she says that all those things are coming right. So we can forget the Money Thingummyjig. Only we mustn't tell because silly people would say silly things like She had Changed her Mind or Reversed her Course. And that would never do for a person in her station.'

'But . . . but . . .' exclaimed Wooh, and he thought of how people would find out and how they would blame it on him, who wasn't to know because he was a Bear of Little Brain. And anyway he was only following orders and perhaps She wouldn't trust him with the money box any longer but give it instead to Nott A. Rabbit or Patrick Jackass who brushed his teeth in the dark – or even to Niglet. . . .

And he couldn't even think of a hum, although Christopher didn't seem in the least surprised by it all. *(21.12.80)*

Behind Brixton's Front Line
George Brock and Robert Chesshyre

In the benign April sunshine Rattray Road is a pleasant street of substantial mid-Victorian terraced houses. The passer-by would say that it is coming up in the world, having fallen for a while on hard times: there are men up ladders painting, and the council, private owners and housing trusts are renovating derelict properties. There's even a hint of 'gentrification.'

There are more black faces than white, but this unoppressive, open street is by no means Harlem. For every abandoned car, there are half a dozen almost new ones. The music – mainly from transistors the size of hi-fi units – was louder and more pervasive than many people would think proper. There are black kids in huge jockey caps riding bicycles down the middle of the road, and middle-aged black men in uniform setting off for a shift on the buses.

Elderly white women gather to gossip, and small children of both colours play football against a wall. The only real sign of blight is a corner house up for sale and abandoned. Rattray Road could be near the centre of any large English city, and a lot of people would be glad to live there.

But Rattray Road is not anywhere; it is in the heart of residential Brixton. Only days ago the roofs reflected the orange glow of flames, and the noise of riot and rage filled the smoke-tainted air. Youths with petrol bombs chased down side streets, and police armed with riot shields and snatched-up dustbin lids chased them back again. Some people got in their cars and fled; others have scarcely slept since.

The vibrations of that night will linger. One hundred yards to the east lies Railton Road, now vested with something of the awful mystique of Belfast's Falls Road. To local people it is the 'front line,' seldom referred to by name, and life on Rattray Road is life behind the front line.

Rattray Road is the real Brixton, much more so than the indelible pictures of arson, looting and stone-throwing that recent events will have inevitably left on the minds of people throughout the country, for whom Brixton has become a place at war.

We were introduced to the street by a young man called Devon Thomas, who has lived in Rattray Road since he arrived with his family from Jamaica in 1959. Then they were one of the first four West Indian families in the street, all related. He is a short, jaunty man of 30, who wears a tweed fly-fisherman's hat indoors and out, and once contemplated professional cricket with Surrey.

He works for Lambeth Council, creating temporary jobs for the unemployed, three-quarters of whom are black. He is one of only two black people in 'management' positions with the council; the other is in race relations. Devon is also a community leader and on the hastily formed 'defence committee.'

He still plays cricket, and a huge cricket bag blocks half the hallway of his home. He has a subtle, sharp mind, pulling one away from the ever-present trap of painting life with too broad a brush. Upbringing and brain have made him something of a social chameleon, at ease with the different languages of the infinitely complex community of Brixton.

A white person going into a black house, he said, sees the furniture arranged in a broadly familiar way, and therefore assumes that he understands what is going on. 'White people in fact know very little about the level on which black people live,' he said, and he was not talking about tastes in music and food, but of the profound psychological differences and hidden social undercurrents that are impossible to gauge from outside.

One crucial result of this is that police techniques for controlling organised white crime in such places as the East End of London – by intermingling with criminals in well-defined and mutually recognised territory and 'trading' as between brothers who understand the nuances of the game they are playing – are of no use to them in Brixton. In the East End, an honest citizen can live, unmolested by the police, cheek by jowl with the grossest villainy.

A white CID officer will never begin to penetrate the equivalently coded and complicated world of organised black crime, such as exists on the front line, and no black man brought up in the area – who *could* do it – would ever think of joining the police. Out of this police impotence grows a frustration which in turn can easily lead to the racist assumption that all black kids are up to no good.

A black youth with a 'sus' conviction told us: 'If there are two or three of you on the road and talking to one another, according to them you're about to go robbing. You always "fit the description" of someone they want. When you get to the station, they accuse you of something different.'

But to understand police frustration, it must be realised that mugging and housebreaking – dreadful though these crimes are – are small beer financially set against organised dealing in drugs, 'having women on the street' and the disposal of stolen goods. Because of the ravine between police and black cultures, a decision to raid or arrest is often taken on very tenuous information.

The implications of a series of cases in which wrongfully arrested blacks have been acquitted are not lost on either side. And some police are widely accused of crude corruption, recycling confiscated marijuana back onto the streets, for example.

As more and more black youngsters fail at school and on job training, so many more go on the front line, leaving homes in streets like Rattray Road for squats. 'They become very tough, having to depend on their own resources, even for somewhere to live,' said Devon, who does not pretend that even he can penetrate all Brixton's hostile intricacies.

'By last weekend there was a feeling here that unless it was stopped now, there would never be any deliverance; it would roll right over you; that you would never be worth being anything. Social conditions have improved in the material sense, but hope has never been so low.' He spoke with great sadness.

It is not a moral judgement he makes. 'I don't tell people not to steal because it is illegal.' He warns them that life on the line is as risky as any other. For every one person like himself who has succeeded as a professional man, there are 20 who have failed; for every flash character gliding round the neighbourhood in an XJ6, there are 20 sleeping rough or doing time.

Just as what happened here was inevitable, according to most blacks in Rattray Road, so it is inevitable that it will happen again unless there are some radical changes. Another man said: 'The police have shown that they cannot combat crime by saturating the area without causing an explosion.' Brixton is not like St Paul's, Bristol, a small, simple village by comparison, where last Easter's violence had a cathartic effect.

Devon said, and others echoed his words: 'Victory over the police has made people feel good, given them a pride that they managed to triumph over a certain part of the system. There is a hell of a lot stored up if the police are still prepared to exert their muscle on the streets. The kids have nothing to lose; they're in a kamikaze frame of mind.'

'Matthew' is a bus conductor, who came from Jamaica at the same time as Devon. 'I don't really want to move too far away from Brixton. I feel at home, you know. You'll be OK if you stay in Brixton.' For Jamaicans, it is a little bit of England that is almost like home, with its extended networks of relatives and friends.

But most people who were born in Jamaica carry the dream of one day returning, and a sense of identity both for West Indian immigrants and black Britons is difficult to achieve. Many blacks live in a vacuum and are far more cosmopolitan than the average Englishman. Most of the first families who bought Rattray Road houses later re-emigrated to other parts of the world. Immigrants tend to feel sad for blacks born here, who have no reassuring dream of an idyllic childhood country to which one day they may return.

Mrs 'Matthew' is absolutely determined to go 'home'; 'Matthew' was less sure. As we spoke, he often flicked his thumb over his shoulder in the direction of the front line: although rioting was clearly far from his scene, he could not resist a certain pride in what had been achieved. 'How are we going to stand up unless something is done that everybody sees? You wouldn't have known nothing about Brixton if there weren't fires. It's good they put it on the map. You've got to have violence to show people.'

For those who have been here long enough, the romantic view of the past encompasses the early years in Britain. A now retired car worker who came in 1945 said: 'Things were wonderful. There was no dole queue. I was happy on £7 a week. When I finished work, I was unhappy on £70 a week.'

The often underestimated strain of being an immigrant had wreaked havoc on his family. He had had to work night shifts, two of his children are in care, his wife has had a breakdown, two other children are out of work. He bitterly regretted that he had not returned to Jamaica 12 years ago.

Bringing up children in Brixton is a constant worry. A mother with an eight-week-old baby had been debating the future with her husband. We asked if they had come up with a solution, and her eyes clouded over. A nurse with a small boy said she hoped to emigrate to Canada.

The future in the ever-present form of the young unemployed is all around. A girl who had done a Government training course in office work sat on the front path sunning herself. She had clearly given up after failing for two years to land a job.

As we talked to her we returned as usual to the police, who ran throughout our conversations like a theme in a symphony. Her boyfriend, one of those arrested in the riots, is constantly being stopped because he has a nice car. 'They search under the seats, in the boot. Looking for drugs? He doesn't smoke, drink or swear. Because he's black, he can't have a car.'

The white people we met in Rattray Road fell into two groups, largely depending on the circumstances in which they came into the street. 'Tim,' a mature student and part-time playgroup leader, is renovating a house. He and his wife came because they could afford nowhere else, but now plan on being there for the next ten years. He also told tales of black people being harassed by the police.

The riots had in many ways possessed a festival atmosphere: 'Tim' had had a bottle of Guinness thrust into his hand. 'There was a "buzz". The police became a bit like a common enemy, though that's probably putting it too strongly.'

'Tim' is under no illusions. He has been burgled once, and his life is organised round the possibility of a mugging; he never takes large sums of money out with him (unlike an imprudent Irishman in the street, who had been hit over the head and relieved of £70 two nights before we met him). 'West Indians love to consume, and they feel a great sense of being deprived. They see ads on TV which raise hopes never to be realised.'

He has tried to work through local party politics but gave up because they were stuffy and decisions took ages to arrive at. 'You've got to speak that particular language, and if I, white lower-middle class, can't do it, West Indians haven't a chance.'

A middle-aged, middle-class white woman sat behind drawn curtains in her front room (most houses in Rattray Road keep their curtains drawn) and told how her family moved out on the night of the riots. Normally friendly black youths were wild with drink, making and throwing petrol bombs. She would like to move permanently but cannot afford it. She thinks schools have gone downhill markedly since black people arrived, but she was generally tolerant.

'Years ago black people used to scare me more. Now we've lived round here so long with them that we've got to know them. The coloured people in this road are OK, we get along. They're very noisy, but then we have parties, too.'

Mrs Thatcher's Britain. 29

It was noise that afflicted two old ladies we met. They, like another elderly white resident, wouldn't open their doors to strangers 'at night,' – so liberally interpreted that they did not open their door at 5.30 p.m. in broad daylight.

Two young blacks were standing in the doorway of a house where we had been told someone might speak with us. As we introduced ourselves, two slightly older men appeared and told us in no uncertain manner to leave. It was our clearest sight of that impenetrable wall of which Devon Thomas had spoken.

We did meet young people, working on a Government-funded temporary employment project. They spoke of their bleakness when on the dole and added: 'We're not asking for a lot; for a reasonable life like everyone else, to be left alone and not picked up for nothing.' One of the older black instructors said: 'With poor housing and no facilities, everyone gets tense after the boring winter, waiting for a bright day to let off steam. Someone provokes them, and that's all it needs.'

That may seem less dramatic than talk of outside agitators, but after several days in and around Brixton, that instructor summed up in simple terms what appears to have happened. Molotov cocktails, after all, don't take much pre-planning when virtually every house is heated by paraffin stoves. 'If it had been planned,' said a black community worker, 'the whole of Brixton would have been devastated.'

The sun was still shining when we left Rattray Road after two days. For a moment we were lulled into thinking again that this might have been anywhere. The harsh clatter of a helicopter's rotorblades broke the illusion. The police who had never left the streets all week were back in the sky. The front line was under observation. *(19.4.81)*

30. Mrs Thatcher's Britain

2.
Two Narrow Escapes

Trail of Hate to St Peter's
Neal Ascherson and a Daylight team

He washed his black hair before he went out, using a special shampoo for greasy scalps he had bought two days before in a *profumeria* in the centre of Rome. Then he put on a new blue shirt, which would suit his brown skin. He could inspect the effect in the mirror, but room 31 in the Pensione Isa, Via Cicerone, was very dim, facing into the court-yard well of the old Palazzo. Two huge eyes, black and solemn as those of a priest before a great ceremony, gleamed back at him.

The next thing was to take the Browning and snap the first round from the magazine into the breech. To do it out there in the open – that little jerk of two hands close together, unmistakable to anyone who has handled an automatic – would not be prudent.

Faruk Ozgun, whose real name was Mehmet Ali Agca, was very prudent. He put on the safety catch, before wriggling the gun into the waist-band of the suit.

Then he had to button the jacket over it. A pity; it was a smart suit, and Wednesday, 13 May, was turning into a warm afternoon. But the bulge didn't show. It merely weighed rather: with its thick grip and 12 9mm rounds, the Browning was a mass-produced officer's pistol rather than the custom-built weapon a professional prefers.

Mehmet Ali Agca went down the three flights of stairs holding himself carefully, to be sure that the gun wouldn't fall out on the pavement. A woman at the reception desk on the first floor saw him go past and wished him good-day. The handsome Turkish boy, with his big eyes and smart clothes, had stayed at the Isa before. He wasn't a problem. He always had money. People telephoned him a lot, trunk calls and even foreign; that was a bit of a nuisance. But he was respectable. An Italian, no foreigner, had taken the trouble to ring up the week before and book his room. Signor Ozgun was not one of those Turks who made trouble. Today, though, he seemed not to hear her. He was thinking of something else. He ran lightly down the last steps and turned into the street.

The Pope had almost finished meeting the 10,000 people in St Peter's Square. The white 'Popemobile' had crawled slowly about the inner track cleared through the crowd.

Pope John Paul II had touched and blessed and kissed his way round. Now he was nearly at the end of the second, wider circuit. In a moment he would have to get out and go to the wooden throne and make his address. It had to be something firm and loving but not too outspoken: the Italians were to vote at the end of the week in the abortion-law referendum. Firmness about life, about the way that it was God who was really murdered when a life was taken by another living human being.

The car began its last, very slow turn close to where the north-east corner of the Bernini Colonnade pushes into the Square. A blond child, very sweet. Those Polish pilgrims again, the cheerful party of working men and women from Poznan who were going on – of course – to see Monte Cassino. A picture of the Black Madonna; they wanted him to take it. A dark child, held out to him but stiff with fear.

Then suddenly a violent blow on his hand, and sounds which cut through 35 years to memories which no Pole can be free of. Somebody was shooting. He was being shot. The wound was in his body somewhere, not just the hand. Blood. Red on white, our flag. He was falling, but 'Staszek' was holding him tightly, very gently, Father Stanislaw Dziwisz who was his secretary from home. Everyone was shouting, screaming; a photographer was crawling up the car at him like a one-eyed ape. He didn't want to look any more. He wanted to pray, not for his life, but for the life which belonged to God, which was God.

How could they do this, how could they not understand what they had done? His head down, his lips scarcely moving, he began: '*Bogurodzico Dziewico* . . .' At first only Father Dziwisz, cradling this heavy man under his armpits and watching the stain spreading like a cloud under the surface of the white tunic, understood that he was talking to the Virgin Mary. The secretary knew several ways for this prayer to go on. One of the new ways said: 'We dedicate to You the

32. Two Narrow Escapes

Holy Father John Paul II, summoned from Poland by God to the throne of St Peter, and we implore You to take him under Your protection . . .' Now this. It was the worst day in Father Dziwisz's life.

It was exactly 20 minutes past five, and everything was happening in fragments. Even the Poznan pilgrims, only 30 feet away, did not understand what had happened at first. The two shots (there were 10 rounds left in the magazine when the police unloaded it) were muffled in the crowd. Only the plain clothes Vatican security men, from the Inspectorate of Public Security, reacted instantly. Some hared off ahead of the Pope's vehicle to clear a way to the Gate of Bells, the exit from St Peter's Square.

Pasquale Navarro found himself looking straight at a swarthy young man, his eyes now dilated like black lanterns, slowly backing from the crowd barrier, clutching a gun.

Navarro and another agent vaulted the barrier. There was panic around them. Men in the crowd jumped at Agca or tried to block his flight; now the screaming was rushing upwards and outwards around them like a squall, roughening the whole Square. The two policemen grabbed Agca before he had run 20 feet and rushed him under the Bernini Colonnade. He didn't try to use the gun, but struggled instinctively to get free.

The crowd, seeing him held, rushed at him with hands tearing at his face; Navarro saw the first blows get home and realised that the gunman would be lynched within minutes. He lugged him forward again and down an arcade to the police point. Somehow the door was shut. 'He really didn't strike me as crazy or as some sort of nut,' Navarro recalled. The prisoner calmly wrote down the name Ozgun, and said that he was a student at the University of Perugia. Navarro sensed that he was lying about the name at least. Then the questions began.

There had been some forethought in the Vatican. With the right-wing killers and the Red Brigades raging up and down the Italian peninsula, the Pope – though an unlikely target for either force – required greater protection. When the white vehicle accelerated wildly out of the Square, somebody already knew how to get the standby ambulance. When the Pope, still conscious, had been transferred to the ambulance, somebody knew where to go. The long journey from the Vatican City to the huge Policlinico Gemelli, the Catholic University hospital in the north of Rome, took only 20 minutes. Somebody had a plan for clearing the route in this emergency, and the ambulance was well on its way as the sirens of the police cars and more ambulances began to wail round St Peter's, where the crowd was now weeping and praying on its knees.

Professor Castiglione is the chief surgeon at the Gemelli. He had chosen Wednesday to go to a conference in Milan and the hospital caught him by loudspeaker at 5.40 p.m., 20 minutes after the shooting, just as he was trooping out of the airport building at Linate. He ran back and took the next flight to Rome.

A police escort hurtled him like a foreign statesman from Fiumicino airport to the clinic. He was hastening into the ninth floor operating theatre in robe and mask just before 8 p.m.

The operation was already in progress. But an hour and a half before, the scene had been bizarre. Professor Crucitti, another of the clinic's chief surgeons, had arrived a few moments after the ambulance – he had been in a private clinic, but 'I dropped everything and rushed' – and found the theatre a jostling mob of doctors, policemen, stretcher-bearers and assorted priests.

Just as eighteenth-century kings died in a crowd of various dignitaries, so the Pontiff seemed to be facing major surgery with a mass official audience. When most of them had been shooed out, the situation turned out to be less chaotic than it looked. By good luck, two assistant surgeons had prepared the theatre for an operation on a small boy which they had decided to postpone only seconds before the phone call from the Vatican came through.

They had time to collect their wits before the ambulance drew up, but neither of the two senior surgeons was on the premises. They were not reassured by the look of Karol Wojtyla, otherwise Pope John Paul II, as he was carried into emergency. There was a lot of blood now – Father Dziwisz had undone his robe – and he was talking hard to himself in Polish. The doorman caught something about 'Maria' but could understand nothing else.

The first examination had been carried out and the anaesthetist was getting to work when Crucitti burst in, a very welcome sight indeed. Castiglione was on his way, they knew, but it would be madness to wait for him and the Alitalia flight. As the world press and at least two Polish bishops dashed into the Gemelli lobby, the surgeons started work.

As they investigated, their spirits cautiously rose. 'There wasn't that moment,' one of them recalled, 'when one feels: there's nothing I can really do about this one.' On the minus side, the Pope had bad lacerations of the small intestine, and the organic matter in the gut had inevitably spilled around.

This meant shortening the intestine; that wasn't in itself a problem, although it might mean (and it did) that there would have to be a colostomy which introduced an artificial by-pass, and that in turn meant a second operation in a few weeks' time to remove the by-pass and join up the small intestine again. The real trouble was the danger of infection from the leakages, not least with entry and exit wounds nearby. Add to that a loss of blood which seemed to have been heavy, and the fact that the patient was 60 years old.

The main plus point was that the pancreas and other delicate organs – to say nothing of bones and arteries – had not been hit. Wojtyla's sheer fitness, his persistence in taking physical exercise, helped too, although not as much as the journalists wanted to believe.

The operation took five and a half hours. They took out 10 centimetres of intestine, by-passed it, and operated on a difficult perforation in the lower colon, also a possible infection centre. That was the real danger. The surgeons had done their best; now it was a matter of nursing and waiting. The Pope had stood the operation remarkably well, but the doctors were not going to say anything firmly optimistic until they were sure they were through the period when infection might develop.

Was Agca a half-crazed megalomaniac or a calculated, cold-blooded killer? The evidence to date suggests something more pedestrian: a neurotic young man who was financed by right-wing political masters to carry out skulduggery which they did not wish to perform themselves. Though they may have used him against left-wing opponents, there is no indication that they meant him to kill the Pope.

Agca's story began on the night of 1 February 1979. Abdi Ipekci, the editor of the respected (and slightly left of centre) daily newspaper, *Milliyet*, was driving home from work. A few hundred yards from his home, the car ran into heavy congestion. A young man darted from the kerb and rained automatic bullets through the wind-screen, killing Ipekci almost immediately. The gunman escaped on foot, astonishingly, by a side street, and was driven away at lightning speed in a waiting car. It was a highly professional selective assassination – and the assassin was Agca.

Agca was born and brought up in the township of Hekimhan in Malatya province – a turbulent region of south-eastern Turkey where Kurds and Turks, Sunnis and Shias are intermingled. In south-eastern Turkey political and ethnic violence is almost endemic, and Agca from his teens carried a gun as a Briton carries his umbrella. His father, who died some years ago, was a peasant, apparently poor but not penniless. Agca was educated at the local school; his mother, a brother and a sister still live in Hekimhan, and are said to be bewildered by what has now happened.

On the strength of local schooling, Agca entered a local teachers' training college – perhaps an ominous step. In the 1970s such institutions were hotbeds of political fanaticism, and Agca got a fistful of extreme right-wing indoctrination.

Then on 1 February came the killing of Ipekci. It took the police some time to get on Agca's trail, and he may have committed a blunder by returning to Malatya to address a gathering of 'idealists' clubs,' i.e. the right-wing commandos who did the dirty work for Alparslan Turkes' Nationalist Action Party (NAP).

Up to this point he was still unheard of. But on 25 June the police arrested him in Istanbul for the murder of Ipekci. He underwent exhaustive grilling – personally attended by the then Interior Minister, Hasan Fehmi Gunes. Gunes formed the impression that Agca was a cold-blooded killer and that his display of theatrical paranoia was a pose.

Agca's trial by an Istanbul military court was bizarre. At the outset, as during interrogation, Agca confessed to the murder of Ipekci – but at the end he claimed to be innocent. Asked why he had changed his mind, he said he wanted to confuse the court and the press.

Agca's most remarkable comment was: 'I have no use for the established order, but I have no links with the established forms of terrorism of right and left. I represent a new form of terrorism of my own.'

On 25 November 1979 Agca, awaiting a death sentence, escaped from the maximum security military prison at Maltepe, Istanbul, aided by five rightist soldiers who gave him a military uniform.

Three days later Pope John Paul was due to arrive in Istanbul for ecumenical talks with the Greek Orthodox patriarch. Agca's first action was to ring up *Milliyet* – whose editor he had murdered – to say he had left a letter in a mail box near the paper's offices. The letter said Agca would 'definitely kill the Pontiff' if his visit to Turkey went ahead.

This was the first hard evidence of Agca's intentions about the Pope, though it is reported that he had earlier included the Pope in his demonolgoy of American imperialists, Communists and Jews.

After escaping, Agca made his way home to south-eastern Turkey, where he probably made contact with his NAP controllers. Around this time he acquired a false passport and made his way to Iran, in whose chaotic conditions he could easily get lost.

Immediately after his escape in November, the Turkish authorities asked all Interpol member countries to look out for Agca. They are bitter about the lethargic response to their appeal.

After a brief stay in Iran, he returned to Turkey, though he was one of the most wanted men in the country. It was at some point in mid-1980 that he made his way to western Europe. The Turkish intelligence service are convinced that he spent much of 1980 in West Germany and their agents claim that he was sighted in Ulm and in West Berlin. It is widely assumed that in Germany Agca was befriended by underground right-wing supporters of Colonel Turkes, who over the years had built up connections with the German extreme right.

In February this year Turkish security men claim they traced Agca to Milan and the theory is that he then visited Rome to reconnoitre the Pope's movements. The Turkish consul-general notified the Italian authorities, but if any action was taken it was unsuccessful, for Agca left Italy a little later, either for Germany or for another European country. He was plainly not short of funds.

On 8 April he checked in at a pension, the Hotel Posta, in Perugia, and proceeded to enrol at the University for Foreigners for a three-month course in Italian. But after paying his fees for the full course, he vanished the next day – and at this point apparently went on holiday to Majorca. On 9 May he flew from Majorca to Milan, and the next day (or possibly 11 May) he arrived in Rome, where he entered the Pensione Isa, on the last lap of the long trail of hate to St Peter's. *(17.5.81)*

A Man of Terrible Honesty
Patrick O'Donovan

The attempt to kill the Pope in front of St Peter's does not come as a true surprise. It is part of a modern pattern of assassination whose chief aim seems to be the infliction of grief. Assassination has long been an instrument of politics. Usually there seems to have been some purpose, however ugly, in the killing; but lately we have had death or attempted death dished out in a way that can change no situation fundamentally, that is evilly futile and a calculated act of contempt for all humanity. From this form of gratuitous death no one is immune and it is coming close to the fact that popularity and eminence are the marks of a likely target. It is a vile predicament for civilisation.

Pope John Paul II was just such an obvious target, except that he seemed hedged by special qualities that added extra dimensions of indecency to attacks on his person. His unique reputation as a public figure owed nothing to the wiles of a politician. He seemed almost to choose to say the unpopular thing and fiercely to maintain the unpopular or unfashionable doctrine. His recent predecessors have been exquisite compromisers in comparison.

He taught the strictest doctrines, renewing a series of negatives that had begun to grow less absolute to the faithful and more preposterous still to non-believers. Thus he could teach vast, teeming crowds of the poor and over-crowded, say, in Mexico, not the virtues of abstinence from birth control but its absolute requirement by God. He taught the evil of abortion to middle-class Catholics who wanted the agonies or at least discomforts of their consciences eased.

The Church is still short of new priests and still losing older ones by acts of laicisation that under his rule have become more rare or uncanonical. There has been no hint of a married priesthood for members of the Roman version of the Catholic Church. And the idea of a female priesthood is clearly not within the powers of the possible. From the Second Vatican Council there was meant to emerge, not a democratic Church, but a collegiate one in which the Pope presided over his bishops and shared a great deal of authority. This Pope has fashioned a conservative and absolute authority.

Such a doctrinal code – and it could be greatly extended – would seem to make for ferocious resentment. Some prelates and theologians, it is true, are resentful, but somehow the resentment is more against the nature of authority than against this man who exerts it. It is extremely odd and one reason may be that Catholics, especially semi-sophisticated ones, have discovered the dignity and authority of their own consciences and this cannot of its nature be taken away from them.

Pope John Paul, all over the world, has taught the strong, distilled spirit of Catholic doctrine. It is not in itself comforting. True, he has also taught a social doctrine in which the rich, particularly in South America, are fools as well as sinners and the poor are not merely God's special people but men deprived of their natural rights. And he has dismissed violence as being the non-Christian method. All this he has taught with a brave clarity.

He can stand on the podium of some temporary high altar, his plain and voluminous vestments flourished into baroque sculpture by the wind, the most exposed figure in the world for an assassin who is prepared himself to pay the full price for his killing, and it is far more than his genius as a public figure, his gift of tongues and his radiance of sincere and Christian love that gets to the people. It is the uncompromising sincerity of the man. If you do not intend to obey him, at least here is a very human man who practises what he preaches and a man in whom all his qualities seem to add up to an ideal and an excitement. He dignifies life. He confers pleasure. He may not noticeably change the societies he visits – except perhaps in Poland. He left Ireland as he

38. Two Narrow Escapes

found it.

But people crowd home from their city parks with their picnic baskets and raincoats feeling that they have seen a man in authority who is logical and seeks nothing for himself. They have been given a glimpse of the impractical made real for a moment. They have seen a terrible honesty at work and the display has been made by an indefatigable man who says hard things for his love of the people looking up at him. All this has made him the most singular public person in the world.

His public appearances have been countless; abroad, in the large and vulgar public audience hall in the Vatican, at the more than ping-pong sized altar that is set up on special occasions in front of the façade of St Peter's. He drives, standing, through unimaginable crowds. He stands alone and defined, still before myriads. A wise courtier of a flourishing and pleasure-conferring monarchy might say that he is over-exposed, too long and too often. A cynical head of security might say that he has been asking for it.

In Rome there is one know-it-all rumour that could not possibly be checked which says that he rushes about because this is the most effective form of modern pastorate that he has found. And he does it in a hurry because he expects assassination. There is even an adornment to this story. It is said that when he was a Polish bishop, he went to visit the late Padre Pio in his remote Franciscan convent in Italy. Padre Pio, it must be said, was a man who appeared to have the bleeding stigmata on his body, which attracted both the disapproval of the Church and hordes of penitents. The most serious and honourable men believed in this fierce old peasant friar.

It is said that, like many dignitaries, Bishop Wojtyla came to see this man who, if nothing else, was a superb clairvoyant. He is said to have told the Pole he would be Pope, and assassinated. It is the sort of story that many Catholics love to believe and I heard it long before the bullets huddled him at the back of his white jeep. I do not really believe it, especially the Padre Pio bit.

But an irrelevant Turkish terrorist has tried to play God at him, and the world has had another example of its sick and silly madness. It is not brutal to write that nothing has been changed fundamentally. That is far from the point of this class of killing. *(17.5.81)*

The Saving of the President
Anthony Holden

'Withdrawn, a loner . . . unable to work steadily in the last year or so before the assassination . . . white, male . . . chooses a handgun as his weapon . . . selects a moment when the President is appearing among crowds.'

The description is that made in 1968, by President Johnson's violence commission, of the likely profile of 'the next assassin to strike at a President.' It is a chilling sneak preview of John W. Hinckley Jnr, the man accused of attempting to kill President Reagan for love of a teenage film star.

In one haunting sentence it distills the feeling that there was something wholly predictable, almost inevitable, about this 'latest' attempt on a President's life. A common remark from bystanders, ineluctably drawn to the scene outside the Washington Hilton, was: 'I thought it would happen, but not this soon.' Even the President's brother, Neil Reagan, said: 'I expected something like this.'

I was lunching a few blocks away. A waiter, knowing my companion and I were both journalists, passed by with apologies for interrupting our conversation: 'Sorry, but I thought you might like to know that the President has been shot.' We left at once; but nobody else did. People got on with their lunch – there was even some laughter – as the news passed around the room.

Later in the day, as the ritualistic messages poured in from foreign leaders, the words 'shocked' and 'stunned' seemed mechanical and inappropriate. Nobody here was feeling that way. Depressed, yes, disgusted, sick at heart, but not surprised. There was none of the dazed horror, the disbelief, which greeted the news from Dallas in November 1963. Just a deep world-weariness, a mood of baffled introspection.

The executive vice-president of Handgun Control Inc., Charles J. Orasin Jnr, was out of town when he heard the news. He immediately called his office – and was astonished to get straight through. When John Lennon was shot dead in New York last December, the switchboard had been overloaded for hours.

'What is it?' Orasin wondered aloud. 'Are people just exhausted by all this violence? Are they so inured to violence in their neighbourhoods that they expect it? Are they so used to seeing national leaders fall that they don't react any more? What's going to get them angry enough to pick up the phone, call their Congressman and demand they pass a gun control law now and stop this madness?'

40. Two Narrow Escapes

Over at the Citizens' Committee for the Right to Keep and Bear Arms, its chief lobbyist, John M. Snyder, gave the appropriately ironic reply: 'Reagan is the best friend we've had in the White House for generations.' He went on: 'What has happened to him proves we've been right all along' – by which Snyder means to say that the 'answer' lies in exploring the motive for crime and imposing steeper penalties, rather than in tighter restrictions on handguns.

Written and telephoned threats against Reagan's life tripled in 24 hours. Suddenly, it was open season for maniacs. As John F. Kennedy once said: 'No amount of protection is enough. All a man needs is a willingness to trade his life for mine.'

There are plenty of such people about, as America now knows all too well. Of the last nine Presidents, six have been fired upon – only one, Harry Truman, by assailants with an identifiable political motive. The solitary, obsessive gunman wandering from cheap motels with his weapon in his pocket and malice in his heart, has become an American stereotype.

It came as no surprise when Hinckley's friends began to recall him reading 'Mein Kampf,' when he was discovered to have 'a history of mental illness,' when letters turned up betraying his own dire intent. It all fitted the pattern. There is now even a phrase used by Secret Service psychologists: 'The Bremer Type,' named after the man who shadowed and finally gunned down George Wallace in 1972. It was used publicly for the first time in 'Nashville,' a film about a 'Bremer Type' who shadowed and tried to gun down a politician.

Nashville – there are always these chilling coincidences – was the town in which Hinckley was arrested last October for trying to board an aeroplane with three handguns in his possession. When asked why the arrest was reported only to the FBI, not to the Secret Service, the airport police said last week it had 'not occurred' to them to link the incident with the presence in Nashville that day of the then President Jimmy Carter.

It was another movie, 'Taxi Driver,' which appears to have given Hinckley his idea. Robert De Niro, withdrawn loner, etc., attempts to kill public figures to impress a teenage hooker, his love for whom is unrequited. The hooker is played by Jodie Foster, to whom John Hinckley wrote at approximately 1 p.m. last Monday: 'By sacrificing my freedom, and possibly my life, I hope to change your mind about me. This letter is being written an hour before I leave for the Hilton Hotel.'

Ninety minutes later, after Hinckley had performed what he himself billed as his 'historical deed,' Reagan was much nearer death than was initially acknowledged. Jerry Parr, the Secret Service man who bundled the President into his car, at first ordered the driver to head for the White House. He then saw a trickle of blood coming from the President's mouth and ordered a diversion to George Washington Hospital.

It was the nearest. Had Parr decided to make for Walter Reed Hospital, where Presidents are traditionally treated, Reagan might not have survived. An eyewitness leaving the emergency entrance as the President 'walked in' said: 'He was gasping for air. He looked like he was in shock . . . then his eyes rolled upward, his head went back, his knees buckled and he started to collapse.'

Once a tube was inserted between Reagan's chest wall and collapsed left lung, two quarts of his blood – between a third and a half of his total blood volume – flowed out at what a doctor present described as 'a rather brisk rate.' His blood pressure was low enough to signify shock, a condition which could prevent a man of 70 from recovering.

Reagan has since, as Ed Meese, the President's counsellor, joked, made great progress for a fifty-year-old. The President's now famous wise-cracks – to the surgeons: 'Are you guys Republicans?'; to a nurse: 'Does Nancy know about you and me?' – seemed deliberately designed to bolster national morale. There was much reminiscence about Theodore Roosevelt in 1912; shot while making a speech, he insisted on finishing it before receiving medical attention.

Meanwhile, back at the White House, the Secretary of State, Alexander Haig, had taken it upon himself to reassure the nation and the world. Those with him in the 'situation room' two hours after the shootings, when he decided to take to national television, said his intent was 'to assure the allies that everything was under control.' That was not the impression Haig gave the nation.

Not only did he promote himself in the 'chain of succession' – an unpardonable error from so high an official, especially after the recent controversy over 'crisis management' – but he sweated profusely, his voice choked with emotion, and his hands shook as they gripped the lectern. He had reacted the same way, said a friend, after an attempt on his own life in Belgium in 1979. It was not the demeanour looked for in a man declaring that his was the finger temporarily on the button.

The button, in fact, was elsewhere. Television viewers may have seen the famous 'man with the black bag' – the military officer assigned to stay within six feet of the President at all times, carrying the coded devices needed to order a nuclear attack or retaliation – sprinting desperately after the fleeing motorcade. He made it; and he stood doggedly in the operating theatre throughout the two hours that the President underwent surgery.

The aftermath of the shooting will be with us for some time yet: most notably in the shape of the invulnerable macho President. Reagan has apparently agreed that he will in future wear a bullet-proof vest on

42. Two Narrow Escapes

some public occasions – there is a new, lightweight variety sometimes worn by Carter and his staff – though it is unlikely that such protection would have helped much this time, when the bullet entered his left armpit. (The .22 'Destructor' bullet had in fact ricocheted off the President's limousine door before hitting him.)

With that in mind, the Secret Service are also aware that these attacks tend to come in spates. It was only 10 days after Sara Jane Moore's bullet whistled over his head in 1975 that Gerald Ford was attacked by Lynette 'Squeaky' Fromme. Said a chastened Ford after Reagan's shooting: 'If we can't have the opportunity of talking with one another, seeing one another, shaking hands with one another, something has gone wrong with our society.'

It was a universal sentiment. Another such attack on a public figure in the near future would have this country on the edge of a collective nervous breakdown. President Reagan's humour for all its John Wayne bravado, always verged on the macabre – but never more so than when a nurse told him he must 'keep up the good work.

'Why?' said the President. 'You mean this is going to happen again?' *(5.4.81)*

Two Narrow Escapes. 43

3.
Questions of Class

Deep Shame of our Class Bias
Richard Hoggart

A few years ago I took part in a television programme about the depiction of class on television. The research for the programme gave reasonably clear indications that the correlations between family, class, school, college and access to some of the main professions were probably still as strong as 30 years before. The BBC seemed to find the film embarrassing and it had no second showing. I was told by three senior officials that I was in error. Britain was now a classless society: to insist otherwise was a Leftist illusion.

Only a few days ago, I gave a lecture to a group of foreign professionals attending a conference about British society today. I said that both the sense and the reality of class were still very strong. The first questioner, a Latin American, asked why I argued thus, since they'd been very confidently assured by a previous speaker that 'class' no longer existed in Britain.

And so it goes on. The more articulately defensive heads of public schools pooh-pooh, in just the right accents and inflections, the idea that privilege still reigns in this country, and in particular that there are excessively strong links between social class and educational and professional opportunities. They claim that their schools are now democratic and open; and then go on to talk about British society and the role of such schools within it in a way that makes you awestruck at the cultural cocoon in which they have been wrapped all their lives.

Now two important studies, by Professors Goldthorpe and Halsey, are going to make it harder for anyone of goodwill to continue talking in that way. They show that, in spite of all the intended reforms of recent decades, 'no significant reduction in class inequalities has in fact been achieved.' We are not becoming much more open, socially or educationally.

Even the meritocracy, about whose human thinness and unforgivingness T.S. Eliot and Michael Young warned us, is not emerging. The new 'service class,' which does to some extent recruit from the working class – some bright fish jump the rapids – looks after its own in much the old manner. The social-educational links remain massively firm.

Put it another way. The 'to-him-that-hath' law still runs strong in this country. Create a new social benefit because it is badly needed, especially by the working classes, and the 'service class' will take best advantage of it. Such reforms usually mean 'increased subsidies to the affluent.' They will fill the Arts Council subsidised theatres; they will take better advantage of the National Health Service because they know how to make their wants articulate and will not be easily bullied or ignored; they will get most from the billions of extra money poured into education, and especially into higher education, in the last 20 years.

Taken all in all, the educational reforms of those years have nevertheless shown that the pool of educable talent is larger than has been conventionally assumed and asserted. But the connections between social class and opportunity remain so tenacious that there is still virtually no more chance for working class people than there was 35 years ago.

Here is a litany for repeating each evening: in the late 1970s the burghers of Sheffield decided to set up their own 'independent' day grammar school; so much for the 1944 Act and the idea of equal opportunity. In 1979, a British Government, in the face of all the evidence of need elsewhere, set up the Assisted Places scheme. We do not have an educational system: we have an educational-and-class system, and that's very different. We are still, at the least, two nations and the crevasses between the main groups are hardly less deep than they were when Disraeli wrote.

What a brave Secretary of State for Education must first tackle is the excessively privileged status of the public schools. He can start by taking away their fiscal advantages by which the tax-payers, most of whom will never see inside such a school, subsidise them. Integration will and must follow. These schools are wasteful of resources and talent needed elsewhere; they reduce the articulate critical pressure needed within the State system; they are socially disastrous because they are monstrously separatist. We need to be diverse but not divided, least of all in this way.

Consider, for instance, the lawyers who go from the cloisters of Eton or Winchester to those of New College or King's to those of Gray's Inn – and then spend their lives straightening the jackets of the rest of us. They do not *know* this society; and no amount of bonhomie with the man they buy their fags from in High Holborn will make up for that lack. This is the fiftieth year since D.H. Lawrence died and the twentieth year since the Lady Chatterley trial. I still remember the appalling impression created at that time by the style and manner of some representatives of the English legal system resisting what they thought was in effect a breach of the bastion, and little has since changed.

Where such tight links exist, the freedom to buy education for your children is not like the freedom to smoke or not, to drink or not, to have expensive holidays or not. Access to good education should be as much a universal social right as access to pure water; and we don't buy better water than the people down the hill.

In his new study, Goldthorpe raises the question of why resentment by working class people to this process has not been more evident, and concludes that it has probably been muffled by the increasing prosperity enjoyed by all classes, at least until recently. I would myself point to the role of the admen and the mass media as opiate manufacturers for the consumer society.

Goldthorpe doubts whether fragmentary reforms via the politics of consensus can substantially alter things; the built-in resistances are too great. Yet he is not looking for blood in the streets. He sees the increasing collective aggressiveness of the unions as a reaction against the whole process he has described, but wants that collective force to be put behind demands for more than simple wage increases, behind a wide and radical range of movements towards a more open and just society.

Halsey has a more specifically educational theme. He doesn't expect the millennium but does see some grounds for hope, particularly now that the 'service class's' educational demands seem to have been substantially met. The current climate certainly doesn't encourage the hope that funds will be transferred to working class needs.

Against such perspectives, we should give overwhelming priority to three areas. First, the 'comprehensive' schools. We must get those right, and in our own best way, which means getting nearer to solving a lot of other related social problems. But there can be movement and progress against all the odds, as Rutter's '15,000 Hours' showed. And comprehensive schools already often do better than most of the Press leads us to believe.

46. Questions of Class

Second, we have to put much more into providing for those 16- to 19-year-olds – more than half of the age-group – for whom education has been such a failure that, after they leave school at 16, they never go back to any sort of educational provision.

Third, we have to recognise the crucial importance of making much more provision for continuing education, as the means of providing better for those of us who realise belatedly, and at different stages in life, that education can have something to say to our condition, professional, social, recreational or spiritual.

We should do all this, not just for economic reasons – because we hope it will help the economy to revive – but for the good of our souls. As long as our educational system is as class-based as these studies confirm, we will be a poorer society in every way, but above all morally. We should be deeply ashamed at the way such bias persists in the national life. It is virtually a case for the European Commission on Human Rights! *(13.1.80)*

Don't Blame the Middle Classes
Lynne Reid Banks

As an unrepentantly middle-class woman, I view with increasing resentment and bewilderment the mounting assault upon my class by commentators such as Richard Hoggart in his 'Deep Shame of our Class Bias.'

Why should I feel ashamed of the indisputable fact that we, the middle classes, fill the better schools with our children and the theatres with ourselves? Mr Hoggart writes as if we elbowed the working people aside, as if, should we step out of their way, institutions of education and culture would at once be filled with working people hungry for self-betterment. They would not, as many another idealistic socialist has broken his heart finding out.

The 1944 Education Act has failed to reduce class inequalities, not so much because the middle classes ruthlessly 'take advantage' as because the working classes, on the whole, spinelessly don't. Mr Hoggart's analogy of pure water, which is available equally to all, is false. We turn on taps and swallow water without personal effort or commitment, but education is quite different.

There is nothing wrong with comprehensive schools except the children. If I, following the sorry example of so many left-wing friends in recent years, withdraw my child from his comprehensive school, it won't be due to any fault I have found with the teachers or the curriculum or the facilities, but becasue he is trying to learn among children who can't or don't care to, and many of whom, in addition, behave like barbarians.

This is basically nobody's fault except theirs and their parents'. The opportunities are there, and have been there now for 36 years. If they don't want those opportunities, or can't use them, I refuse to be blamed.

Incidentally, Mr Hoggart should try being an 'articulate' and 'critical' parent at such a school. My articulate criticisms have so far been either totally ignored, or, in the case of a piece I wrote for the Parents' Association newsletter, stifled by the teachers, who refused to distribute it.

I know middle-class parents who, having started from a point of idealism, faith in humanity and a sense of guilt at their own privileges, have gone all-out to make the State system work in just the way Mr Hoggart recommends. One by one, they have been forced to give up; what drives them to it is the awful realisation that the working people of this country, on the whole, are not interested in educational or cultural self-improvement. They have no ambition for their children apart from material ambition. If Mr Hoggart is waiting for the trade unions to turn their energies to demanding better cultural status for their members, as distinct from higher wages with which to improve their material living standards, he will wait in vain.

It would take more than Acts of Parliament, or the destruction of the private sector, to alter the deep resistance of British workers to all the values and advantages that Mr Hoggart longs to give them, because most of them don't give a damn. The few who do care move into the middle classes anyway. They were probably middle-class in their values and aspirations to begin with.

Oh yes, we are an 'us and them' society. But whose doing is that? The genuine liberalism of the Sixties among my class has turned itself inside out in its disillusionment.

Nevertheless, one must salute Mr Hoggart's courage. He dares to speak of morality and of the soul, and of the benefits which would accrue to both by removing class bias from our education. Yes. But you cannot do it from the top. You can't force people to want to learn, to expand, to improve the state of their spirits.

In 1960, Arnold Wesker (one, I imagine, of the aforementioned broken-hearted ones) made his working-class heroine Beatie Bryant say:

> 'Education isn't only books and music – it's asking questions all the

time . . . no one, not one of us, is asking questions, we're all taking the easiest way out. We're so mentally lazy we might as well be dead. Blast, we are dead! And . . . it's our own bloody fault!'

She continues, in one of the most powerful speeches in modern drama, to castigate her own class for not caring, not trying, not bothering to want anything better than the 'slop' and 'squit' that the commercial world sees fit to dish out to them. She might have added that an even worse crime is to ignore what the non-commercial world is striving to offer them, the education which is there for them and which could change the face of this nation if they would only rouse themselves to lay hands and minds upon it, but which they leave lying about for the much-abused, over-privileged middle classes to pounce on. *(27.1.80)*

Back to Champagne
Katharine Whitehorn

'Life in London is a party forever,' said the Iranian who has lived here for eight years, since she first moved in with a kettle, a mattress and a racehorse. 'It is café society.'

'I can't remember when there were so many parties,' says the editor of the *Tatler*. 'I suppose people think there's no point in saving the money any more.'

There's a return to manners: someone who gave a party for 400 received thank-you letters from just about all of them; a return to evening elegance: a man who reports such things for *Vogue* spoke almost with tears in his eyes of the Feathers Ball: 'The whole room in white tie and tails, the girls beautiful, everyone dancing cheek-to-cheek; not a drug in sight – and you're too old at 17.'

Some young men again go to Lobb's and Lock's for handmade shoes and hats, 'girls put on proper ball dresses for quite ordinary parties.' Among them, certainly, there is upper-class punk gear, but apparently that gets classed as fancy dress: 'Of course there are punks!' said this reporter. 'They're beautiful! If I was younger I'd dye my hair pink myself!' Depends, I suppose, on how you look at it: as another *Vogue* commentator wrote, 'When a handsome prince changed into a frog, from frogs' point of view it was a definite improvement.'

Our incomplete social revolution has been like an earthquake:

there's been a shake-up, all the pieces are now settling back again – but not into quite the same places in the same way.

After an upheaval, people search first for the old foundations, and there is a fashionable nostalgia around, perhaps most clearly to be seen in Oxford. It is embodied in such all-male dining clubs as the Vile Bodies, in which each member takes on an Evelyn Waugh character; they wear boaters and blazers and do such things as shooting off to Calais for May Day instead of attending the traditional dawn singing on Magdalen Tower.

One of the most spectacular clubs is the Piers Gaveston, which holds fantastic fancy dress parties – one man turned up in just a fur jock-strap, another painted all over in gold. One party last year was 'Dress Penal' – which meant chains and broad arrows for some, a different interpretation of the word for others. Its title shows its original avo-cation, but they now invite not only women but heterosexuals to their parties: 'Four years ago,' I was gravely informed, 'it was very in to be gay or bisexual; now it's OK to be straight.'

Traditional clubs like the Bullingdon, which has its own point-to-point, will hold large dinners where the guests don't pay, so each member will finally have to cough up about £200. A Commemoration Ball costs £50 a double ticket (£75 next year). The clubs get the help of college servants whose pay has just gone up to £1.38 an hour, though they may get tipped at the end of the term.

Another throw-back to the Twenties is the revival of the scavenger hunts, fleets of taxis rushing about collecting a St Hilda's scarf, a Somerville blanket, a secretary. And *Cherwell*, the undergraduate newspaper, tells of 45 teams vomiting their way round 11 pubs, starting at the Turf and ending at the Roebuck. For charity.

Drugs have rather faded from the scene, though opium seems to be on its way back – that's traditional too, perhaps: look at de Quincey. 'Oxford's main drug is alcohol,' I was told. 'Pimms and champagne for choice.'

And sex? With the enormous relaxation in the rules that used to keep the young apart, plus women in most of the men's colleges, it may be a surprise to learn that, according to a *Cherwell* survey, a third of Oxford youth are virgins – but as they only got 76 replies, we do not know how many of those who didn't answer were busy doing some-thing to rectify their condition.

The launching upon society of a dew-bespangled deb is not really a 1980s happening – 'How can you launch a girl when she's already launched herself before she's 16?' said one mother. But some forms exist: a cocktail party at Daddy's club – Cavalry and Guards, Brooks's, Boodles – and it's real champagne again. 'For several years it was just that white fizzy stuff.'

50. Questions of Class

In the country there is more control over the young than in London: one girl was sent packing for stubbing out a cigarette on a 400-year-old lawn, and when another girl lit up a cigarette after the soup her hostess said icily, 'We seem to have finished,' and led the entire party from the room. That was the end of dinner.

In London, much of the action goes on in clubs and restaurants; there are OK places to go – Eleven Park Walk, San Lorenzo in Beauchamp Place, the clubs Wedgie's and Tramp. Langan's Brasserie is in, surprisingly – after all, there was that incident when a hysterical woman waved a dead cockroach she'd found in the Ladies in front of the owner's nose and he just swallowed it and washed it down with a glass of Krug.

The *jeunesse dorée* who make up the centre of the whirlpool have a hidden but none the less intense rating system which all but the most innocent understand. You score points *against* for talking about money, for talking about what's in and what's not, for trying too hard and, beyond a certain point, for rudeness and getting drunk. Much, however, is forgiven the man who rings up and apologises next morning.

Points in *favour* come from being amusing, or very pretty, or having facilities – Daddy's jet, a vast swimming bath, a chic car. You score most points of all for who you are with. I was assured, against all disbelief, that a girl will score far higher for arriving with the right gay than for hanging on the arm of the wrong boyfriend of her own.

What do they use for money, these young things? 'They all, without exception, say they're desperately hard up,' said David Litchfield, who resents fiercely being asked out to a birthday party, getting stuck with his share of the bill and watching all the males quarrelling noisily over who had what. He says (shades of Graham Greene's 'Dr Fischer of Geneva') that the rich will do anything for a free handout: those who despise the Playboy Club will still queue for three-quarters of an hour for free meals chez Victor Lownes in the country.

None the less there has to be money around. One struggling Old Etonian (OEs still dominate the scene) complained that he took his girl for a hamburger and then 'a couple of drinks' at Tramp and the evening cost £56. Flats cost upwards of £100 a week, however many other bright young things you cram in, however fiercely you dodge paying the phone bill each quarter. Cocaine, too, is expensive. 'I'm wretched to say,' said one party-giver, 'that parents often take the line they used to take about cannabis – "so long as he's not on heroin I don't mind".'

At something like £2,000 an ounce you wouldn't have thought many could afford it, but apart from the slightly sinister figures who are known to push it around, there are plenty of 'ouncers' – those who buy an ounce of cocaine and take it home and mix it with something else.

Questions of Class. 51

'When you've seen two well-known MPs kneeling down beside a glass-topped table snuffing the stuff up you realise it's considered a socially clean drug. Half the time what they're sniffing is dried milk and they don't know the difference.' Sadly, the girls often get hooked for good while the young men pass through drugs as a phase.

Allowances from the family, for some; interest from family trusts for others. There is also 'this great tide of bills wafting across the rooftops to come to rest on Father' – and, of course, overdrafts. No one has yet quite succeeded in designing the tax-loss son to match the tax-loss farm, but many an affluent Papa has come extremely near it.

What is certain is that these young have abandoned the pretence of being have-nots; and are being as gay, ebullient and decorative as they were in the Thirties – when we also had a strong pound and two million unemployed. And one might ask how many young people, punk, comprehensive, small grammar or polytechnic, would actually turn down the chance of a life – or at least a night-life – like this if it was on offer.

It's worth remembering, though, what some cracker-barrel American sage once said after he had listened to tales of the glittering doings of New York's café society for some time. He took his corncob pipe out of his mouth, spat, and said: 'In New York, you may be café society. Back home, you're just the town drunk.' *(27.7.80)*

52. *Questions of Class*

4.
Questions of Sex

Grunts of a Sexist Pig
Anthony Burgess

Cleaning out my son's bedroom the other day (he has gone to Paris to work as an apprentice fish chef in the all-male kitchens of Le Fouquet) I came across a partly eaten pig in pink marzipan. It had come, apparently, in the Christmas mails and was so ill-wrapped that neither its provenance nor purpose was apparent. My son thought it was an eccentric gift from one of his friends.

Now, quite by chance, I discover (a matter of an old *Punch* in a thanatologist's waiting-room) that it was a trophy sent by the Female Publishers of Great Britain to myself as one of the Sexist Pigs of 1980. I forget who the others were, but I think one of them published a picture book on the beauty of the female breast. What my own sin against women was I am not sure, but I'm told that it may have been a published objection to the name the Virago Press (women publishers publishing women) had chosen for itself.

Now all my dictionaries tell me that a virago is a noisy, violent, ill-tempered woman, a scold or a shrew. There is, true, an archaic meaning which makes a virago a kind of amazon, a woman strong, brave and warlike. But the etymology insists on a derivation from Latin *vir*, a man, and no amount of semantic twisting can force the word into a meaning which denotes intrinsic female virtues as opposed to ones borrowed from the other sex. I think it was a silly piece of naming, and it damages what is a brave and valuable venture. The

Virago Press has earned my unassailable gratitude for reprinting the 'Pilgrimage' of Dorothy Richardson, and I said so in *The Observer*. But I get from its warlike officers only a rude and stupid insult, and I cannot laugh it off. Women should not behave like that, nor men either.

It has already been said, perhaps too often, that militant organisations pleading the rights of the supposedly oppressed – blacks, homosexuals, women – begin with reason but soon fly from it. On this basic level of language they claim the right to distort words to their own ends. I object to the delimitation of 'gay'. 'Chauvinistic' stands for excessive patriotism and not for other kinds of sectional arrogance. 'Pig' is an abusive word which libels a clean and tasty animal: it is silly, and it can be ignored. But 'sexist' is intended to have a precise meaning, and, on learning that I was a sexist pig, I felt it necessary to start thinking about the term.

As far as I can make out, one *ought* to be a sexist if one preaches or practises discrimination of any kind towards members of the other sex. In practice, a sexist is always male, and his sexism consists in his unwillingness to accept the world-view of women in one or other or several or all of its aspects. This means, in my instance, that if I will not accept the meaning the Virago Press imposes on its chosen name, I qualify, by feminist logic, for the pink pig. But I cannot really believe it is as simple as that. The feminists must have other things against me, but none of them will speak out and say what they are.

In the *Harvard Guide to Contemporary American Writing*, Miss or Mrs Elizabeth Janeway, discussing Women's Literature, considers a book by Mary Ellmann called 'Thinking About Women.' She says: 'It is worth being reminded of how widespread and how respectable has been the unquestioned assumption of women's inevitable, innate, and significant "otherness," and Ellmann here collects utterances on the subject not only from those we might expect (Norman Mailer, Leslie Fiedler, Anthony Burgess) but from Robert Lowell, Malamud, Beckett, and Reinhold Niebuhr.'

Note both the vagueness and the obliqueness. There can be no vaguer word in the world than 'otherness.' The vagueness is a weapon. Since it is not defined, the term 'otherness' can mean whatever its users wish, rather like 'virago.' The position of people like Mailer and Burgess and Fiedler vis-à-vis this 'otherness' does not have to be defined either: we have an intuitive knowledge of their qualities, and, between women, no more need be said.

That women are 'other,' meaning different from men, is one of the great maxims of the feminists. They are biologically different, think and feel differently. But men must not say so, for with men the notion of difference implies a value judgement: women are not like us, therefore they must be inferior to us. I myself have never said or written or even thought this. What I am prepared to see as a virtue in myself (as also in Mailer and Fiedler and other pigs) is – because of the feminist insistence on this damnable otherness – automatically transformed by such women as read me into a vice. I mean the fact that I admire women, love the qualities in them that are different from my own male ones, but will not be seduced by their magic into accepting their values in areas where only neutral values should apply. Here, of course, the trouble lies. Women don't believe there are neutral zones: what males call neutral they call male.

I believe, for instance, that in matters of art we are in a zone where judgements have nothing to do with sex. In considering the first book the Virago Press brought out – the masterpiece of Dorothy Richardson – I did not say that here we had a great work of women's literature, but rather here we had a great work which anticipated some of the innovations of James Joyce. I should have stressed that this was a work by a woman, and the womanly aspect of the thing didn't seem to me to be important. I believe that the sex of an author is irrelevant, because any good writer contains both sexes.

But what we are hearing a lot of now, especially in American colleges, is the heresy that 'Madame Bovary' and 'Anna Karenina' can't be good portraits of women because they were written by men. These are not aesthetic judgements: they are based on an *a priori* position which refuses to be modified by looking at the facts. The feminists just don't want men to be able to understand women. On the other hand, women are quite sure that they understand men, and nobody finds fault with the male creations of the Brontes or of Jane Austen.

Let's get out of literature and into life. I think I am quite capable of seeing the feminist point of view with regard to men's sexual attitude to women. I am strongly aware of the biological polarity, and it intrudes where women say it shouldn't. I am incapable of having *neutral* dealings with a woman. Consulting a woman doctor or lawyer, shaking hands with a woman Prime Minister, listening to a sermon by a woman minister of religion, I cannot help letting the daydream of a possible sexual relationship intrude. That this diminishes the woman in question I cannot deny. It depersonalises her, since the whole sexual process necessarily involves depersonalisation: this is nature's fault, not man's.

Women object to their reduction into 'sex objects,' but this is what nature decrees when the erotic process gets to work. While writing this I am intermittently watching a most ravishing lady on French television. She is talking about Kierkegaard, but I am not taking much of that in. Aware of her charms as she must be, she ought to do what that beautiful lady professor of mathematics did at the University of Bologna in the Middle Ages – talk from behind a screen, meaning talk on the radio. But then the voice itself, a potent sex signal, would get in the way.

This awareness of the sexual power of women, I confess, induces attitudes which are, from the feminist angle, unworthy. At Brown's Hotel a woman porter proposed carrying my bags upstairs. It was her job, she said, but I could not let her do it. Old as I am, I still give up my seat to women far younger when on a bus or tube train. This is a protective tenderness wholly biological in origin. How can I apologise for it when it is built into my glands? Women are traditionally (but this is, I admit, possibly, a man-imposed tradition) slower to be sexually moved than are men, and this enables them to maintain a neutral relationship with the other sex in offices and consulting-rooms.

I believe what women tell me to believe – namely, that they can do anything men can do except impregnate and carry heavy loads (though this latter was contradicted by the woman at Brown's Hotel). Nevertheless, I have to carry this belief against weighty evidence to the contrary. Take music, for instance. Women have never been denied professional musical instruction – indeed, they used to be encouraged to have it – but they have not yet produced a Mozart or a Beethoven. I am told by feminists that all this will change some day, when women have learned how to create like *women* composers, a thing men have prevented their doing in the past.

This seems to me to be nonsense, and it would be denied by composers like Thea Musgrave and the shade of the late Dame Ethel Smyth (a great feminist herself, the composer of 'The March of the Women' as well as 'The Wreckers' and 'The Prison,' which the liberationists ought to do something about reviving). I believe that artistic creativity is a male surrogate for biological creativity, and that if women do so well in literature it may be that literature is, as Virginia Woolf said, closer to gossip than to art. But no one will be happier than I to see women produce the greatest art of all time so long as women themselves recognise that the art is more important than the artist.

I see that most, if not all, of what I say above is likely to cause feminist rage and encourage further orders to pink-pig manufacturers (did the Virago Press search for a *woman* confectioner?). But, wearily, I recognise that anything a man says is liable to provoke womanly hostility in these bad and irrational times. A man, by his very nature, is incapable of saying the right thing to a woman unless he induces the drag of hypocrisy. Freud, bewildered, said: 'What does a woman *want?*' I don't think, despite the writings of Simone de Beauvoir, Caroline Bird, Sara Evans, Betty Friedan, Germaine Greer, Elizabeth Janeway, Kate Millett, Juliet Mitchell, Sarah B. Pomeroy, Marian

Ramelson, Alice Rossi, Sheila Rowbotham, Dora Russell, Edith Thomas, Mary Wollstonecraft and the great Virginia herself, the question has yet been answered, except negatively.

What women *don't* want is clear – their subjection to the patriarchal image, male sexual exploitation, and all the rest of it. When positive programmes emerge – like the proposed 'desexualisation' of language – we men have an uneasy intimation of the possible absurdity of the whole militant movement. I refuse to say Ms, which is not a real vocable, and I object to 'chairperson' and the substitution of 'ovari-mony' for 'testimony.'

And I maintain (a) that a virago is a detestable kind of woman and (b) that feminist militancy should not condone bad manners. If that pink pig had not been thrown in the garbage bin I should tell the women publishers of Britain what to do with it. *(21.6.81)*

What do Men Want?
Katharine Whitehorn

'What do women *want*?' said the plaintive Freud, quoted by Anthony Burgess; and he (Burgess) goes on to confess that, despite the writings of Simone de Beauvoir, Juliet Mitchell, Mary Wollstonecraft etc., etc., he doesn't know the answer.

Suppose I asked, with an equally despairing wail, 'What do men *want*?' and confessed that, in spite of the writings of Flaubert, Shakes-peare, Anthony Burgess, St Augustine and the Two Ronnies, I still didn't know? He might point out, with that politeness for which he so eloquently begs, that it is possible that not all men want the same thing; and that the entire progress of mankind has been devoted to trying to find out what men want, so far without definitive success.

Anthony Burgess was enraged by being sent the Sexist Pig of the Year award by the feminist publishers, Virago: he wrote a witty piece about how stern convictions don't excuse bad manners, which includes sending people pink pigs. He thinks Virago were too touchy by half when he criticised their name; and denounces the idea that those who have noticed the difference between men and women must be con-sidered sexist.

I admit my first impulse is to shrug off what he says in a slap-you-on-the-shoulder manner. Oh, come on, you know it isn't like that; things seem quite different when you're the underdog yourself. You're far too intelligent to rank with the people who say they've nothing against blacks except the chip on their shoulder, that they wouldn't mind the working classes if they didn't eat with their mouths open, that they'd sympathise much more with feminists if they weren't so rude. All sorts of things can sting when it's the attitude behind them you hate: this isn't just a question of words, and you know it (come to that, how come a world-famous literary gent gets so steamed up about a pink pig?).

There's a much deeper point than manners, though, which I think he misses. What Virago and other such feminist writing outfits are trying to do is to upgrade the quality and amount of attention that gets given to the things women do. For just exactly what they are up against, read Auberon Waugh (all pigs are sexist but some are more sexist than others) on the trouble with women novelists: 'They seldom have much to write about except various domestic crises, marriage break-ups, unimportant and strangely unconvincing love affairs leading to child-birth, or abortion, or nervous breakdown.'

Waugh would presumably regard as important such things as the fate of nations, wars and statesmen, dictators and even painters. Yet he does not regard as even interesting the forces which might shape such men of destiny – the state of their parents' marriages, for example, the resentments and privations of their upbringing, or whether, and how often, they were dropped on their heads as babies. I know that all his class get sent away to boarding school, so that everyone can thankfully assume that what happens to Master Moseley and Master Benn, once they are out of rompers, concerns no one but Winchester and Westminster; but surely, since Freud, this is a some-what limited view – a view that Virago and Co. are doing their best to expand.

They also want conventional subjects – language, history, anthro-pology – to be studied from two alternative viewpoints, not just one. Whatever you may think of the women's movement, I would have thought that one thing for which anyone might be thankful is the research it has provoked: the second side of the picture in huge areas of scholarship. For scholarship has never been as 'neutral' as Burgess suggests.

For example, there was a book by Elaine Morgan (recently backed up by the Richard Leakey TV programme) suggesting that explan-ations of our ancient past that talked only about Man the Hunter didn't give a true picture, since Woman the Gatherer grubbed up a good 60 per cent of the food. There's the fascinating 'Women and Words' by Casey Miller and Kate Swift on language, which traces back feminine endings to show that 'brewster' was a female brewer, quite common in the Middle Ages, and that 'chairperson' is indeed an abomination (as

Burgess feels) since 'man' originally meant the race, not the sex: there were two kinds of it, the carl-man (male) and the wyf-man (female).

There was a book (hideously named, I admit) called 'The Wise Wound,' in which Shuttle and Redgrave explored the deep feelings of fear and revulsion felt by males towards menstruation. This is not more important, perhaps, than their revulsion against spiders or Vietcong but it was a subject that had simply never been investigated before.

Until Anne Oakley started to research it, there was virtually nothing to be read on the history of housework – how many volumes and volumes have been written on such subjects as armour, or guns, or the training of priests and princes, while what just about all women were up to was so ignored? Burgess started his article by pointing out, quite casually, that his son is working as an apprentice in the all-male kitchens of Le Fouquet. Everybody knows that the one thing girls are always told to be good at is cooking. Try that one the other way round. How would he feel, if he were brought up in the idea that all good boys should write, that he wouldn't be a proper male at all unless he could write, but that (well, naturally) all the really top jobs in writing had to be taken by women? *(28.6.81)*

Questions of Sex. 59

5.
The Other Island

A Kind of Mourning in Dublin
Conor Cruise O'Brien

At the time of the funeral of Bobby Sands in Belfast, a moderately large crowd of mourners assembled for a vigil outside the General Post Office in Dublin.

The GPO was the headquarters of Pearse and Connolly during the Easter Rising of 1916. To Republicans, it is a holy place. It is in fact the central shrine of the cult into which Bobby Sands was initiated by his mother, for which he took up arms, and for which he starved himself to death. The cult is that of Ireland, as a sentient being calling for human sacrifice – and also of those who heard that call, and died. And killed.

'Irish men and Irish women' begins the Proclamation of the Republic – 'in the name of God and of the dead generations from which she receives her old traditions of nationhood, Ireland, through us, summons her children to her flag, and strikes for her freedom.'

'. . . Ireland unfree,' said Patrick Pearse, 'shall never be at peace.' That saying has become the watchword of the Provisional IRA: I saw it written in large letters on a Dublin wall the other day. It is, of course, more than a prophecy: it is a licence to kill, with a valid and commanding signature. And it also legitimises voluntary death by hunger, with an authority which, in the eyes of the Irish Catholic Republicans, is greater – in this particular sphere – than that of any Pope.

Thursday in Dublin was a dark, clammy day, with low clouds and occasional heavy rain. The weather made a good topic of conversation:

that is, a good way of avoiding another topic. Dubliners went about their business more warily and quietly than usual, but they did go about their business, most of them. The IRA – speaking through the 'National H-Blocks Committee,' and also through some ominous pickets, wanted a general closure and National Day of Mourning, but they didn't get it, this time. There were a few young men and boys around in the streets with black arm-bands. The citizens gave them a wide berth. On Monday, after the first GPO vigil on the news of Sands's death, similar mourners had smashed the windows all along Dawson Street, including the windows of Dublin's Mansion House.

Dublin was getting a whiff – as it does intermittently – of lurking violence, of hatred and fear: of what the North has lived with for more than 10 years. Dublin didn't like it, at all.

People didn't talk about Sands: not in public at any rate. This was only partly circumspection, I think; contradiction came into it too. For, after all, if you were to talk about Sands, what on earth could you say? You didn't want to mourn him, and you earnestly wished his scary-looking mourners would go away, back to the North or wherever, and stay there. *But why didn't you want to mourn him?*

Not a point you'd want to argue with a Republican, even a quiet one. The dialogue:

'"Ireland unfree shall never be at peace," do you agree with that, or don't you?'

'I suppose so.'

'Are the Six Counties part of Ireland, or part of England?'

'Part of Ireland.'

'Right then, that's what Bobby Sands believed, and fought for, and died for. So why aren't you in mourning?'

The political culture of the Republic, drawn from the Irish Catholic nationalist tradition, reinforced by the official cult of 1916 and of past Republican heroes, precludes any coherent answer to that question. Bobby Sands died in the same way as Terence MacSwiney, and for the same cause. Why is he not honoured in the same way?

Again, there can be no coherent answer, within the bounds set by the tradition of the cult. True, the IRA has no democratic mandate from the people for their 'war.' But what mandate did Pearse or Connolly have? Less, in fact, than Bobby Sands, who, unlike either of them, was an elected public representative.

Awkward, very.

Out of the tradition, the cult and the awkwardness, the IRA has got its strength and durability in Catholic Ireland (South and North). They *really* believe what everyone is *supposed* to believe, and they act on their belief.

'Everyone' in this context means all Irish Catholics. Protestants don't count, unless they agree with Catholics in wanting a United Ireland. If they don't agree, then, to Republicans, they are 'England's garrison' and have no right to be in Ireland, or to live. This applies to almost all Ulster Protestants, a majority of the population in the area which the IRA is bent on 'liberating' with the approval of so many of the world's vocal freedom-lovers.

Very few Irish Catholics would push the logic of Republicanism to that grim end. But it is the logical ones, who push it there, who are now making the pace.

The *Irish Press* – the organ of the De Valera family, and of the greener shores of the Fianna Fail party – has been regularly predicting during the hunger strike that, if a hunger striker died, we would see again a great wave of popular Republican emotion, like that which followed the 1916 executions: a terrible beauty would be born, again. (Yeats, like Pearse, contributed to the construction of our infernal machine.)

Watching that Belfast funeral on television, I could believe that something of the kind might be happening among the Catholic youth of Northern Ireland, but walking and driving in the streets of Dublin – the capital city, not only of the real Republic, but also of Pearse's republic, and therefore of the IRA – I didn't think that a terrible beauty was being born, down here.

Paradoxically, I think that there was less indignation in Dublin about his death than there was in Paris, let alone New York. *We* after all knew that the Dublin Government – *any* Dublin Government – would let IRA hunger-strikers die, and would be totally deaf to all humanitarian appeals, genuine or other, in such a matter.

When we watch Sile De Valera busy about her humanitarian errands, we can recall that her famous grandfather – whose name is her political stock-in-trade – not only let IRA men die on hunger-strike in the jails of his republic (not Pearse's) but hanged IRA men. If Miss De Valera does not know that, everyone else does. *Politically*, of course, there is a vast difference between a De Valera decision on such a matter, and a Thatcher decision. But in *humanitarian* terms – if that were really what it were all about – the balance tilts, not against Thatcher, but against De Valera. It is less cruel to let a man kill himself, for not getting his own way, than it is to kill a man in cold blood.

We have to know therefore, in our hearts, that this is *not* a humanitarian cause; it is a political one. And we know what the cause is about: not about prison conditions, but about forcing Northern Ireland out of the United Kingdom, against the will of a majority of its inhabitants: forcing that, through the use of any weapon available: the gun, the bomb, propaganda, blackmail, humanitarianism, liberalism, penal reform or a rusty garden fork.

We know that cause and we don't like it, not really. It frightens us, and we don't want Northern Ireland anyway. And yet – in our pro-found, historically-formed ambivalence – we let our politicians go on saying on our behalf that we must have a united Ireland: like the doggy in the window, nothing else will do.

And so that famous 'aspiration towards unity' goes out, from Dublin and New York, across Northern Ireland, in a great windy current, fanning flames in which other people die. *(10.5.81)*

IRA's Distorting Mirror
Editorial

Bobby Sands and the other hunger strikers – sacrificial victims to the IRA's need to revive international interest in its cause – have achieved a propaganda coup. When Mr John Bowers of the International Long-shoremen says in New York that 'all people of Northern Ireland want is to be reunited with the rest of Ireland,' it is no use pointing out to him that the election results of the past century show the opposite. As ever in Ireland, myths are the only truths.

Many people in Britain, as well as outside, are anguished by the charge that their Government is 'letting men die because they want to wear their own trousers'; and, more generally, that maladroit security policies are obstructing political progress. These charges need to be answered.

First, the hunger strikes are not to improve prison conditions in Northern Ireland, which are better than in most European prisons. They are for political status – the right of convicted terrorists to run their own camp compounds; to train, discipline and punish their own members, as both IRA and Protestant paramilitaries did in the early Seventies.

Ironically, the much reviled internment (1971–1975) was a form of political status: when the police and army convinced a Minister that a man was a terrorist, he was arrested, with the intention of holding him, as prisoners-of-war are held, until the end of hostilities. Internment had been an effective weapon against terrorism, in both the Republic and Ulster, in previous IRA campaigns. But this time the Provisionals made it a potent propaganda weapon, and British and Irish politicians who, privately or publicly, had advocated internment, resiled and talked of 'phasing out.'

Detention without trial is an odious procedure, which has been barbarously misused around the world too often this century for politicians willingly to defend it. But 'phasing out' and political negotiation also failed to bring the peace which had been promised. Indeed, the first nine months of 'phasing out,' after Direct Rule, in March 1972, were the bloodiest of the whole Ulster crisis. Nor was the intellectual – as distinct from the political – case for relying on the courts to deal with terrorism ever effectively made.

Conservative and Labour Governments in succession set up committees under two distinguished jurists, Lord Diplock and Lord Gardiner, to study what could be done. Both declined to recommend that internment should be abandoned at once. Lord Diplock's remains the classic statement of the difficulties. After describing intimidation of witnesses and juries and how IRA 'godfathers' operate, he wrote:

'The dilemma is complete. The only hope of restoring the ability of criminal courts of law in Northern Ireland to deal with terrorist crimes is by using an extra-judicial process to deprive of their ability to operate in Northern Ireland those terrorists whose activities result in the intimidation of witnesses. With an easily penetrable border to the south and west, the only way of doing this is to put them in detention by an executive act, and to keep them confined until they can be released without danger to public safety and the administration of criminal justice.'

The Government adopted Lord Diplock's proposal for terrorist cases to be tried by a High Court judge sitting without a jury (because of intimidation). As security allowed or politics demanded, successive Secretaries of State continued to 'phase out' internment. But two years later – though Lord Gardiner acknowledged that internment was providing 'a recruiting agency and a school for terrorists with all expenses paid,' and that it created 'a myth of repression which is becoming part of the terrorist legend' – he declined to say when it should end. Violence was widespread, the future unpredictable; Government must decide.

Mr Merlyn Rees ended internment in December 1975, announced that there would be no 'special category' for crimes subsequently committed, decided that terrorism must be dealt with through the courts, and therefore established the 'primacy of the police,' since policemen, not soldiers, are trained to gather evidence.

But the propaganda battle has continued, since the IRA and its apologists are not concerned with civil liberties or legal reform, but with victory in their terrorist campaign. With the courts taking over from internment, yet no civilian witnesses prepared to risk murder or maiming, the police rely chiefly on confessions. New allegations of ill-treatment of suspects in custody led to the Bennett inquiry, which found some cases manufactured, but others true. The result was stricter interrogation procedures, fewer confessions and fewer convictions. Terrorism has continued, though at a lower level.

Now the wheel has come full circle: the IRA and, increasingly, Catholic politicians reject the 'Diplock courts' (though similar no-jury courts operate in the Republic). That rejection is made the excuse for the hunger strikes and the campaign for political status.

On that issue, as on others, the Republic's own attitude is ambiguous. A British Army intelligence report in 1978 made clear that victory against the IRA was impossible while the Republic provided 'the classic safe haven so essential to any successful terrorist movement,' and pointed particularly to freedom from extradition for crimes committed in the North.

Not only is this a grave practical handicap in the fight against terrorism. It also provides apparent justification from Dublin for the IRA's demand for political status, for the excuse given by the Irish Supreme Court for refusing extradition is that IRA men are charged with 'a political offence or an offence connected with a political offence.'

Much is made in Dublin of the special relationship with Mrs Thatcher, of the search for closer links with Britain. Faced with a campaign of terror and murder by an organisation the Irish Government has made illegal, Britain ought to receive greater support from Dublin in this matter. Is extradition still unthinkable? Or, failing that, is detention in both North and South of a small number of IRA leaders, known to be responsible for this long-drawn-out campaign, also unthinkable?

If the answer to both these questions is, as we suspect, 'Yes,' then the talks with Dublin on friendship and co-operation are hypocritical posturing, an offence to the memory of more than 2,000 people who have died in Northern Ireland in the past 12 years. Mrs Thatcher ought not to continue the talks without raising these matters again. The Republic is not behaving as a friendly neighbour should. *(10.5.81)*

6.
In and Out of
the Oval Office

The New Sheriff
Martin Amis

Here is a brief and tendentious selection from the 60-odd films featuring the new President. The titles have been chosen for their redneck tang, the obviousness of their aspirations, and the impression they give of steep upward mobility.

'Cowboy from Brooklyn,' 'Angel from Texas,' 'Sergeant Murphy,' 'Swing Your Lady,' 'Brother Rat,' 'Brother Rat and a Baby,' 'Bedtime for Bonzo,' 'Hellcats of the Navy,' 'She's Working Her Way Through College,' 'The Winning Team,' 'Law and Order' and 'All American.'

'Bedtime for Bonzo,' in which Reagan co-starred with a baby chimpanzee, was one of his biggest hits. When a sequel, 'Bonzo Goes to College,' was offered to Reagan he turned it down – showing the probity and pragmatism on which the Western Alliance will learn to depend over the next four years. 'Who could believe a chimp could go to college?' asked Reagan sternly. 'Lacked credibility.'

In his screen heyday, Reagan was always the bluff good-guy, not too bright or too glib, but manly and dependable, a sound man to have on your side. As his career declined during the Fifties, though, Reagan found himself playing smaller and steadily more repulsive parts. Do you remember, for instance, the mottled mobster in 'The Killers,' roughing up Angie Dickinson and two-timing John Cassavetes?

Reagan would not now be President if he had continued down that road. There is no political future for the likes of Dan Duryea, Lee Van

Cleef, and all the other serial mass-murderers. When the news of the Reagan landslide came through, however, one was irresistibly reminded of a famous moment in a recent American horror film, 'The Shining,' when the crazed villain chops his way into the family apartment.

As it happened, Reagan's image didn't have time to become tarnished in American eyes. Towards the Sixties he prudently repaired to the homelier confines of the small screen. For three years Reagan was the genial and craggy front-man for the Western anthology series 'Death Valley Days.' He then had a much longer stint as MC and guest-star for 'General Electrics Theatre of the Air.' Part of his job was to tour the country giving stirring lectures.

This was Reagan's introduction to the mass-reassurance business. His highpoint on the circuit was a televised speech in praise of GE's latest product, the nuclear submarine. A trio of Californian businessmen were impressed by Ronnie's TV know-how. With their backing he ran for Governor.

Reagan's 'mastery of the medium' tells us as much about American television as it does about the President. In New York a TV technicians' strike threatened a blackout of the Democratic Convention. Had the strike gone through, it would have been doubtful whether the Convention could be said to have 'happened' at all. Carter would certainly have argued as much. The four nights of free air-time translated, willy-nilly, into a 15-point climb in the polls. You'd have thought that four nights of Carter (with his references to Hubert Horatio Hornblower, and so on) would have been the last thing the Democrats needed. But this is to misunderstand the place of TV in American life. It is, simply, the medium.

What is this mastery of Reagan's? It is a celebration of good intentions and unexceptional abilities. Reagan's most familiar pose is a kind of hammy bashfulness, a stoical dismay about his own talents and their sudden elevation. There is even something honest and naïve about his bodily movements, resembling the dignified, thumb-in-belt awkwardness of John Wayne. 'I'll never lie to you,' lied Carter in 1976, trying the same pose himself. Carter didn't dare repeat this act in 1980, against an opponent who had been playing the part for 50 years.

Meanwhile, it is not entirely frivolous to view the 1980 campaign as the outline of a vanished Reagan Western. Carter is the canting weakie who keeps the store. Anderson is the gesticulating frontier preacher who just holds up the action. But Reagan is the man who comes riding into town, his chin straight and true, not afraid to use his fists – well-prepared, if need be, to become the next sheriff of the free world.
(9.11.80)

Laid Back in the White House
Simon Hoggart

President Reagan is now, 12 weeks after he was shot, one of the most popular leaders America has had since the Second World War. His advisers are already talking about a second term, which means that he would quit the job at the age of 78. One Congressman I met said: 'What scares me is that this man is so popular that he could announce a nuclear war, and everyone would say "That's just great, Mr President".'

One secret of his popularity is his remarkable relaxation. Americans call it being 'laid back,' though a closer English translation might be 'lying down.' His team said that when they took office they would 'hit the ground running,' which they certainly have. Reagan himself hit the ground fast asleep.

Jimmy Carter used to get up at 5 a.m. Reagan's chief aides don't meet until 7.30, when the President is still snoozing. He turns up around 8.45 most days and, after a tough morning's decision-taking, goes back for a nap. If it's a working afternoon, which it often isn't, he'll be back in the Residence at six for some much-needed rest before facing a strenuous reception or dinner party. Then he's back home to greet the Sandman for the final visit of the day.

This hectic schedule has, of course, had to be toned down since the attempt on his life. He doesn't, for example, work quite so many afternoons, but the basic outline remains the same. It always has. During the election campaign, the hours between one and three were euphemistically listed as 'staff time.' It became quite a popular phrase. Mothers would call their children in of an evening, saying: 'C'mon honey, it's staff time.'

He is the first man for 20 years to make the Presidency a part-time job, a means of filling up a few of the otherwise blank days of retirement.

There is no evidence that the American people mind this. Reagan came to power promising to get the Government off the backs of the people, and he has begun with himself, getting on to his own back instead. Carter behaved like the school swot, who had to know everything and to read every memo and every briefing. He even used to read the list of people using the White House tennis court each day. Reagan, by contrast, doesn't read much at all. Memos to him are short and give the general gist of an argument or a position. Details are left to other people.

I called in at a Reagan Press conference to see at first hand the technique of government by somnambulism. It was fascinating. No

British politician would dare to try it.

It was only the third Press conference he has held since coming into office. Carter had one every fortnight for his first two years. One of those firm yet oily voices which sounds as if its owner gargled with a dry Martini every morning announced: 'Ladies and Gentlemen, the President of the United States!' and we all stood up.

Reagan himself looked a little shy, even unsure of himself, as if not quite certain why all these people were here. First he read out a statement which had clearly been written for him about the necessity of tax cuts. Some Congressional committees, he said sternly, were trying to get around the cuts. One committee had agreed to cut suppers at day care centres but had decreed that lunches could be served instead at supper time. This, he said, using a favourite word of the new Administration, was 'unconscionable,' which I suppose it is, unless you rely on the free meals.

The whole statement sounded uncharacteristically tough. The true Reagan emerged in the later questions. His most frequent answer, employed three times, was: 'Well, I don't really have the answer to that.' There's no way you can harry a man who simply admits that he doesn't know.

The folksiness can get a trifle wearing. At one Press conference he was asked a fairly hostile question about the effects of his policies on the poor. He asked: 'How can you say that about a sweet guy like me?' Another time he was asked if he had a message for the Russians. He replied: 'Roses are red, Violets are blue, Stay out of Poland, And El Salvador too.'

This kind of sophisticated global thinking has made some people wonder exactly what the Administration's foreign policy is, so last week he took the opportunity to fill us in. 'I am satisfied,' he announced, 'that we do have a foreign policy. Already I have met eight Heads of State and the representatives of nine other nations.' This, of course, scarcely amounts to a foreign policy, but then politicians the world over confuse meeting people with taking action.

When he was asked about his health, he looked genuinely pleased that someone should be interested. We inquired about gun control. Well, it turned out that he had had a 'very nice talk' with Senator Kennedy on this very topic. Did we know that there were some 20,000 gun control laws in the various states, and that some of the toughest were right here in the District of Columbia? But they hadn't stopped a fellow at the Hilton Hotel. This is no kind of answer, of course, but no one picked him up on it. You don't shoot at such kindly gents, whether they have come in to help with the gardening or are President of the United States.

This general air of a lovable old grandpop is carried into all his dealings. I talked to two people who had had separate meetings with him recently. One, a Democrat, said: 'The guy is really dumb. There are a whole lot of questions you ask him, and he does not know the answers. He has to be told.' The other man, a conservative, found him 'most impressive. He was full of jokes and anecdotes about the old Hollywood, and he put us completely at ease. We asked him a bunch of policy questions; some he answered very fully. Others he'd say: "I don't really know about this, but Ed does," and Ed would talk. You came away thinking: "The guy's all right".'

'Ed' is Edward Meese III, the White House counsellor, and one of the three or four most powerful men in America. He is the most important of the 'triumvirate' who quite simply are the Presidency during the long hours that Reagan is in bed. Meese has been with Reagan since the 1960s, when he joined him as legal secretary to the Governor of California. His views on almost everything, from the Communist menace to the urban poor, match Reagan's exactly.

His greatest passion is law enforcement. His idea of relaxing is to curl up at home with a good book and the police radio blasting out. Meese is powerful because he not only has the ear of the President, as and whenever the President is awake, but because two of the most powerful offices in the White House – the National Security Council and the Office of Policy Development (basically foreign and home affairs) – report to him.

The next most powerful man to Meese is James A. Baker III (these American dynasties seem to stop at IV; you never meet someone called Frank N. Furter XXVI). Baker's title is Chief of Staff, and he is nominally in charge of staff and organisation. In fact, he works on policy, where his opinions are especially valuable, because he is one of the tiny handful of people who actually understand how Washington works. It was Baker who persuaded Reagan to lift the Soviet grain embargo just in time to get votes from the farming states for the Budget. His reputation was made during the televised debates with Carter. Baker handed the candidate a small card marked 'chuckle,' and when Carter began criticising, Reagan chuckled and said: 'There you go again.' Amazingly, this was thought to be the key, brilliant answer of the campaign.

The third of the Big Three is Michael Deaver, who has no Roman numerals at all after his name and is thought to be the least significant. But he is a close friend of the Reagan family and is trusted, even loved, by both Reagan and Nancy. He manages the little details, some of them extremely little. For example, Vice-President George Bush changes his watch strap to match his suit. During the campaign, Deaver kept the small supply of straps to offer him.

The point about the Triumvirate is that, unlike Nixon's Haldeman and Erlichman, they are exceedingly nice. People seem to like them and to trust them, though whether they will when things start to get rough remains to be seen. Already some of the hardline right-wingers are beginning to grumble that Reagan is being led astray from the true path by his more pragmatic advisers. This is the familiar sound of extremists the world over getting ready to complain 'our policies didn't fail; they were never tried.'

Reagan himself is a committed right-winger who came to office determined to alter the whole structure of the American economy and American society. Yet the easy-going nature which made him so popular with the voters also means that he is perfectly capable of ignoring the right-wing's writ at any time. This gives his ideological backers, who at last thought they had their own man in the White House, occasional pause for thought.

One highly placed official who admires Reagan greatly said: 'For the first time since Eisenhower, we have a President who is not driven by a terrible demon inside himself. He doesn't have to prove anything to anybody. We're actually working with a guy who doesn't mind the fact that he is sometimes wrong, and I cannot tell you what a relief that is.' (21.6.81)

Nixon Comes to Town
Donald Trelford

Like a bad penny, former President Nixon turned up in town last week, fitting London between France and Spain on a promotion tour for his timely new book on World War Three.

His publisher, Lord Longford, anti-pornographer-royal and friend of the criminal classes, gave a dinner to honour the visit ('The Honorable Richard Nixon,' said the invitation) in the ballroom of the Hyde Park Hotel. Sir Charles Forte, the catering king, who owns both the hotel and the publishing firm, sat beaming on his left.

The assorted diplomats, tycoons, editors and other representatives of the demi-beau-monde were fed on the best that Trusthouse Forte could offer: Mousseline de Truite Saumonée Pol Roger and Noisettes d'Agneau Jussière, washed down with Graacher Domprobst Beeren-auslese 1976 and Chateau Montrose 1966. I sat between Margaret, Duchess of Argyll, and Colonel Jack Brennan, Nixon's self-styled

Chief of Staff. She was a vision in red gauze, diamonds and pearls, with a gold handbag and a sprained wrist. The Colonel wore black; no diamonds, no handbag.

The Duchess professed herself an unashamed admirer of the former President. 'I love the man, I love him,' she enthused. She told him so before dinner. 'Do you remember a crazy Englishwoman sending you cable after cable of support?' The former President thought hard. 'No,' he said finally, with characteristic wit, style and grace (and unwonted honesty).

The Duchess kept turning to me throughout Nixon's set speech with ecstatic stage whispers, like antiphonal responses. 'Ours is not just a Western alliance, but a global alliance,' said Nixon. 'He's awfully good, isn't he?' whispered the Duchess. 'We need to unite against terrorism – joint force, joint response,' said Nixon. 'Don't you love him, don't you love him?' trilled the Duchess.

Nixon's hazy rhetoric rolled on. 'The Russians don't want war' . . . [long pause] . . . 'but they want the world.' The Duchess was now beside herself. 'Kiss, kiss!' she cried. Nixon looked up in alarm. (Afterwards someone offered an explanation for this enigmatic cry. 'She was trying to say "Kiss-Kiss-Kissinger",' he suggested – perhaps to acknowledge the intellectual source of Nixon's remarks.)

Hers were not the only noble tributes. Lord Longford referred to 'President Nixon's wonderful book.' ('I'm glad they're calling him President,' the Duchess said.) Longford went on (rather ambiguously, I thought): 'A child could understand the message of this book, but it would take a person of considerable intelligence to interpret the message.' Nixon, he revealed, 'is an established favourite with the British public.'

Lord 'Alf' Robens, former head of the Coal Board and much else – and once proposed as a leading candidate for the Boardroom of Great Britain Limited – waxed lyrical. 'After a long day,' he declared, Mr Nixon appeared before us 'with a freshness as though it was bright morning.' And indeed the famous ski-jump nose, the Herblock jowls and the five o'clock shadow were strangely muted, as though his features had been drained of definition by the loss of power. The teeth looked different.

Lord Alf was 'lost in admiration,' he said, at Nixon's 'outstanding career.' He had achieved 'more than any statesman anywhere in the world.' By this he evidently meant things like ending the Vietnam war and opening the door to China – rather than, say, other aspects of his presidency.

Part of Nixon's appeal to the audiences who still turn out for him – people who, given the choice, would probably prefer a strong bad man to a weak good man in power – is the contrast with the hapless Jimmy

Carter. When the loyal toast was extended to 'The President of the United States,' a bluff businessman added loudly: 'God help him!'

As if in reproof, the telephone rang outside. It was the White House on the line. Colonel Brennan took the message: 'It's Brzezinski. Shall I talk to him or will you?' The ex-President pondered this grave decision. A finger shot out firmly: '*You* talk to him. But I'm available.'

Eventually Nixon went out himself, followed by his bodyguard in a blue buttoned-down shirt, a Special Branch man with a fat cigar, Colonel Brennan – and a buzz of excited speculation. Something momentous was clearly going on.

When they returned, Nixon took the microphone. 'You may be wondering why I went outside.' Irreverent titters in the audience. 'Not for the usual reason. It was Mr Brzezinski from the White House to tell me personally that a new Secretary of State has been appointed – Senator Ed Muskie of Maine.'

Already Nixon looked a different man, more alert, less crumpled. Plugged in again to the power supply, he began visibly to shine. The old adrenalin was on the move.

Next to me, Colonel Brennan began to unwind. For a moment he had thought it was the President himself on the line, since Nixon kept saying 'Sir.' He had worked for Nixon for 12 years and had no complaints. 'He's been good to me. I don't argue with people who disagree.'

I confessed that my wife was among those who disagree. She disapproved of my going to the dinner. He sympathised sadly: 'It's always the women. Whenever we get the old guys together for a Watergate reunion, it's the wives who try to stop them. Kalmbach made us pretend we'd bumped into him accidentally.'

Did they still meet, then? 'When we can. We saw Bob Haldeman recently – he's doing well in business now. No, not Ehrlichman – he's dropped right out. Did you know Chuck Colson was in London this week to preach a sermon? I hear he's gone to Ireland.'

An air of unreality was taking over, like a buzz in the ears. Emma Soames was ushered into the presence: Alice in Wonderland meets the Mad Hatter. Nixon suggested that her father might mediate with the Ayatollah (an intriguing prospect), presumably on the grounds that handling one Third World nut is much like handling another and that Iran is a place much like Zimbabwe (or 'Boogieland,' as Ms Soames recently described it in *Tatler*).

Nixon fielded questions from the audience, mostly slow lobs that gave him a chance to demonstrate his genuine grasp of foreign affairs. Then a bearded man from the *Sunday Express* tried to bowl a faster one. Lord Longford's voice cut in loudly: 'I don't know who this chap is, do you?'

Finally, Lord Robens rose to give fulsome thanks. 'It's almost,' he said wistfully, 'as if you were a candidate.' Suddenly, the creeping sense of unreality was overpowering. Time to go home. *(4.5.80)*

The Man from Nowhere
Anthony Holden

. . . and this time it vanished quite slowly, beginning with the end of the tail, and ending with the grin, which remained some time after the rest of it had gone.

Like Lewis Carroll's Cheshire cat, Jimmy Carter's presidency lingers only in the shape of that grin, defiant in defeat, self-confident still beneath the landslide. The rest of it was snuffed out with unexpected brutality at the climax of the year of the interminable campaign.

The story of 1980 is that of the most protracted, laborious and expensive disappearing act in American political history. The image of the year – symbolic, in harsh hindsight, of the Carter presidency – has to be those eight burnt-out helicopters spreadeagled across the Iranian desert.

As the dust settles on a radically altered political landscape, one central truth is already clear. Carter proved above all what Americans do *not* want their President to be. Their dramatic repudiation of him says as much about the office as about the man.

On paper Carter can (and will) muster a passable list of accomplishments. In foreign policy: above all the Camp David accords – an historic, if now faltering, step towards Middle East peace. The Panama Canal treaties, the normalisation of relations with China. The emphasis on human rights abroad.

Biggest plus: keeping American troops out of combat. Biggest minus: failure to secure Senate ratification of the second Strategic Arms Limitations Treaty.

Achievements at home: development (at the fourth attempt) of a national energy policy, deregulation of business and industry, reorganisation of the civil service, even-handed judicial appointments, establishment of a separate Department of Education.

The list of failures, alas, is considerably longer. Inflation, inherited from Gerald Ford at 4.7 per cent, stood early this year at an annual rate of 18. Unemployment, which he promised to 'cut in half,' stands where it was at eight per cent. Other 1976 campaign promises, all unfulfilled: to balance the Budget, reform the tax system, cut down the bureaucracy, reduce Federal spending, institute a national health insurance programme, reduce defence spending.

Abroad, the Carter presidency became a familiar and sorry saga of vacillation, inconsistency and U-turns, best characterised perhaps by his naïve astonishment that Brezhnev might dare to tell him a fib. An 'unacceptable' Soviet combat brigade in Cuba was meekly accepted. The Russians, despite the anger of Olympic athletes, remained in Afghanistan, and the US hostages in Tehran.

Americans, deeply humiliated by their impotence against Iran, were also acutely aware of the murmurs of discontent from Europe. Chancellor Schmidt became something of a hero for his open contempt of Carter's unpredictability. Mrs Thatcher, whatever she was doing to the British economy, was seen as displaying positively Churchillian qualities of leadership.

All occasions informed against Jimmy Carter, however ruthlessly he used the incumbency for personal electoral advantage. His shoddy autumn campaign insulted the voters' intelligence, reminding them only how much he wanted to remain President, without explaining why he deserved to.

History, at first flush, seems likely to bracket Carter with Herbert Hoover, remembered 50 years on as a well-intentioned flop. A kinder fate would cast him as an accident of history, elected from nowhere amid post-Watergate disenchantment to a job he simply couldn't master.

Was he elected to a job, as his apologists argue, that has grown too big for any man? Carter cannot be held to have proved that. It is not the fault of the office that this President behaved with such misguided arrogance towards Congress, or that he chose to entrust such power to rude Georgian mediocrities.

Nor can any President hope to function effectively while remaining aloof from the mainstream of his party, while failing to preserve the broad coalition which elected him. The insular, self-obsessed Jimmy Carter was his own worst enemy, so rapt in the agonies of making decisions as to ignore the more important agonies of getting them implemented.

No President, moreover, can carry the people with him unless he can communicate a grand and common vision. If Carter had such a vision, such a political philosophy – which must remain in doubt – he certainly couldn't communicate it. The man who began with fireside chats and phone-ins, bringing the presidency closer to the people, leaves office regarded as a cold fish, one of the most distant, least-known American leaders of recent memory.

In and Out of the Oval Office. 75

When his presidency was on its knees, in the summer of 1979, his remedy was to summon the readers of entrails to a mountain-top, then lecture the country about its supposed 'malaise.' He was at his most impressive, by contrast, in one-to-one conversation, displaying his mastery of the fine print of any available issue – at the level, in other words, of a skilled administrative aide, drafting memos of pros and cons for a more ideological master.

The Carter years, in short, provide archetypal proof that there is more to the art of governance than merely managing the Government.

President Reagan will be much less visible, less eager in his search for instant crises to discuss in grave tones on network TV. He will seek to restore to the White House, as to the nation, the air of grandeur and prestige it has surrendered in recent years.

This is all a clear part of Reagan's mandate from a nation in sombre conservative mood. Four short years after embracing Carter's brand of populism, America seeks a return to the imperial presidency, in style if not Nixonian substance.

This, ironically enough, is Jimmy Carter's immediate legacy. His place in history may ultimately depend on which, if any, of his accomplishments Ronald Reagan chooses to leave intact. *(28.12.80)*

Born-Again America
Martin Amis

Ronald Reagan, Jimmy Carter and John Anderson are all 'born-again' Christians. They are not alone. One in three Americans take the lesson of Nicodemus in John 3: 'Unless one is born anew, he cannot see the kingdom of God.' The latest surge in Evangelical activism is entirely new. Like so much else in America, it is to do with money, power and, above all, television.

There are 36 wholly religious TV stations in America (and 1,300 radio stations). Jerry Falwell's 'Old-Time Gospel Hour' is seen on 374 stations nationwide, outstripping 'Dallas.' Pat Robertson's daily devotional chat-show has more viewers than Johnny Carson. The TV preachers turn over billions of tax-free dollars every year. (Falwell alone raises more than a million dollars a week, $300,000 of which goes on buying more air-time). Their mailing-lists are kept on guarded computer-tapes. The electronic ministries have a combined congregation of 115 million people, attending every week.

The political wing of the movement has developed only in the last 15 months. Its names are legion: Moral Majority Inc., Religious Round-table, Christian Voice, Christian Voters' Victory Fund, Campus Crusade for Christ, Christians for Reagan – all loosely grouped under the pro-family banner. American religion has always been popular rather than hieratic in character, concerned not with theology but morality; and it has always, until now, been politically quietist, with low registration and a tendency to vote for the incumbent. The Evangelical message is plain – 'out of the pews and into the polls.' 'Not voting is a sin,' says Falwell. 'Repent of it.'

'And the Lord turned to him and said, "My precious child, I never left you in your hours of trial. When you look back along the pathway of your life and see only one pair of footprints in the sand – why, that was when I carried you . . .".'

This wasn't the ghost of the Reverend Billy Sunday: it was a close-to-tears Ronald Reagan, winding up his address to the 15,000 Evangelicals (10,000 pastors, 5,000 lay) at the Reunion Arena in Dallas. Reagan is taking these people seriously all right: he has hired a Moral Majority operative to liaise with the born-again community. 'Religious America is awakening, perhaps just in time,' said Reagan hopefully. He praised the freedom fighters of Poland and their leader the Pope – 'just the son of simple farm folk.' He tied himself up in knots to pronounce 'Solly Neetsin' and his friend 'Archie Pelaygo.' He spoke of the dream of all true Americans to attain 'that shining city on the hill.' But this was mild, hammy stuff compared to the shoot-'em-dead oratory of the electronic preachers.

The Rev. Jerry Falwell is the most powerful, most convincing, most committed – and the least vulgar – of all these electronic Evangelicals. He is without the messianic stridency of James Robison (with his talk of 'prophets' and 'new Jeremiahs'), and without the frank hucksterism of Pat Robertson. Falwell will last when the others are too bored, frightened or mad to continue usefully on the political wing. And if you ask *him* about his colonial mansion in Lynchburg, Virginia, his private aeroplane and airport, his tax-avoiding loans within his corporation, his bodyguards and gofers, he will tell you that material wealth is 'God's way of blessing people who put Him first.'

'I know Jerry Falwell since he was knee-high to a duck,' said the old Lynchburger in the bar (which took some finding). 'Knew his daddy too, biggest bootlegger ever hit this State. I seen Jerry Falwell so drunk he couldn't stand up – 30 years back, must be. But don't you trash Jerry now, you hear? Bet he earns more money than you ever will.'

In and Out of the Oval Office. 77

Thomas Road Baptist Church is more like a cinema than a place of worship, with its scalloped stalls sloping downwards to the stage, and the TV cameras wedged into the balcony. I mingled unobtrusively (I hoped) with the 4,000 Lynchburg faithful. Everyone opened their much-thumbed, much-underscored Bibles. It was 7 p.m. The two-hour service began.

We memorised a verse from the Book of Psalms, slyly invited by a Falwell sidekick to insert the names of Carter and Reagan wherever we thought it appropriate: 'God is the judge: he putteth down one and setteth up the other.' We heard a spiritual from an Isley Brothers-style trio (among the few dark faces in the house) and a squawky ballad from five local sisters on violin. Falwell preached with avuncular cheer – don't listen to the media, God loves you, my little wife, Judgement Day we'll all be bigshots, sometimes you're up, sometimes you're down.

A pro-family propaganda film was screened. Doubters filed up and then filed back, all born again. Then Falwell asked us to join in little groups of two and three, and pray together, out loud.

Until that moment I had been performing a nervous, if quite passive, imitation of a devout Virginian. When people jotted down apophthegms, I took notes; when they sang hymns, I mimed along; when they prayed for salvation, I prayed for a Winston King Size and a large gin and tonic. But suddenly the young man on my left, who had kindly shared his Bible with me during the readings, turned to me and said: 'You wanna pray together?' – and I, for some reason, said: 'Surely.'

We hunkered down, hands on brows. 'You wanna go first?' he asked. 'No. You go first,' I said. And as he stuttered on about the Lord helping America in its hour of etc., etc., I thought of the burly young champions of Christ all about me, and of my own blasphemous intrusion. In five minutes, I thought, I'll be dangling from the rafters – and quite right too.

The voice beside me trailed off with some remarks about Sue-Ann's rheumatism and Joe-Bob's mortgage; I turned to see his bashful, expectant face. In rocky Virginian I babbled out something about our people in Tehran and the torment they must feel in their hour of etc., etc. My prayermate wished he had thought of this too. We squeezed our frowning foreheads and nodded together for a very long time.

Falwell is innocuous in his home pulpit, smiling, sensible, protective: he understands the American spiritual yearning, which is the yearning to belong. But my first reaction when I met and talked to him, back in Dallas, was a momentary squeeze of fear. With his people milling about him in the futuristic foyer of the Hyatt Regency Hotel, he reminded me of the standard villain of recent American fiction and film: the corporation man.

78. In and Out of the Oval Office

Jerry Falwell (born in 1933; born again in 1956) is six foot and then some, with the squashy-nosed face of the friendly policeman. He wore a suit of some incredibly plush and heavy material.(taffeta? theatre curtains? old surplices?), adorned with a small gold brooch in the characters of Jesus Christ, the terminal 't' stretched into a cross. (The same thing happens to the 't' in VOTE on his supporters' banners.) A huge aide brought us coffee. We began.

Doggedly I began to rehearse the obvious liberal objections to his platform, mentioning that he had called the Equal Rights Amendment 'a vicious attack on the monogamous Christian home.' 'That's right,' he said blandly. 'I don't believe in equal rights for women. I believe in superior rights for women.' (This is consistent enough: Falwell has always wanted to kick women upstairs). 'You know, the Women's Lib movement? Many of them are lesbians, you know. They're failures – probably married a man who didn't treat them like a human being,' he added, completing the machocentric circle.

'If you were President,' I said, eliciting a brief smirk, 'how would you stop people being homosexual?'

'Oh, they've got to live, have jobs, same as anybody else. We don't want any Khomeini thing here. It's the sin not the sinner we revile. It's anti-family. When God created the first family in that Garden, he created Adam and Eve, not Adam and Steve.

'Besides, I want influence, not power. But I want global influence. We can't buy more air-time in America, no way. But we'll start buying it worldwide. South America, Europe, Asia. . . .'

His aides signalled. I asked my final question.

'Yes, sir, every word, quite literally, from Genesis to Revelations, which says there will soon be nuclear holy war over Jerusalem after which Russia will be a fourth-rate power and Israel will astonish the world. Nice talking to you. Now if you'll excuse me, I have a radio show to attend. . . .'

Easy prey, perhaps. British liberals enjoy being panicked by commotion on the American Right; we also tend to indulge our vulgar delight in American vulgarity. Although the Evangelicals have made an appeal to something old and fierce in the native character, it will take years to develop this into any kind of consensus. The movement constitutes a genuine revolution from below, however, and will have to be heeded. To dismiss the beliefs of the Evangelicals is to disdain the intimate thoughts of ordinary people.

Nor is their critique of American society contemptible in itself. One of Falwell's TV specials is called 'America, You're Too Young To Die.' It shows leathery gays necking in Times Square, sex-aid emporia, child pornography, aborted foetuses in soiled hospital trays. A predictably alarmist collage, certainly. But some of us who have been born only once find plenty that is cheerless here, and fail to buy the 'humanist' package entire.

'All the ills from which America suffers can be traced back to the teaching of evolution,' wrote William Bryan in 1924. 'It would be better to destroy every other book ever written, and save just the first three verses of Genesis.' The anti-intellectual content in Evangelical feeling is, by definition, a source of pride to its leaders. But it will either ruin or deform the movement eventually. No book but the Bible; Genesis or Darwin, one or the other. This is why the movement will have to be contested. This is why the movement is so wide-open, so abjectly vulnerable, to authoritarian thought. *(21.9.80)*

80. In and Out of the Oval Office

7.
Worlds Apart

The Old Men in the Kremlin
Edward Crankshaw

Too often and too easily, hypnotised by sheer quantity, we think of Russia as an unfettered giant; her Government's freedom to move in any direction it likes inhibited only by fear of nuclear incineration.

In fact, like every other country in the world, she is the prisoner of her own history, traditions, preconceptions, immemorial fears. Perhaps *more* than any other country, because Russia's history has been so special to her, her traditions so ingrown, her preconceptions so deliberately exalted into articles of faith, her fears so ancient and frequently well founded.

Certainly the Government of Russia, more than any other, shivers at even the most distant prospect of any departure from the status quo, sitting on the lid so heavily that it takes an explosion on the scale of the 1917 Revolution to bring about any effective change. Even then, when the dust has settled it is soon discovered (thankfully?) that ancient customs have not died.

One of the troubles with Russia is that almost any useful change in the status quo is bound to be giving something up: so often her ingrown habit of taking hold of more than she can comfortably manage, simply because if she does not somebody else may, produces a situation in which the slightest change of grip means that something escapes. This is not to be borne! So the grip is not changed, even when it hurts.

At the same time the age-old principle of over-insurance, which drives her internally to push absurdly extended frontiers ever farther outwards, continues to operate in an unco-ordinated and opportunist manner (which she invariably seeks to rationalise as some sort of a crusade), making that grip still more convulsive.

There is some excuse for this. The vast bulk of Russia, the Soviet Empire, on the map so frightening to Western eyes, looks very different when you are sitting in the middle of it. Then you are conscious not of protective bulk but only of an extravagant and terrible length of highly vulnerable frontier.

To be in Moscow, as I was, when Hitler had sliced through that frontier and watch on the map the sinister black arrows marking the armoured spearheads of the German advance snaking ever closer, with no natural obstacles in their way, until they were actually beginning to curl round the city itself, was to understand something of the depth of the compulsion to push that frontier away, even if this made the land still harder to defend.

In the light of Russia's past the only thing new or revolutionary about the march into Afghanistan was that we allowed it to happen. Ever since the days of the wretched Tsar Paul, there have been Russians in high places who have hankered after control of that wild country, the gateway to India – and there have been others, more influential, who have said enough was enough. Until lately, Britain put up a warning notice on that gateway; but this has been taken down, and it was only to be expected that sooner or later Moscow would be moved to gild the lily by 'making sure' of Kabul – whether as a vaguely defensive move against nameless dangers from Iran or Pakistan, or as a potentially useful jumping-off ground for further adventures, I imagine Mr Brezhnev himself would be hard put to it to say.

In the light of Russia's past, also, it is clear that as the old, old men in the Kremlin contemplate the goings-on in Poland and wonder what on earth to do, they must be visited by a sad sense of *déja vu*. The great Lenin himself burnt his fingers over Poland in the early days of the Workers' Paradise, while Stalin, never an optimist, seems really to have believed that he had destroyed Polish independence once and for all when he murdered practically the entire Officers' Corps in Katyn Forest and elsewhere – and then invited the Germans to massacre the Home Army, the Resistance Army, in Warsaw.

But in 1956 the Poles bobbed up again, and Khrushchev (or his advisers) knew enough about history to realise that Soviet tanks could not smash the Poles as quickly as they could smash the Hungarians, or quietly subdue them, as they were later to subdue the Czechs. Brezhnev and his advisers still know that.

This does not mean that they might not decide that a destructive combination of civil and national war is the lesser of two evils. It does mean that they are having to think very hard indeed – not theoretically and irresponsibly in a void, which comes naturally to them, but practically and with reference to an immediate issue – the sort of thing which goes against the grain of these incorrigible doctrinaires.

So although there is nothing to stop them crushing Poland, as Hitler crushed her 41 years ago, and Tsar Alexander II before that in 1863, and Nicholas I before that in 1830, and Catherine the Great before that in the eighteenth century, they know that they would be facing a nation in arms, that the fighting would be bitter and perhaps protracted, costly, *and very close to home* – that to invite the East Germans to fight Poles would (there is no other way of putting it) bring the house down: the house being the Warsaw Pact.

Even without East Germany, Russian intervention would bring the house down anyway. The bogus fabric of the Warsaw Pact would be in tatters. I say bogus because the Warsaw Pact exists only, as it were, by courtesy of ourselves. We imagine it. What on earth are all these peoples, held together by the Soviet Army, supposed to have in common except mutual hatred? And the mutual hatred of the Russians and the Poles is something special: even that free and liberal spirit, the great poet Pushkin, was tainted by it.

Of course the Soviet Army is all lined up and ready to move at a signal from Moscow: it is no good thinking about using force if you are not in a position to apply it when needed (a lesson we have still to learn). But, the more fire-eating marshals notwithstanding, I don't think the signal will be given unless and until Brezhnev sees the very foundations of the Communist order, the security police, being seriously threatened. If that happens it will.

The trouble is that Russia cannot take Poland without reducing it to the condition it was in after the agonies of 1863, and Brezhnev knows it. He may be compelled to do this if the Poles can't stop in time. His tougher and sillier advisers even now may urge him, hoping that the West will undertake the feeding of the Poles (Moscow certainly cannot) once the Soviet marshals have had their fun and the country is in ruins. I doubt it. Russia would be left a moral leper, with a ruined 'grand alliance' and a crippling economic liability.

This is the sort of thing I mean by Russian vulnerability. The Soviet Union is in such a pickle with a limping economy (one of the differences between Russia and us is that we can sometimes publicly recognise our failures; the Russians cannot), shortages of the most elementary foodstuffs, a dead hand of a political system, and the appalling burden of armaments, apparently considered necessary to show how up to date they are, and to stare America, Western Europe and China in the face. To what purpose? Even Mr Brezhnev must sometimes ask that question. *(7.12.80)*

Red Garbo's Last Scene
Jonathan Mirsky

Sex, Madame Mao once observed, is initially interesting, but what really endures is political power. That was in 1972.

Now Madame Mao, in the words of the official indictment, is merely 'Jiang Qing, female, 67, of Zucheng county, Shandong province. Member of the Tenth Central Committee of the Communist Party of China and its Political Bureau prior to her arrest. In custody.'

In custody, but still centre-stage at Peking's Special Court. Centre-stage because of the amazing contrast between her public persona and her private life.

At the height of the Cultural Revolution, it is now known, the fervent advocate of revolutionary theatre was memorising (in an English she could not understand) Garbo's lines from 'Queen Christina.' Dressed by day in a Liberation Army uniform, she slept between silk sheets in her private jet.

The limit was reached, as the Chinese people have learned, when the woman who summoned up millions of screaming disciples confided in 1972 to the American historian Roxanne Witke that 'the masses' terrified her. The present leadership will never forgive Jiang Qing's 60 hours of intimate revelations to a foreigner about her life at the top.

A complex woman – victim, actress, demagogue – Jiang Qing is also a murderess. Even allowing for the rhetorical hyperbole of the prosecution, the evidence of her guilt is clear. Horrifying in scope and chilling in detail, Jiang Qing's worst acts emerged in the Special Court from a torrent of signed documents, tapes and telephone logs whose authenticity she has hardly contested.

As the tapes show, Jiang Qing was responsible for the events leading to the death of President Liu Shaoqi and other leaders. Nor can there be much doubt, from the evidence produced at the trial, that she bore a heavy share of responsibility for the fate of thousands of lesser people who died or were falsely imprisoned during her years of power. Included in their number are thousands of teachers, scientists and doctors whose convictions led in many cases to suicide.

On 6 October 1976 it all ended. The woman who had said, 'I want to maintain my political youth forever,' was arrested with the rest of the Gang of Four.

Mao had 'gone to meet Marx' (his euphemism for death) in September, and the coup was directed by his successor, Hua Guofeng, once the Gang's Minister of State Security, who is nearing the end of his own long slide from the top.

Jiang Qing has always riveted those close to her. Even at 68 she still makes audiences catch their breath. (In Nanking, I heard a Chinese audience gasp and pull up its chairs with a screech when she made her first televised court-room entry).

Already in 1944, the *New York Times* correspondent at Yanan, Mao's wartime headquarters, described Jiang Qing as 'a Chinese painting come to life,' while the writer Robert Payne, who met her in 1945 when she was 31, 'realised that her face possessed more beauty and expression than the face of the considerably more famous Mme Chiang Kai-shek.' Even her critics today note her smooth skin and flashing eyes.

But her 'towering crimes' apart, Jiang Qing appears in Peking's Special Court saddled with China's traditionally most disabling characteristics: she is a woman, an actress, and the consort of a ruler who cast off his legitimate wife to take up with a temptress. What was – and remains – unacceptable was her female independence.

Despite her early membership of the Party (1933) and her eight-month imprisonment the following year by Chiang Kai-shek's police, she never became respectable. The best she could do for decades was to be an obscure fourth wife, as the strait-laced Party demanded. Only after 27 years of marriage to Mao did she make her first public speech.

Her father was a carpenter and cart-builder from whom her mother fled when Li Jin (Jiang Qing's real name) was 13. By then 73, her father was a desperate and violent man who broke one of his daughter's teeth as she shielded her mother from being beaten with a spade.

It was a frightening childhood. She remembered wandering about in the dark at the age of five searching for her mother. Also remembered were the daily gunshots as innocent people were shot against the city wall, and the decapitations signalled by rounds of applause from 'the rich.'

But by 1929, and for the next eight years, Jiang Qing (then known as Lan Ping, 'Blue Apple') had made her way into the urban world of acting, teaching, observing factory conditions for the YWCA, and Communism.

It is in that period, centring on Shanghai, that her darkest secrets lurk: of numerous lovers and husbands, of despair as an actress, and of humiliation at the hands of the intellectual establishment.

Witness after witness, including her elderly servant from long ago, came into the Peking court to link the beatings and killings of the Cultural Revolution to Jiang Qing's years in Shanghai.

Once during her trial, faced with accusations from a Shanghai intellectual, Jiang Qing suddenly shouted that he was a spy. After refusing to be silent, she was bundled from the chamber. She had earlier been ejected after calling the whole court 'spies.' But generally she preserved her composure.

What has even more maddened the authorities has been her not unsuccessful efforts to link herself tightly to Chairman Mao.

She had begun living with him in 1937, after he packed off wife number three (a soldier and veteran of the Long March) to Moscow 'to get well.' (In the Fifties, Jiang Qing was herself to languish for years in Russian sanatoria, undergoing painful tests and treatments for mysterious ailments.)

The Party, displeased by Mao's marital vagaries, decreed that his new wife was to remain apart from all official activities. From time-to-time after 1949 she attempted forays into the politics of China's cultural life, and found her way blocked. Only in Mao's last decade, when he required allies for his Cultural Revolution, did the Chairman free Jiang Qing to display the powers which, unseen, had surged within her.

It was then, in the Sixties, that her husband's distrust and envy of intellectuals found a ready instrument in Jiang Qing's resentment. Neither the Shanghai intellectuals, who thought of her only as a pretty face from the northern provinces, nor the Party hierarchy, had ever respected her.

She 'fixed' them throughout the Cultural Revolution, in their dozens, hundreds and thousands. About 1,000 relatives and associates of an ex-husband were persecuted for knowing too much about Lan Ping, the Shanghai actress.

Like Mao, Jiang Qing seized the hour and the means to crush her enemies. Her past penetrated her present. The violence of her childhood, her loneliness as an actress and as the Chairman's consort, her fear of the Party's scorn and, probably, of her husband's penchant for eliminating those closest to him, all underpinned Jiang Qing's dramatic flair and political convictions. She admired and studied Han and Tang empresses of early Chinese history, ex-consorts who rose to individual eminence.

Now the Party, embarrassed by its role in the Cultural Revolution, and unsure of how far to lower Mao from his plinth, is confronted by the Garbo-loving daughter of a carpenter, an actress who ran off with its Chairman and, increasingly deranged, eliminated many of its members.

Mao Tsetung wrote to Jiang Qing in 1976: 'You could reach the top. If you fail you will plunge into a fathomless abyss. Your body will shatter. Your bones will break.'

The prosecution has demanded her execution. In China this usually means a bullet from a pistol in the back of the head. *(4.1.81)*

86. Worlds Apart

Hero of the Lenin Shipyard
Mark Frankland

Like many of the best heroes, there was something mysterious about Lech Walesa's first appearance.

On 14 August 1980, the early shift at the Lenin shipyard in the Baltic port of Gdansk went on strike demanding higher wages – and a monument to the workers killed on the Baltic coast during the suppression of strikes in 1970.

The news from Gdansk alarmed the Polish Government. Strikes had broken out all over the country in a quite unco-ordinated way since meat prices had been raised on 1 July, but most of them had been settled easily enough with promises of more money.

Gdansk was different. The authorities knew that workers there were angry about bad living conditions. They also knew that the memory of the 1970 killings gave that anger a special bitterness.

Not the least of the Government's worries, though at first this may not have been so well understood, was the fact that later on that August morning a man in a nondescript grey suit, open shirt and sandals had climbed over the shipyard wall.

He was at first glance not a daunting figure, rather slight of build and with a heavy moustache hiding a withdrawn lower lip. But when he climbed on to an excavator to interrupt the shipyard director who was trying to get the men back to work, he was immediately accepted as the leader.

Few people in Poland outside Gdansk and a small circle of intellectual dissidents in Warsaw who published an illegal (because uncensored) workers' paper had then heard of Lech Walesa. He became a public figure and a budding hero only 17 days later, when he appeared on Polish television with a deputy Prime Minister for the signing of the Gdansk agreement, whose first points created a potential revolution in the Soviet bloc by recognising the Polish workers' right to form free trade unions.

A rosary round his neck and a huge ballpoint pen topped by a model of the Polish Pope John Paul II in his hand, Walesa was not the sort of person Poles were used to seeing on their television screens. He sounded different, too, saying in his rapid, almost stuttering, way that the two sides had agreed because they had both talked 'as Poles talk to Poles.'

His openly displayed Catholicism and patriotism and his nimble manner at once delighted people. A few weeks later a Polish Catholic weekly, writing in a new and freer atmosphere, tried to analyse

Worlds Apart. 87

Walesa's popularity and decided that 'the secret lies in the fact that he is a "worker," but at the same time a "little knight," unimpressive only in appearance.'

There is no questioning his working class credentials. He was born in 1943 and left school at 16 to become an electrician. What is interesting about those dates is that they make him – like most of the young working class created by post-war industrialisation – a true child of Communist Poland.

Like many Polish workers, he accepts the basics of the system he grew up in. 'In our country,' he said recently, 'things are simpler than they are in the West, because we all form the State and we are closer to responsibility. There is no one between us and the State, no factory owner.'

But this apart, the remarkable thing about Walesa and the Poles of his generation is how little influenced they were by those decades of propaganda reinforced, intermittently, by pressure and sometimes terror.

He seems always to have been a bit of a rebel. When he was an eight-year-old schoolboy, a priest, shocked by the way the young Walesa expressed forcible views of his own, warned him he would end up in prison. Since that time, he says, 'when I have seen something wrong, I have fought.' But this strong character fits into Catholicism as though it were the most natural thing in the world.

His bodyguard, a benign-looking bruiser who fought in the wartime resistance, wakes him up at six every morning in his flat in a working class suburb of Gdansk so they can attend early Mass. Both men wear on their lapels miniatures of the ikon of the Black Madonna of Czestochowa, Poland's most holy image.

Walesa openly reveres Cardinal Wyszynski, the Primate of Poland, and speaks of him as 'a man who is forbidden to lie, who must know the truth and must show it to others.' Part of the attraction of the Church for a man like Walesa is its truth-telling in contrast with a Government that in the past entangled itself in half-truths, evasions and lies.

The experience and beliefs Walesa shares with Polish workers explain the ease with which he talks to them and their trust in him. But this does not explain why he and not someone else became the leader of Solidarity.

It was partly thanks to his experience in Gdansk. He was working at the Lenin shipyard at the time of the December 1970 strike and shootings and was a junior member of the strike committee set up then.

Fighting against the erosion of the concessions made then to the workers eventually cost him his job at the shipyard. He was sacked from two more jobs, because he was too active and outspoken, and was out of work when the 1980 strike began. Eventually, with a handful of other workers who are now also leaders of Solidarity, he set up an embryo free trade union for the Baltic Coast.

The authorites gave them a hard time, but this has marked Walesa less than the others. He understands compromise. Some of them believe the Government responds only to unyielding toughness.

It was during these years that Walesa came into touch through the illegal workers' paper *Robotnik* with a wider world. Walesa is by no stretch of the imagination an intellectual. He doesn't read much. But *Robotnik* was part of a loose society of intellectual dissidents grouped round KOR, the organisation set up to help workers arrested after more food price riots in 1976.

The result was that Walesa was, by last summer, both prepared to be a workers' leader and in Gdansk already recognised as one. But he was not prepared, nor for that matter was anyone else, for the speed of events. Six months ago he was, for the Gdansk police, a jobless trouble-maker. Today, he is the leader of two-thirds, perhaps more (Solidarity's statistics are still approximate) of Poland's 12 million blue and white collar workers. He has had a private meeting with Stanislaw Kania, Poland's Communist leader. He will soon have a private audience with the Pope.

His life has become bizarrely hectic. After the meeting with Kania, he rushed off to receive the leader of Japan's largest trade union grouping, to whom he announced that Poland could become another Japan. This is one of his favourite ideas. Another is that the West's riches are not good for it.

His wife, with six children to look after, finds that he brings home handfuls of strangers to breakfast after Mass, though these days he is often travelling round the country attacking crises with the (so far) wonder-working dash of a comic strip hero. His wit and skill at story telling help here, but so do his appeals to patriotism. 'Every one of us is first a Pole and only second a member of Solidarity.' A Walesa meeting usually ends with singing the national, and then the Polish Church, anthem.

The question is whether Walesa is more than 'a brilliant symbol' (the words of Jacek Kuron, KOR's leader). He is often criticised for his lack of interest in organisation, which did not matter in the dramatic days but arguably does now that the union is trying to consolidate.

He is the sort of man who either breaks off a conversation after five minutes or talks for two hours, chain-smoking cheap 'Sport' cigarettes. He seldom stays put when chairing a meeting. Secretaries despair of him. Colleagues have to fight for his attention.

And without developed ideas of his own, how can he guide Solidarity? At the moment he gets advice from many people, starting with the almost invisible counsellors assigned him by Cardinal Wyszynski and ending with far more radically minded young workers and intellectuals. 'Sometimes I must calm the radicals,' he says, 'and on other days encourage the timid.'

But what Walesa does have, and which is perhaps worth more than all his possible defects, is a very human common sense that is almost startling in a part of the world where the drums of ideology have been beaten so long and so hard.

'It is not a question of being Communist, or Socialist or Capitalist. What matters is that each system should be human, should be for the people and with the people.' There are the makings of a quiet revolution in that remark alone. *(28.12.80)*

Does Anyone Speak English?
Shyam Bhatia

My introduction to the Mujahiddin guerrillas of Afghanistan came when our convoy of 16 motor coaches and an oil tanker was ambushed just south of Ghazni City.

Eleven coaches managed to get away, but the rest, with the tanker, were stopped and set on fire by 15 Mujahiddin armed with rifles.

We passengers were then forced to run for about an hour across fields covered in thick snow, with the sound of gunfire in the background and the shouts, kicks, curses and rifle butts of the Mujahiddin encouraging us to move still faster.

By 1.30 p.m. we were all inside the mosque of Bakshir village, where we sat out an afternoon's bombing by Russian helicopter gunships on a search and destroy mission.

Thirty died in Bakshir that day and eight were injured.

I still have a piece of the shrapnel with me. It is triangular with a letter from the Russian alphabet like an English 'B' the wrong way round etched on one side.

The village council debated for three hours whether I should be killed or employed to teach English in the local school.

I was terrified when they were debating my future. I tried to remember the Lord's Prayer, but the words came out topsy-turvy.

Later that evening our group was divided into two. The larger number were sent off to the mountains under armed escort for 'deep interrogation.' A smaller group, consisting of three young Afghans and myself, now accepted as a reporter from a sympathetic country, were sent in another direction to see the Mujahiddin Commandant.

The three young Afghans were subsequently shot, I was told later, for belonging to the Communist Party.

From Bakshir we moved to the mosque of a neighbouring village and from there, soon after midnight, we tripped and ran across frozen fields until we reached Jamalkhel.

It was a hazardous journey because guns started firing behind us, helped by rocket flares that kept bursting ahead. It was the prelude to another day's bombing. Two local men were killed by bombs outside their houses.

We finally met the Commandant the next morning, in a small village near the town of Qaraba. A tall, impressive-looking man with a shaven head and long beard, he told me through an English-speaking interpreter that he was determined to 'finish' Communism in Afghanistan.

Later the Commandant, known as the Haji, pressed me to accept money to help me on my way to Kandahar. He also asked me if anything had been stolen from me. I said 'No,' although my personal bodyguard, Mohammed Ghoul, had helped himself to my wrist-watch and about 3,000 afghanis (about £30) 'for Allah's sake,' as he told me.

Ghoul, who later also took my transistor radio and a St Christopher medallion chain, was then deputed to leave me by the main road the next morning.

For most of the day we walked towards the road, stopping in the evening at his home village. There we ate long strips of dry bread with tea and slept in a small room near the family kitchen.

The next morning the family blindfolded me and led me across fields for about two hours. When the blindfold was removed I was told not to look behind but to walk straight ahead until I reached the main road.

I walked along the road for two hours before seeing a group of men clustered around a crane and two lorries. They were part of the mixed Russian-Afghan first battalion, based a short distance away in Azzakhel.

Two of the men had their guns trained on me as I approached. I raised my hands slowly and shouted: 'Do you speak English, for God's sake does anyone speak English?' *(2.3.80)*

Shooting Shadows in the Hindu Kush
Colin Smith

Shah Mohammed was as good as his word. On Whit Sunday, at precisely 6.30 p.m. local time, his guerrillas opened fire from about 800 metres at the piled stone sangars of the Afghan Army outposts which constitute the forward defences of the Barikot garrison in the Nuristan mountains of north-east Afghanistan. At first the Army were slow in replying. Then the tempo of their shooting picked up, like an engine spluttering into life.

Lazy blobs of red tracer floated across a dying sun. Anti-tank rockets exploded harmlessly against a rocky hillside. White smoke, something like the musketry clouds in eighteenth-century battle prints, billowed up around Shah Mohammed's positions as trees and scrub caught light. There was the occasional *bop bop bop* of automatic fire, but mainly from the Army because the Mujahiddin did not have the ammunition for such indulgences. Some mortars came into play, but the light was fading fast now, and it was difficult to see where they were exploding.

Abdur Rahman – named, I suppose, after that same Afghan king who converted the Nuristani kafirs to Islam at gunpoint in 1895 – leaned against a rock, strumming the stock of his Kalashnikov, as if he would rather be making love than war. He was well over average height, languid and darkly handsome. His headgear was a baseball cap with 'Tomorrow Awaits' stencilled on its long peak. He had learned his English at the Intercontinental Hotel in Kabul, where the guests had called him Johnny and he had eventually risen to working on the reception desk. But his body had become soft, and when he came back to his mountains it was hard going at first. Now he liked it.

He had found an old man to guide us to a ringside seat a hill away from Shah Mohammed and his men. From there we could observe the pyrotechnics in relative safety, since all Afghans are good shots and nobody was going to hit the wrong hill.

When we reached our perch, which was covered by some low bushes, we lit cigarettes and settled down to watch the shooting. A state of armed truce existed between the Barikot garrison and the Mujahiddin, occasionally broken by the sort of peppering we were now witnessing. The officers of the brigade stationed there previously had even been negotiating with the rebels, offering to withdraw and leave their heavy weapons behind, when the deal collapsed due to a schism typical among the rebel tribesmen where the scent of booty often destroys fragile alliances.

As it became dark, the firing subsided to a couple of single shots every other minute. It was moonlight, but Shah Mohammed had no night sights. They must have been firing at shadows. 'Now the Mujahiddin go closer,' said Abdur Rahman, who had been doing his best to give us a running commentary.

But if they're going closer why did they fire before? Why did they alert the Russians? (Out of politeness we called the enemy 'the Russians,' although there were no more than four or five advisers with the Barikot garrison.) 'Perhaps Shah Mohammed saw somebody,' said Abdur Rahman in reply.

The mosquitoes had built up to squadron attacks, and I was squandering cigarettes as a repellant. I could also feel my lice multiplying. 'Let's go back down,' I said. At the foot of our hill, where the white foam roar of the Chitral river almost drowned out the occasional shot, a group of men were sitting on a tree platform built over the water serving tea and goat's cheese.

Twenty-two Afghan resistance groups have their headquarters in Peshawar, the capital of Pakistan's frontier province, where summer dust storms swirl like smoke screens and cram fragments of central Asia into every orifice. Peshawar, once the winter capital of Afghanistan, is an army town.

Much of it exists in a time warp, not so much Kipling as Paul Scott: a hint of Twenties suburbia about the officers' bungalows, polo fanatics lunching at the Peshawar club, now sadly deprived of their sundowners by President Zia's Islamic ordinances; barracks with everything that doesn't move whitewashed and corps signs up in English.

The Russians have constantly attempted to justify their invasion of Afghanistan by alleging that the Americans, Chinese and Pakistanis are arming Radio Moscow's 'reactionary bandits.' This is not entirely untrue but very nearly so. A trickle of arms is getting through to the Mujahiddin: Egyptian-made Kalashnikovs and Finnish ammunition for them. The Chinese may be sending a bit more down the narrow Wakhan panhandle in the extreme north-east, territory forced on the evolving Afghan kingdom by the buffer-obsessed Imperial British, although one glance at the map shows that this is a relatively easy loophole to block. The village gunsmiths in this frontier district, who for years have beaten out exact and sometimes reliable facsimiles of the old British .303, are now turning their hand to AK-47s and even anti-tank rockets.

Peshawar is not crawling with green berets or SAS men trying to look like tourists, although in one Mujahiddin office I discovered a military textbook called 'Total Resistance – the Swiss Army Guide to Guerrilla Warfare and Underground Operations.' The only Westerners the rebels see are reporters and, on the Pakistani side, relief workers, and they welcome both with open arms.

Anwar, about 40 and like many Nuristani guerrillas clean-shaven below the upper lip, laboriously prepared letters of introduction in Farsi. He wrote by the light of an oil lamp, while we squatted on carpets eating grilled fish and rice in a room full of staring people. We had met the military commander of the Flag of Islamic Nuristan in the Pakistani village of Naga which sits near the roof of the world just south of the old mountain kingdom of Chitral. It is about 150 miles north of Peshawar and impossible to reach by road until mid-May, when the snows on the Lewari pass begin to melt and a Jeep can squeeze through.

Guides were appointed, two of Anwar's nephews called Muzzafer and Abibrarahman. Muzzafer, who was in his mid-twenties, was a dapper young man in a rust-coloured, baggy-trousered suit. An indication of his wealth was the fact that he wore socks with his brown suede desert boots. He had a wispy moustache and slightly Mongolian features, as befits a people who claim descent from the hordes of Genghis Khan and Tamburlaine.

Abibrarahman was much younger, about 18, and wore Western clothes most of the time – a check shirt and jeans. He looked quite rotund at times, but I discovered later that this was because beneath his shirt he wore a strange corset-shaped garment in which he kept his most treasured possessions: cartridges, hashish, knife.

Anwar insisted that we leave immediately to avoid border patrols. The Pakistani police are usually quite sporting about reporters they catch trying to get across, although it is mandatory that those who land on the wrong square are returned to Peshawar.

With about 30 minutes of our first night march behind us, zig-zagging crazily up an even steeper goat track, we begged for a rest and collapsed, utterly winded. Our guides took this opportunity to gaze at the stars and roll joints. Many of the Nuristani Mujahiddin used hashish. It enabled one to forget hunger and aching limbs and the lice, collected from sleeping on farmhouse quilts, doing their own route march around your waist.

After that first halt the pace was set and we were treated with the respect due to journalists on the nursery slopes of middle age. Russian conscripts might fare a little better, but I find the Soviet reluctance to use infantry in the mountains perfectly understandable. Abibrarahman was particularly solicitous and proved a genius at scrounging food, running off to hilltop farms to reappear with bowls of fresh milk and cottage cheese.

We crossed the border in daylight, having rested for three hours in a shepherd's hut. Muzzafer demanded 200 rupees 'to bribe the police,' then proceeded to avoid all checkpoints by leading us up a thickly wooded slope – tall conifers flourish at well over 7,000 feet. From the summit a dyspeptic woodsman with a conical-shaped wicker basket on his back and carrying a long-handled axe, guided us, belching loudly, into the Afghan village of Gavadesh, or what was left of it.

For this was one of the villages destroyed by ex-President Taraki's Communist militia almost two years before. A substantial mosque had been gutted by fire, and most of the houses were in ruins. But the fields were under cultivation, irrigated by an elaborate system of hollowed out logs, like miniature dug-out canoes, which divert the mountain streams to where they are most needed, and there were cattle and sheep grazing among the dandelions on the springy meadows.

Our letters of introduction were examined by a distinguished looking old gentleman with a white beard who was introduced to us as Dostagear Tong, President of the Nuristani Mujahiddin. The President and a considerable staff, including a bespectacled secretary, lived with about 10 million flies in a house built into the side of a cliff. Flies never seemed to worry the Mujahiddin, who were rarely without a halo of them.

The front, which was at the end of a river gorge, was still six hours' walk away. En route Abdur Rahman, who had been sent to collect us, pointed out a huddle of graves which he said belonged to Mujahiddin who had died fighting Taraki's men.

We had heard talk of a Russian build-up around Barikot, but it was obvious from our first view of the rebels that they were unaware of it. At a bend in the river there was an old mulberry tree on whose lower branches the leading Mujahiddin hung their rifles and under which they sat, talked, slept and ate and – not very far away – defecated.

The nominal leader of these guerrillas was Gulam Mullah. He was a grey-bearded man with a couple of fingers missing from his right hand who carried an elongated Kalashnikov. He asked me if I knew the Robertsons, referring to Sir George Robertson, Victorian hero of the siege of Chitral and explorer of Kafiristan in the 1890s.

When I asked him what kind of Afghanistan he was fighting for, he paused and then said that he thought he would like his children to grow up under the sort of Islamic government they had in Saudi Arabia. All the Mujahiddin seemed very devout and lived an almost monastic existence. Their day was punctuated by prayers, with much ritual washing beforehand, and meals. No women were around. I surprised two young men having a cuddle under a rock, but I was more embarrassed than they were.

The grey hairs in Gulam Mullah's beard might have made him senior to Shah Mohammed, but there was no doubt that he deferred to the younger man who commanded about 50 youngsters, almost all carrying Kalashnikovs, from different villages. Shah Mohammed was clean-shaven, about 30 years old, with eyes that drilled you.

When he was not talking business, he gave the impression of being a taciturn man, but the night before the action, with Abdur Rahman interpreting, he opened up a little. He knew they were fighting alone, he said. All Washington and London did was talk about the Olympics. At least, that was what they heard on their radios. Not, he added diplomatically, that they were not grateful for any pressure that was brought to bear on the Russians.

We asked him what he most needed, and expected the usual request for SAMs and anti-tank missiles. Shah Mohammed was too much of the realist for that. What he would really like, he said, was a decent pair of field glasses. He needed to see what was going on in the trees.

Before they went into battle the Mujahiddin prayed together on the river bank, the urbane Abdur Rahman committing his soul to Allah as devoutly as the rest of them. We said our goodbyes to Shah Mohammed – us to our opera box and him to his firing position. They said that they were about to rendezvous with scores of other Mujahiddin and insisted, to our great relief, that it was much too dangerous for us to accompany them. I think their real concern was that we would see how small their numbers were.

My last memory of the guerrilla leader is a figure standing on the skyline with his rifle raised in farewell. It may have been something he learned from the last reel of a Western in Peshawar, but I doubt whether Shah Mohammed has ever been further than Chitral. I would like to get him those binoculars. A man should know what's going on in the trees. *(16.6.80)*

Claret and Cordiale
Editorial

'The English, are they human?' was the challenging title of a popular book in the Thirties written by a Frenchwoman who had lived in Britain for many years. It was a light-hearted account of English eccentricites as seen through French eyes.

The French and the English (French relationships with the Scots and Irish are historically different) have been questioning each other's qualifications for membership of the human race – not always so lightheartedly – ever since the Norman Conquest. They have been at it again with increasing vigour in the past few years.

In the hope of pouring some oil – or at least claret – on these troubled waters, 150 British and French politicians, journalists, scholars and businessmen are meeting in Bordeaux to discuss the state of the world and of Anglo-French relations.

Mrs Thatcher came to the party in conciliatory mood to assure them that she wasn't preparing another Hundred Years War or planning to recover long-lost Acquitaine, whatever British holiday settlers might be up to in the Dordogne.

Few other peoples of Europe have had such a long, intimate and complex love-hate relationship as the English and the French. Intense rivalry has been coupled with close friendship, periodic war and inter-mittent alliance. Popular chauvinism has co-existed with intellectual admiration. Real differences of temperament and tradition have been distorted into monstrous national stereotypes.

These media manifestations obscure the more important underlying historic trends which bring Britain and France inexorably together.

Since their last titanic struggle in the Napoleonic wars, Britain and France have been forced willy-nilly, whatever their temperamental or cultural differences, into alliance in Europe (though often remaining in sharp competition in Africa and the Middle East).

The rise of German power in Europe, and of new centres of world power in America and Russia, encouraged the British and French to seek a partnership which was expressed in the Entente Cordiale and in their alliance in two world wars.

France's defeat and occupation in the Second World War left a legacy of distrust on both sides, as well as a mutual admiration. De Gaulle struggled to restore French independence, which he saw most theatened by the domination of a weakened Western Europe by the new world power of the United States. For this and for domestic political reasons, to gag the French Communists, de Gaulle turned to Moscow. Britain he saw as an appendage of the United States, the agent of Anglo-Saxon hegemony in Europe and as a threat to France's remaining empire, especially in the Middle East, North Africa and Indo-China. In fact, both the British and the French empires were doomed. But it took two long and bloody wars in Algeria and Vietnam and the joint disaster of Suez to convince both countries that their imperial days were really over.

De Gaulle's return to power made this change more acceptable in France, but for Britain it meant the long French veto on British entry into the Common Market. The General still saw the British as America's Trojan horse in Europe. To reaffirm French independence he withdrew from NATO and developed the French nuclear deterrent. He accepted the Common Market but opposed supra-nationalism, claiming for France the leadership of a European league of nation states in close association with the growing economic power of Western Germany.

It was this German power which eventually led Pompidou, de Gaulle's successor, to lift the veto on British entry into the EEC in order to balance German influence in Europe. Pompidou's move towards better relations with the United States and Britain was continued by President Giscard d'Estaing. But Britain's entry into the EEC did not bring the harmony with France that was hoped for.

France continued to be the biggest beneficiary from the expensive Common Agricultural Policy, the main financial burden of which was borne disproportionately by Britain. Under the impact of world recession, Britain was rapidly becoming one of the poorest countries of Europe, while France had become one of the richest.

British attempts to renegotiate the terms of their membership of the Common Market led to accusations by the French that Britain wanted the benefits of membership of the European club without paying the dues. The British, it was said, were confirming continental fears that they were not truly 'European.' Yet after a year of acerbic negotiations the French, albeit reluctantly, accepted the Brussels compromise which met most of Britain's budgetary demands.

The European top political triumvirate envisaged by Pompidou – France, West Germany, Britain – has shifted, however, towards a more exclusive Bonn-Paris partnership. This has been the result partly of the mutually admiring personalities of Giscard and Chancellor Schmidt, and partly of the economic decline of Britain and the political decline of the United States under President Carter.

Gladstone once said, in defending the Anglo-French alliance of his day, that Britain and France could never combine for an unjust purpose in Europe. French cynicism and British hypocrisy are still liable to be demonstrated outside Europe, especially in such things as arms sales and military intervention in Africa and the Middle East. But if Gladstone's claim is still largely true, it is not simply because of the new European balance of power. It is also because of the broad attachment of both peoples to the humane values of a free, just and orderly society.

It is by building together the European and world communities on this basis, rather than by chauvinistic vituperation about French apples or British lamb, that Britain and France will once more become real partners, and the spirit of the Entente Cordiale be restored. *(21.9.80)*

98. Worlds Apart

It's Not So Easy Being a Jew
Donald Trelford

A new Israeli joke. A member of the ruling party is haranguing his colleagues: 'Things have come to a terrible state, my friends. The whole world is against us. The Arabs are getting stronger every day. Our economy is in ruins. Inflation is over 100 per cent. Strikes, demonstrations, everywhere. I tell you,' he concludes, thumping the table, *'none of this would be happening if Begin was alive!'*

It is a curious fact that the Israeli Prime Minister, whose name has been denounced in every language on earth, seems almost invisible inside his own country. Nobody seems to know him well. I asked one of his closest associates, a leading man in the Herut Party who has worked with him for nearly 40 years, what Begin is really like. 'His wife knows him,' he said. 'Nobody else.'

Israeli Cabinet meetings must be the longest and leakiest in the world: Rabin, when he was Prime Minister, once tried to make his Cabinet take a lie-detector test. Every member has a right to speak, so they go on for about 10 hours. Begin's handling is said to be patient and self-effacing, with the iron will under control. But he can't shut his Ministers up, either during or afterwards.

Dissatisfaction with the Government is expressed loudly on all sides. On the day I arrived the Peace Now movement had a protest that linked arms all the way from Haifa to Jerusalem. Then 4,000 settlers, taking the opposite view, marched on the Knesset (Parliament) demanding formal annexation of the West Bank. Twenty started a hunger strike.

And that was just Israelis. Palestinians had their own marches and demos in Nablus, Hebron and Jerusalem. When I referred to all this on a journey through the West Bank, my military escort was subdued. Then he heard a radio bulletin in Hebrew – and his face lit up. 'Not only riots in Nablus,' he chuckled, 'but in Britain too!'

Another Israeli joke. Two old friends meet in Tel Aviv. One is very depressed. 'I'm thinking of leaving, Moshe, back to New York.'

'But why, Elie?' his friend asks.

'For two reasons. This Government is hopeless. They can't solve our border problems, they can't keep prices down, they can't do anything.' His friend interrupts. 'But Elie, all this will soon change. Begin's Government can't last. Then we'll have Shimon Peres and the Labour Party back again.

'And that's my second reason for leaving.'

Worlds Apart. 99

Peres met me in the Labour HQ – as if to prove a point, since his hold on the Labour leadership is not secure. The main threat is from Rabin, his old enemy, who snatched the leadership from him in 1974. The relationship between Peres and Rabin is an interesting one: they hate each other. In his memoirs Rabin sees the hand of Peres raised against him at every stage of his career, including his ignominious fall from office three years ago over his wife's illegal bank account. It's a bit like Thatcher and Heath.

Rabin is a slow, dignified man, with a rather weary air, given to careful exposition. He is said to be bad at nursing politicians and to see too many sides to every question. He smokes non-stop. When he was Chief of Staff before the Six Day War, he seized up at a crucial time and blamed it on nicotine poisoning.

Peres is a wary, quick-witted man, as hard as the floor, with a steady stream of quotable quotes. Here are a few from my notebook:

'The Middle East threat is to the oily places, not the holy places.'
'Resources are more important than geography.'
'The West spends more on women's cosmetics than it does on defence.'
'Iran is rich enough to support revolution as an industry.'
'I believe in a Palestian home-land. It's called Jordan.'
'Hussein is a smart man. He uses PLO language and Jordanian power.'

And so on.

Peres keeps a colourful portrait of Ben-Gurion over his desk, a reminder of his great days in Defence under the first Israeli Prime Minister, when he virtually invented the country's aircraft industry. The problem for Peres is his image. People don't trust him: they see him as a tricky wheeler-dealer. He is not an easy man to work with.

There is a sad sense in Israel, especially among intellectuals, of '13 wasted years.' A professor told me: 'We are a talented ingenious people – we should have found a way in all this time of giving Hussein his land back on reasonable terms.'

Dayan is blamed for this failure, for having effectively vetoed promising chances. Golda Meir is also abused for her inflexibility. I was astonished to hear one Israeli politician, a kindly man, suddenly burst out in uncontrollable rage: 'Golda's soul should be burning in Hell! She was stupid, she didn't understand.'

Labour's most articulate spokesman is the former Foreign Minister, Abba Eban, who wrote a stinging reply to Dayan, his successor, in the *Jerusalem Post*, saying that Israel's occupation of Palestinian land 'has failed both as an idea and as a reality.'

Much heat – in Israel as well as the United Nations – has been provoked by the Begin Cabinet's narrow decision to open a Jewish college at Hebron on the West Bank, thereby asserting a sovereign right over the biblical Judea and Samaria.

Hebron, 'City of the Fathers,' figures strongly in Jewish history. I met a woman who had been dramatically saved from the Jewish pogrom there in 1929. I drove to look at the town, which lies south of Bethlehem on the road to Beersheba. Apart from an Israeli soldier on a roof-top on the way in – and an obstetrician whose sign-board proclaimed a Dublin degree – the town was overwhelming Arabic. I could well believe a journalist who told me: 'It would be suicide for an Israeli to walk alone in the alleys of Hebron.'

Outside Abraham's tomb there I saw a group of Arab boys calling out and laughing after a young Israeli soldier. He smiled uncertainly back, fingering his gun, not sure of the Arabic, not sure what to do – not sure, perhaps, why he was there.

The Mayor of Bethlehem, Elias Freij, is a Christian Arab of alder-manic demeanour, portly, shrewd and polite. Outside his elegant office in Manger Square air-conditioned buses unload pilgrims at the Church of the Holy Nativity.

One of the buses proclaims: 'Nazareth Tourist and Transport Company,' while a sign on a building reads: 'Bethlehem Hotels Incor-porated' – both institutions filling a social need once felt acutely in these parts.

Freij is known as a 'moderate,' a reliable barometer of Arab opinion on the West Bank. Moderates now talk PLO. He declares the Begin-Sadat autonomy talks 'bankrupt.' 'We accept the PLO as our respre-sentatives.'

The West Bank Palestinians seem content to let the PLO, the men in Beirut, make the running for them. But they can oppose the PLO – as thy did when they went to greet Sadat in Israel; and there are strains within the PLO. Jordan still pays official salaries on the West Bank and Hussein keeps himself informed. There is a pull towards the PLO and a pull towards Jordan: too soon to know which will prevail.

As I left the Mayor's office I asked: 'If I come back here in five years' time, will I find a Palestinian State?' Freij answered carefully: 'No, but you won't see any Israeli soldiers out there either.'

By road through the Jordan valley. The heavy rains have brought patches of green to the bony Judean hills. The Holy Land is in bloom: plum trees, strawberries, irises, poppies, anemones. Past the Inn of the Good Samaritan, now a police station. The ravens that fed Elijah swoop down from the Qumran caves, where the Dead Sea scrolls were found.

A swim in the Dead Sea, the lowest point on earth. It's true what they tell you at school: you can't sink in it because of the salt, which is very bitter. You can hardly swim in it either, because your legs float to the top. The floor is a black mud that Cleopatra sent for as an early beauty treatment. The tourists smother themselves in it obscenely.

Past bedouin encampments and the odd mangy camel. Ahead of us an Israeli Volkswagen smashes into the back of an old Arab jalopy, scattering pans across the road. Peace negotiations open noisily.

Then the Jordan itself, a disappointing trickle. When Kissinger saw it he remarked: 'What public relations can do for a river!'

As we head north, heavy rains obscure the Sea of Galilee. The best guide-book to these parts is the Bible, but we have to rush past. Guns everywhere. Soldiers thumbing lifts, an ice-lolly in one hand, an automatic weapon in the other.

In the Golan Heights I visit a bleak Israeli outpost in the driving rain, near the Rafid triangle where Nicholas Tomalin, the *Sunday Times* journalist, was killed by a Syrian-fired Sagger missile in the 1973 war. Our escort, Major Hillel Ashkenazy, had given him his last briefing on the day he died. Ashkenazy's nephew was also killed that day in the same battle zone.

As we leave, I admire the profusion of flowers on the Golan Heights. 'They're all mined,' he said.

Back in Jerusalem, it is the Passover, an austere time. We attend a family *seder* and join in a reading of the Haggadah, which describes the Jews' release from bondage in Egypt.

The message of the Haggadah is that God abhors slavery for all mankind. Some lines leap off the page: 'You should not oppress a stranger, for you know the feelings of the stranger, having yourselves been strangers in the land of Egypt' (Exodus 23.9). The Jews are uncomfortably aware of the moral paradox this presents in their relations with the Palestinians.

Peres invited the Egyptian Ambassador, Saad Mortada, to his family *seder*. They evidently coped with the anti-Egyptian passages. Mortada is lionised by Israeli hostesses, unlike his Jewish counterpart in Cairo, who has a hard time.

No bread can be eaten in the eight days of the Passover. It is burned in the streets. No beer. The hotel can let me have a gin but no tonic. The pool is closed. A Jewish woman sympathises: 'It's not so easy being a Jew.' After a week of these minor deprivations, I have a mad vision of stuffing myself with bread, washed down with tonic, then hurling myself into the hotel swimming pool.

We escape to an oasis called 'The British Pub' and eat in a Chinese restaurant called 'Mandy.' Intrigued by the name, I ask about Mandy.

Could it be the notorious Mandy Rice-Davies? I am informed politely: 'Mandy was a famous and successful lady in England.'

The ultra-orthodox Jews live in Mia Sherim, a warren of narrow streets that clog the centre of Jerusalem. It is virtually a no-go area, even for Israelis. By mistake, we find ourselves lost in this quarter on the holiest of days, the Sabbath in Passover week. We are shouted at angrily by men in black hats and ringlets. We are told later that, had we rounded the next corner, our car would have been stoned.

Teddy Kollek, the Mayor of Jerusalem, fights a running battle with Mia Sherim, which has threatened to put a curse on his life if he goes ahead with plans for a new road and sports stadium nearby. Kollek, a warm expansive personality, doesn't seem to mind.

An early-morning drive round Jerusalem with the Mayor is a rare experience. When he meets traffic he plunges down side-roads or through prohibited entrances that lead past rubble and backyards to find a way through. Startled police reverse out of his path when he darts the wrong way down a one-way street. They grin and wave: 'Shalom, Teddy.'

The same greeting from a little girl in pigtails in the Old City, who is clearly thrilled to see him. Arab workers rise from their tasks and shake his hand. An Arab shopkeeper rushes out and yells that the repaving of Old City streets is taking too long and driving business away. Teddy yells back in Arabic and the two men part happily.

He plainly loves the city. He seems to know every tree, every new building plot. He is hurt by the criticism of Israel's stewardship of Jerusalem, some (but not all) of it badly misinformed. He cannot visualise the city being divided again. He has plans for a Greater Jerusalem – possibly including Bethlehem – where authority could be shared. But he worries that, because of the Begin Government's policies, his work may 'all go to pot.'

Saul Bellow described Kollek as 'Israel's most valuable political asset.' He is an asset to the human race, a force of nature.

Mild culture-shock after a visit to the Dome of the Rock, where Mohammed ascended to Heaven; the El Aqsa mosque, where Hussein's grandfather was murdered; and on to the Wailing Wall (which is segregrated).

The Church of the Holy Sepulchre, the most sacred of Christian shrines, is a shambles, covered in builders' rubble. The Golden Gate, where the Messiah is expected to come, has been sealed up for centuries. St Stephen's Gate, where the Israeli troops broke through in 1967, is about 20 yards from Bethesda, the birthplace of the Virgin Mary. On the Via Dolorosa tee-shirts are on sale: Billion Dollar Man and Wonder Woman. Life goes on.

To open a door in Israel is to be drowned in a gale of noise, chatter, questions, analysis, gossip and jokes. How to make sense of it after 10 days? You can't. You can only listen carefully and do your best.

When I was last in the country in 1971, I was besieged everywhere by the same expectant question: Well, what do you think of Israel? The questioners were confident of the answer, proud of their achievements after the stunning victories of the Six Day War. The question is still being asked, but with less confidence now. They don't expect the same answer. Negative comments are met with a shrug: 'It's not so easy being a Jew.'

I met a businessman in Tel Aviv, who asked: 'Are they filling you with propaganda – or telling you what it's really like here?'

'Tell me what it's really like.'

'It's like I imagine South Africa is. We're going nowhere. There's nowhere to go. You take your country for granted all your life, then you travel and find there are better places. That's why people are leaving. They're depressed.'

At the heart of this man's problems is the economy. Inflation is running at 140 per cent a year (some say more). Interest rates are 10 per cent a month.

The economic crisis may partly account for the mood of disenchantment in the country. The peace euphoria brought on by Sadat's historic visit has largely evaporated. Many Israelis fear Sadat has out-manoeuvred Begin and usurped Israel's special relationship with America. The wonder of going to Cairo is also wearing thin: Israelis come home complaining of the poor hotels and dirty streets. But such moods are ephemeral. I may have caught them at a bad time.

To test the mood I went to the country's artists. There was an exhibition at the Israel Museum on the theme of 'Borders.' The images were vivid: a man's head as a map, the cease-fire lines as a dress pattern, photos of a dog marking out its territory, flowers on barbed wire.

Grim, certainly, descriptive, even matter-of-fact, compared with the stark horror of Yad Vashem, the Holocaust museum. Israel cannot be undersood without the Holocaust. Everyone in the country either lost someone or survived it; just as every family in Israel has survived or lost someone in the four wars since independence. After the Holocaust museum it was unnerving to see a hotel porter with a name-tab: 'George Nazi.'

One emerges from Yad Vashem with a powerful sense of fundamental sickness in the human psyche. The experience has shaped Israel's attitude to the world and conditioned its relations with the Arabs, who also come in the night to kill them. It is a terrible irony that the Jews should have come together for refuge in one of the most dangerous spots on earth.

And yet, even in bad times, there is an energy about Israel, a desperate will to survive, that can be found nowhere else. It is partly the sense of shared national purpose that sweeps it along; partly, perhaps, a special sense of being in the mainstream of history. 'Happy the nation whose annals of history are boring to read' (Montesquieu).

Everyone you meet in Israel has an amazing personal story. I met a taxi-driver whose aunt had arrived in Israel the day before from Minsk in Russia: she hadn't seen his father for 60 years. Many of the Soviet Jews don't stay; they go on to America. But the immigrant mix seems to be working better than people feared. There are black Jews from Ethiopia. The South African and Indian Jews play cricket together.

Can Israel make the mental adjustments that will gain it acceptance in the outside world? There are problems that will have to be faced, quite apart from the atavistic distrust of outsiders built into the Jewish consciousness.

Israel gave back Sinai to Egypt in return for an offer of peace; the return of the West Bank is being demanded without an offer of peace. For the return of Sinai the Israelis spoke direct to Sadat: they could look into his eyes and judge his sincerity. In the autonomy talks they also deal with Sadat, but they know that one day they will have to talk to Palestinians, maybe the PLO. Whatever they concede now to Sadat will be the starting-point for the next negotiations.

There are hopeful signs. The *Jerusalem Post* tells the awkward truth day after day. On West Bank settlements: 'A more striking feat of irrelevance could hardly be conceived.' On the PLO: 'Israel can no longer ignore the fact that the Palestinian State idea has become not only respectable but by now entrenched in world opinion.'

This sounds like the beginnings of a new wisdom. I found it paradoxical that Israel should be in such a disenchanted mood when, after 32 years, a genuine peace may be in sight. Perhaps, I thought, the country has embarked on a mental migration and this mood may be just part of the painful process of coming to terms with new realities. Perhaps.

Professor J. L. Talmon, of the Hebrew University, has said: 'It is the fate of the Jews to serve as a testimony, as a living witness, a touchstone, a whipping block and symbol all in one.' It's not so easy being a Jew. *(20.4.80)*

King of Moon Mountains
Nick Worrall

High in the Rwenzori mountains of western Uganda – the fabled Mountains of the Moon – women and children sang to the beating of the drums as their king walked slowly down from his palace in the clouds to meet the first Western journalist to visit his kingdom for 17 years.

His Majesty King Charles Wesley Erima-Ngoma, of the United Kingdom of Rwenzururu, was dressed in brilliant white uniform, the badges of a field-marshal, peaked cap decorated in green, blue and yellow Rwenzururu colours and a sheathed silver dagger. Beside him walked his small, pretty Queen Zeuliah followed by 10 members of the Cabinet. On the surrounding grass women sang the Rwenzururu national anthem and applauded the royal approach.

It could have been pure Gilbert and Sullivan, but for the 300,000 Rwenzururians their independent kingdom is a serious matter. It contains the 60-mile long Rwenzori mountain range, higher than the Alps and straddling the border between Uganda and Zaire.

Rwenzururu declared its independence from Uganda 18 years ago and its people, mostly from the diminutive Bakonjo tribe, fight on today for recognition. The struggle of the Bakonjo and Bwamba people has lasted for 150 years.

During that time they have fought the people of Toro, in whose defunct kingdom the Rwenzoris were placed, they have fought the British and Belgian colonists and the post-independence governments of Milton Obote and Idi Amin.

Rwenzururu is a classic example of the way the British carved up parts of traditional Africa without heed to the claims of the less-vocal peoples. The Bakonjo's home mountain region was simply split down the centre by the 1910 Anglo-Belgian agreement which declared the 30th meridian and the Congo-Nile watershed to be the boundary between the Belgian Congo (now Zaire) and Uganda.

Possibly because they found the people more immediately attractive, the British then propped up the ailing kingdom of Toro, subduing the angry Bakonjo whose land they gave to the Toros.

It all came to a head in 1962 when the Bakonjo received no mention in the Ugandan independence constitution. Unilateral independence was declared on 30 June, 1962, by Isaya Mukirane, the father of the present king.

Obote sent troops under British officers to 'deal with' the rebels and he even enlisted the aid of a British journalist, Tom Stacey, who had known Mukirane eight years earlier. The mediation attempt failed when Stacey was unable to convince the Rwenzururians of official Ugandan sincerity.

Idi Amin sent troops into the mountains as well. Walking the steep slopes in search of the king, I was shown deserted huts and small-holdings amid lush surroundings where Amin's men had burned, pillaged and murdered the people.

My guides Eric and Eryeza told me how their region, one of the richest in Africa, had been neglected by the men who developed Uganda. Meanwhile foreign currency had been earned from the abundance of coffee and minerals, particularly copper which is mined at nearby Kilembe.

I had called at Kagando hospital before setting off up the mountains. It is run by the British-based Evangelical Alliance Relief fund, and an average 500 people queue for treatment each day. A British doctor, Robert Morris, and his staff carry out operations under extraordinary conditions. Many casualties are brought in with bullet wounds from tribal fighting.

Near the hospital I was vetted by the Rwenzururu Chief Judge Kainabu Yonasani and two Cabinet Ministers. After two sessions lasting eight hours over two days, permission to go on was given and my guides assigned. I would meet the king in the mountains – though not at his palace – the next morning.

So that night, after an exhausting climb of more than 6,000 feet through dense tropical vegetation, mountains streams, banana plantations and cassava fields, and pursued by fierce black flies, I was rewarded by a breath-taking view of the dry plains far below at the equator and of Lake Edward glittering through the haze.

King Charles Erima-Ngoma sat at a bench on the long grass and introduced, one by one, his Prime Minister, members of the Cabinet, Justices and the Royal Chamberlain. They were not politicians, he explained: 'I was appointed by God and they are appointed by me. There are no politics in Rwenzururu.'

The King told how his people, friendless and with no outside assistance, had held off the entire world. The Rwenzururians had few guns, little clothing and no money. Messages sent to the United Nations, the Commonwealth and Britain for help had never been answered.

'Our fighters have suffered for 18 years,' he said, 'and they will continue to fight for the human rights of the United Kingdom of Rwenzururu.'

The proceedings were kept for posterity on the royal cassette recorder produced with great ceremony by the Royal Chamberlain.

Until they achieve legal autonomy and measurable social and economic advances, the Bakonjo will continue to proclaim their independence from both Uganda and Zaire, neither of whom will ever be able to force the Rwenzururians from the Mountains of the Moon. *(27.7.80)*

8.
Royal Occasions

The Greatest Show on Earth
Clive James

With camera shutters crackling around her like an electrical storm, Lady Diana Spencer, as she then was, had a little crisis. Off she went in tears with the world's media in pursuit. Perhaps the whole deal was off. Perhaps she would become a nun.

Next day in Windsor Great Park Prince Charles told ITV that it was all nonsense about his betrothed not liking polo. 'Not much fun watching polo when you're surrounded by people with very long lenses pointing at you the entire time.' The place to be in such circumstances, it was made clear, was on horseback. 'Well, Sir,' asked Alastair Burnet, 'what makes you play polo?' With the first chukka awaiting the swingeing thwack of the Royal mallet, Prince Charles was eager to be away, but he gave the question his serious consideration. 'I happen to enjoy horse activities because I like the horse.'

An hour or so of horse activities duly ensued, apparently for the specific purpose of mystifying Mrs Reagan. 'Prince Charles with the ball . . . Prince Charles out on his own . . . playing for England against Spain just three days before his marriage . . . typically British . . . you can't get anything more British . . . and it's there! Prince Charles has scored for England.'

It became increasingly clear that Prince Charles had scored for England, Britain, the world, the solar system and the galaxy. Every human frailty manifested by Lady Diana only increased the universal conviction that the entire script was being written by the Brothers Grimm and that the heir to the throne had picked himself a peach. 'Are you looking forward to Wednesday?' the Beeb asked Mrs Reagan. 'I certainly yam. Isn't everybody?' The possibility was small that she would have said: 'I certainly yam not, it's just another wedding,' but the enthusiasm was plainly genuine, although she still looked puzzled, perhaps from thinking about the horse activities.

Thames News (ITV) and *Nationwide* (BBC) both covered the coverage being laid on by the American NBC network. 'They've managed to bag these plum positions,' said *Nationwide* rather bitterly. All the rest of the world's television organisations were there too, including the Fuji company, now faced a thousand times daily with saying the two English words most difficult to a Japanese, 'royal family.' It comes out as 'royaroo famiree', but not immediately.

In *A Prince for Our Time* (BBC1) it was explained that 'Prince Charles is Colonel of ten regiments.' As a consequence he was well in command during *HRH the Prince of Wales and Lady Diana Spencer in Conversation with Angela Rippon and Andrew Gardner* (BBC and ITV), an all-channel, all-purpose interview in which the four participants demonstrated various methods of looking uncomfortable in canvas safari chairs with high arm-rests. Lady Diana's pretty shoulders ended up around her ears, which might have helped her cope with the fatuity of the questions by making them inaudible.

It was made clear that sacks of mail had more or less jammed the corridors of the palace, so that you had to take detours through pantries. Angela pretended to be stunned that children had baked cakes. 'Tremendous boost,' said Lady Diana tinily from between her shoulders. 'So many children crawling on top of me.' Prince Charles signalled his hopes that married life would be a calming influence. 'Getting interested in too many things and dashing abate, that is going to be my problem.' Lady Diana would help him solve it, but that wouldn't start until Wednesday. First there must be an evening of ritual separation. 'Not allayed to see me the night before, even by the light of exploding fireworks.'

Before the fireworks filled the sky, however, it first had to be filled by Frank Bough fronting *Nationwide* (BBC1). Frank was on top of a tall building, like a weathercock. He referred proprietorially to 'that famous old Cathedral here behind me.' Meanwhile Bill Kerr-Elliot pumped Lady Diana's famously unforthcoming flat-mates. Still behaving like members of M16 – except, of course, that they are almost certainly not working for the Russians – the flat-mates nevertheless let slip the odd scrap. 'We often came back and found her dancing around the flat on her own . . . bopping.' The flat was a non-event without her. 'There's a general lack of Diana, really.'

110. *Royal Occasions*

The Royal Fireworks (BBC1) were laid on in Hyde Park by Major Michael Parker, First Gentleman of the Rockets and Sparkler in Waiting. Raymond Baxter supplied the commentary, excelling even Prince Charles in the strain he put on a certain vowel, or veil. 'The Queen and 20 craned heads from other lands . . . bonfire built by Boy Skates . . . the Boy Skates, Sea Skates and Air Skates . . . the fuse darts ate across the grass.' Up went the rockets, but not so as to take your breath away. Billed as 'the most tremendous fireworks display since 1749,' it looked a bit sedate.

Early next morning ITV stole a march by getting Leonard Parkin into position outside Lady Diana's window while the Beeb was still clearing its throat with a Bugs Bunny cartoon. 'She's just peeped out of her window . . . the famous hairstyle . . . The Dress is in there.' The BBC's coverage began with Angela Rippon sitting in a vast flesh-coloured Art Deco salesroom for pre-war cosmetics. 'We'll be speculating on The Dress,' said Angie.

Both channels evoked a huge dawn security operation featuring underground bomb-sniffing Labrador dogs at large beneath the city, but already it was apparent that ITV, with a less elaborate studio set-up and more flexible outside coverage, had the legs of the Beeb, which was interviewing boring old buskers while the other side had successfully tracked down the people who had made The Dress. Plainly they would reveal nothing even under torture, but it beat looking at a man with a mouth-organ.

On ITV, Andrew Gardner was with Barbara Cartland. 'What I believe in, of course, is Romance.' Twin miracles of mascara, her eyes looked like the corpses of two small crows that had crashed into a chalk cliff. They were equalled for baroque contrivance by the creation decorating the top lip of the BBC's next guest, Sir Iain Moncreiffe of That Ilk and That Moustache. 'No time is known,' he explained, 'where there weren't these magic royal people.' On ITV, Judith Chalmers had the job of being enthusiastic about The Dress, sometimes called That Dress for purposes of emphasis. 'That Dress . . . The Dress . . . I'm looking forward to it.'

Sandy Gall tuned in from Hyde Park Barracks, where the Blues and Royals of the Escort were already providing a formidable example of horse activities. Prince Charles was Colonel of every regiment in sight but actual power resided in the glistening form of Regimental Corporal Major Lawson, who would be the senior NCO on parade. 'The majority on parade,' rasped Corporal Major, 'will never ever see a parade of this enormity.' Filling the close-up, the hirsute extravaganza adorning the Corporal Major's top lip made That Ilk's paltry ziff look like a dust-bug.

ITV explored St Paul's to a well-written voice-over from Alastair

Burnet, although later on he slightly spoiled things by calling it the Abbey. Katherine Yochiko of Fuji TV was interviewed. 'Royaroo famiree . . . so exciting reahree.' She predicted that The Dress would be 'just rike a fairy tayaroo.' 'It's just after nine o'clock,' said Andrew Gardner, 'so we've only got two hours to wait now before we see That Dress.' Aloft in the ITV airship, a camera watched the first soldiers march away to line the route. The air shots were destined to be a big plus for ITV throughout the day.

Back with Angela at the cosmetics counter, Eve Pollard the fashion expert was asked to predict what The Dress would look like. 'Cinderella dress . . . real fairy-tale.'

The Beeb's chief commentator, Tom Fleming, clocked on for a long day. 'Once upon a time . . . what you will see now is no fairy story, but the story of two very real young people.' Never appearing in vision, Tom yet wears a morning suit in order to get himself in the right mood for dishing out the hushed tones of awe. 'Daunting journey that will carry her through this gateway . . . a new life of Royalty. . . .' But ITV had caught the Earl Spencer, a natural star even in his infirmity. 'Are you a little apprehensive about today?' 'Not in the least.'

With fine young ladies poised beneath them, big hats were floating into the Cathedral like pastel Frisbees flying in slow motion. 'I think it's going to be the most amazingly chic wedding of the century,' burbled Eve on the Beeb. 'It's because *she's* such a knockout . . . endless huge hats.' For ITV Alastair Burnet did a voice-over about the buildings on the route. Gracing the proceedings with a touch of wit, his commentary was yet another plus for the commercial channel's coverage, which by now was making the Beeb's look and sound sclerotic.

But Tom Fleming ploughed on. 'Queen Elizabeth, like Prince Charles, loves horses.' Spike Milligan, who loves whales, showed up after all: having learned at the last minute that Prince Charles was responsible not for whales but for Wales, he had temporarily shelved his protest on behalf of the threatened cetaceans and made it to Moss Bros. just in time. 'Here is the King of Tonga,' said Tom Fleming, neglecting to add that the King of Tonga is roughly the same shape as the much-missed Queen Salote but lacks the bounce. Nevertheless the King of Tonga was an acquisition, looking rather like Lord Goodman giving one of those interviews in which the face is kept in shadow for security reasons.

The Queen's carriage left the Palace accompanied by the cheers of the multitude. 'There they are, all waving their flags,' said Tom Fleming as the people waved their flags. 'Hats,' he said, as the screen filled with hats. Lady Diana was dimly visible through the window of the Glass Coach. Tom was ready. 'A fairy-tale sight . . . that shy smile we've grown to know already . . . these bay horses look hale and hearty.' Lady Diana alighted to mass agreement that she looked like a princess in a fairy tale. 'Ivory pure silk taffeta!' cried the Beeb's Eve in triumph, her predictions fulfilled. 'Isn't it a fairy tale?' asked Judith Chalmers rhetorically.

At least one viewer thought that The Dress had been designed to hide the outstanding prettiness of its occupant's figure as thoroughly as possible, but to say so would have been treason and anyway the lady had only to smile in order to remind you that she would look good in a diving suit.

With all those present in the Cathedral and 700,000,000 viewers throughout the world dutifully pretending that her father was guiding her instead of she him, the bride headed down the aisle towards the waiting groom, Charles Philip Arthur George, shortly to be addressed by Lady Diana as Philip Charles Arthur George, a blunderette which completed the enslavement of her future people by revealing that she shared their capacity to make a small balls-up on a big occasion.

'Here is the stuff of which fairy-tales are made,' drivelled the Arch-bish, adding further fuel to the theory that he's the man to hire if what you want at your wedding is platitudes served up like peeled walnuts in chocolate syrup: he's an anodyne divine who'll put unction in your function. But the soaring voice of Kiri te Kanawa soon dispelled the aroma of stale rhetoric. Singing a storm, she even managed to make you forget what may have been the only surviving example of the Maori national dress.

Spliced at last, the Prince and Princess headed for the door with Tom Fleming's voice helping you master the details. 'The cap-holder appears with cap and gloves,' said Tom as the cap-holder handed Charles his cap and gloves. Off they went down Ludgate Hill in the landau. While Tom told you all about the bells of St Clement's ('the bells that say oranges and lemons') Alastair Burnet recalled that Dr Johnson had defined happiness as driving briskly along in a post-chaise beside a pretty woman. By that definition Prince Charles was the happiest man alive, but Tom didn't want the horses to feel left out. 'These horses . . . certainly not reacting to the cheers . . . and yet perhaps . . .' ITV snatched the best shots of the bride. The policemen who were all supposed to be facing outwards spent a lot of time facing inwards. It would have taken a saint not to drink her in. 'And so, slowly,' intoned Tom, 'the horses find their way home.'

In an open carriage weighed down with rose petals and buoyed up by balloons, the newlyweds headed for Waterloo. The Princess of Wales, wearing the kind of tricorne hat in which Edward VII's Alexandra was wont to wow the public, looked good enough to eat. 'It would be good,' said ITV's Alastair without any real hope, 'if people didn't intrude on their privacy at Broadlands.'

Royal Occasions. 113

As the only clean train in Britain set off on its journey, the Beeb's Tom was ready with the words whose solemn gravity so exactly failed to sum up the occasion. 'Throw a handful of good wishes after them . . . from the shore as they go . . . may they carry these memories . . . to cheer them on their journey into the unknown.' But the people were less frivolous. Having put off the tone of portent until the inevitable day when it would come in handy, they were dancing in the streets. *(2.8.81)*

Few Airs but Many Graces
Alastair Forbes

'You must have been a beautiful baby!' they sang to the Queen Mother from the stage at the last Royal Variety Show, an annual ordeal which few others could bear with the genuine grins she herself, with the empathy of one important branch of showbiz to another, always manages to bestow upon it. A very beautiful baby is exactly what she was, having luckily avoided the somewhat formidable noses her Bentinck (shades of Lady Ottoline Morell!) mother and Bowes Lyon father bequeathed to her many elder brothers and sisters and even to her favourite brother, David.

At the National Portrait Gallery Exhibition to celebrate her eightieth birthday we encounter 'yon wee Lyon lassie' luring us through the picture frame into a sort of private world in which readers of E. Nesbit and Frances Hodgson Burnett will immediately feel at home. Two photographs cast upon me a spell that makes my head dizzy and my eyes dazzle. In one, the lovely candid glance of the seven-year-old child compellingly predicts her compassionate adult character while in the other, where she is using a large fur muff for some stage 'business', she seems already fully mistress of all the arts of seduction.

Indeed, when I mentioned this to Lord David Cecil, who has remained her life-long friend, he exclaimed: 'Can you wonder that I fell in love with her at that age at a children's party?'

By the time Elizabeth was nine, Mr Neill, the bearded dancing master, who would in traditional fashion bring a fiddle to accompany his lessons at the castle, had found in her the perfect pupil whose infectious delight in her ballroom footwork and rhythm is still in her eightieth year a joy to watch. She had also established seigneurial rights over an embroidered rose-coloured brocade ball-dress from the dressing-up box which, accompanied by much expert manipulation of a fan, she wore with such an air that it was hardly surprising that she should have been nicknamed 'Princess' by her family more than a dozen years before she was to acquire that rank, style and title from the Sovereign.

Love and happiness, she likes to say, were always in the air she breathed in all her three family homes and a sundial would have seemed sufficient to count the hours of her girlhood. Love and happiness, too, were what she exhaled as well as breathed and boys galore were to be bewitched (How many hearts Elizabeth will break! was an early prophecy that failed to take into account her gentle touch for mending them afterwards) before James Stuart, the bonny descendant of King James V of Scotland's bonny bastard Moray, was to introduce to her his shy young Royal master. Stuart had been appointed first Equerry to Prince Bertie, the King's second son, whom he confessed to finding 'not an easy man to know or handle.'

'I loved her *madly,* but really madly,' one of my oldest friends has often told me, his eyes misting at memories of the magic of the Glamis of his youth, adding, 'You've no idea what a *wag* she was, so full of witty teasing and captivating jokes.'

'You'll be a lucky man if she accepts you,' Prince Bertie had been told by his quarter-deck-stern Royal father, George V.

Bertie indeed had to swallow one refusal which she had intended to be final; and during the long months in which he patiently continued to press his claims to acceptance, he nevertheless told his parents, with whom he continued to live up to the morning of his wedding-day, on 26 April 1923: 'Elizabeth is very kind to me.'

Elizabeth's sweet and discreet mother felt very sorry for a man of whom she affectionately and perceptively wrote: 'I like him so much and he is a man who will be made or marred by his wife.'

It was while Elizabeth was still trying to make up her mind that the Prince of Wales, who had welcomed her 'lively and refreshing spirit,' had one day turned to her and out of the blue urged her to 'marry Bertie and go on together to Buck House' – but this line of argument from the heir to the throne seemed merely a fanciful aberration at the time. It was certainly the last motive in view when she finally decided to become Duchess of York and take up what Queen Victoria's last surviving granddaughter not long ago rightly called 'an arduous profession. . . . None but those trained to such an ordeal can sustain it *with amiability and composure.'*

Though discovering a genuine vocation for it, she had to fight an habitual unpunctuality that her martinet father-in-law, who was manic on the subject, forgave her only for the sake of her charm. Elizabeth had also to fight and overcome a certain tendency to an easygoingness that some of her circle came near to calling laziness. (Of the slogan on her desk DO IT NOW she had disarmingly remarked: 'I don't know why I keep it. I never do, you know.')

In the event, the marriage proved both a distinct love-match and a great Royal partnership. 'They reminded me of us,' Duff Cooper wrote to his Diana, 'holding hands and whispering private jokes in the passage'. Another friend of mine, a recently married fellow-guest with the Yorks at Belvoir Castle, accompanied them one foggy night after dinner by special train to Leicester. 'We boarded in evening dress at Grantham where a considerable crowd had gathered. The Duke was very shy and rushed along the carriage pulling down the blinds. I was very impressed by the way the Duchess snapped them up again immediately, saying to her husband, "Bertie, you must wave".'

Public speaking remained, in his own words, 'absolute hell' for poor Bertie (K for King and Q for Queen being by a curious irony the Chair Fences among the consonants that it threw him to pronounce), though for all his naturally nervous and highly-strung disposition – in such contrast to his wife's unrufflable calm – his speech was perfectly natural and normal in ordinary conversation. The gifted Australian specialist Lionel Logue had helped him to overcome his difficulties almost completely by the time of his brother David's succession.

During the old King's first brush with death in 1928 – when the Prince of Wales was far away on tour – Bertie had cheerfully ridiculed the rumour circulating that 'just like in the Middle Ages . . . I am going to bag the throne in your absence in the event of anything happening to Papa', so safely and permanently destined for the head of the 'Smiling Prince' did the Crown then seem.

The wonderfully happy and, offduty, almost carefree life the Yorks were able to lead for several years with their two daughters was shortly to be threatened by the besotted Edward VIII's 'affair'. In February 1936 Harold Nicolson, entering Lady Maureen Stanley's London drawing room, found 'a dear little woman in black sitting on the sofa and she said to me: "We have not met since Berlin." I sat down beside her and chattered away all friendly, thinking: "Obviously she is English yet I do not remember at all. Yet there is something about her that is quite familiar." While thus thinking, another woman came in and curtsied to her and I realised it was the Duchess of York.'

Shortly thereafter, her husband would 'break down and sob like a child' in the presence of his mother at the thought of the thunderbolt and lightning his spoilt and self-indulgent brother had so suddenly hurled at him. (In fact, Bertie was less often given to weeping than to gnashing of teeth, and the outbursts of ungoverned, but fortunately quickly passing, rages to which, like the other Bertie, his grandfather

King Edward VII, and his mother's father Franz Teck, he was given, were dubbed 'gnashes' by his entourage, who knew that his wife's soothing 'Bertie, Bertie!' and restraining stroking of his hand or arm would quickly calm.)

A year after his failure to recognise her, Harold Nicolson was at Buckingham Palace detecting on her face 'a faint smile indicative of how much she would have liked her dinner party were it not for the fact that she was Queen of England,' and one who 'teased me very charmingly about my pink face and my pink views.' He could not 'help thinking what a mess poor Mrs Simpson would have made of such an occasion' and went on, with surely rather Osric-like hyperbole, to dub Elizabeth 'the most amazing Queen since Cleopatra.'

Soon the Crown seemed no longer 'the intolerable honour' she had earlier confided it to be to an old friend visiting her at Windsor. It was the Coronation ceremony itself on 12 May 1937 that had chiefly done the trick. The great historian George Macaulay Trevelyan, who witnessed it, had said that 'no ceremony on earth could equal it for splendour, history, religion and Englishry, all blent into a unique thing. . . . The Queen was the most moving thing in it all – and the King the finest.' Trevelyan thought him 'like a medieval King.' I thought him even more like Van Eyck's Arnolfini in the National Gallery than usual. And, as Mary Soames has written, 'at the moment when Queen Elizabeth was crowned as Consort, after making vows of utmost solemnity and receiving tokens of grace for her special task [sacraments incidentally in which she, like her eldest daughter after her, most piously believes] Winston turned to Clementine, and, his eyes full of tears, said: "You were right. I see now the 'other one' wouldn't have done".'

The Queen and her husband had been enthusiastic supporters of Neville Chamberlain and would have preferred Edward Halifax to Churchill as his successor, but both soon came to admire and even cherish their wartime Premier. Later, as I discovered, it was to be Queen Elizabeth who first told Churchill to be sure to study Arthur Koestler's 'Darkness at Noon', which had so deeply impressed her, a book he then proceeded to make Must Reading for his entire Cabinet.

Her taste in books has always been eclectic, as one would expect in a friend of the Sitwells and of David Cecil, whom she still sometimes enjoys listening to as he reads aloud to her from Jane Austen, Max Beerbohm, Walter de la Mare and others from among his favourite writers. And when she heard that P. G. Wodehouse was too ill to cross the Atlantic to claim his better-late-than-never knighthood, she immediately volunteered to 'go over myself to dub the poor man.' It was a characteristically spontaneous offer not taken up by a Palace ('up the road' as she calls it) notoriously stuffier than Clarence House – whose atmosphere is now much nearer to what it was when it echoed to the laughter of the four lovely Edinburgh granddaughters of Queen Victoria as they slid down the backstairs banisters.

Clemmie Churchill herself was a woman famously hard to please, but in 1943 she perceptively described an hour alone with the Queen, who 'looked very sweet and soignée, like a plump turtle-dove,' as passing 'like a flash because she is gay and amusing and has pith and point', and five years later, was writing to her, after a stay at Windsor: 'I can truthfully say that I have not enjoyed a weekend party so much for what seems an immeasurable space of time. After 'Clumps', [the game] which I had not played for 40 years (or more) and then in a much more sedate fashion, I felt nearly 40 years younger. It was moving and stimulating to feel the pulse of Britain beating strongly in Your Majesty's family and to feel "here firm though all be drifting".'

One recalls that Prince Charles has lately referred to his adored grandmother's house as 'a haven of cosiness and charades.' The fact is that the Queen Mother, Queen and Prince of Wales are all first-class amateur actors and exponents of the arts of impersonation and mimicry. In the case of the Queen and her eldest son, that talent for mimicry may be a double genetic heritage, for I know at least one other direct descendant of Queen Victoria, herself a Queen, who is also a brilliant mimic.

Of all her 200 portraits, few if any can give more than an inkling of what Noël Coward once well called 'the charm, humour and deep down kindness' that 'leaves behind her gibbering worshippers'. At least they do hint at what she has all her life undoubtedly remained: a great lady with no airs but many graces. *(22.6.80)*

9.
Labour's Split

A Skipper who Likes Fast Bowling
Alan Watkins

'Much as I admire Denis Healey,' said the Welsh MP, 'I'll have to vote for Michael Foot because, when you come down to it, Michael's one of us.'

Foot could certainly be described accurately as the son of a teetotal Methodist lay-preacher, but such a description would have more than a touch of *suggestio falsi*. For Foot's father, old Isaac, was a solicitor, a privy councillor, a Liberal MP on and off – more off than on – and the possessor of one of the largest private libraries in the United Kingdom.

Foot himself was educated at Leighton Park, Reading (a Quaker establishment), and at Wadham College, Oxford, where, as a young Liberal, he was President of the Union and took a Second in Philosophy, Politics and Economics. (Perhaps it was a good thing that Foot's later interests, history and English literature, were not prejudiced through being crammed into him at the university.)

Nor is Foot Welsh. An article in another Sunday newspaper lately referred to his 'Welsh romanticism.' Certainly he is a romantic, sits for a Welsh seat, and was the friend, worshipper and biographer of Aneurin Bevan. But he was brought up in Plymouth, his mother was Scottish (he is Michael Mackintosh Foot) and the family outings were almost always to Cornwall. If anything, he regards himself as a Cornishman. And though he has a genuine affection for the people of Tredegar and Ebbw Vale, he has been known privately to deplore the

Welsh characteristics – if they are characteristics – of indolence, pro-
crastination and nepotism.

Yet it is easy to see what the Welsh MP meant when he said he was
going to vote for him because he was 'one of us.' For Foot has no
snobbery, no side. His speaking style is highly mannered – some would
call it affected – but as a man he is without affectation. Perhaps
snobbery of a kind plays some part in the esteem in which Foot is
almost universally held, even by his political opponents, in This Great
Movement of Ours. We are a funny old country, after all.

'Shall I tell you why I'm going to vote for Michael?', a Labour MP
(not the one referred to earlier) volunteered. 'Because of all the four
candidates, he's the only one who's a gentleman.'

A gentleman, yet one of us. Is it a paradox, even a contradiction?
Perhaps not. Foot is accepted by everybody because he is rarely wholly
at ease with anybody. His private manner is usually diffident and can
be positively awkward. But he has a kind of sweetness, even innocence. He seems to be one of that small company referred to by his
favourite writer, Hazlitt:

'Happy are they who live in the dream of their own existence, and
see all things in the light of their own hope; to whom the guiding star of
their youth still shines from afar, and into whom the spirit of the world
has not entered! They have not been "hurt by the archers," nor has the
iron entered their souls. The world has no hand on them.'

Some commentators may say – have said – that we do not pay our
politicians to be either romantic idealists or nice chaps. But it is to
Foot's basic niceness that people at Westminster continually return. If
that is the case, niceness is a quality of political importance.

Then there is his relationship with Mr Enoch Powell. This is not
solely a matter of their common opposition to British membership of
the EEC; of their somewhat mystical regard for the House of Commons; or of their successful campaign to thwart the late Richard
Crossman's reform, if reform it was, of the Lords in 1968-69. Mr
Powell reveres, even loves Foot. 'I love him,' Mr Powell once said,
'because he speaks beautiful English.'

It is difficult now to recall the degree of hatred which Mr Powell
aroused in 1968 following his 'rivers of blood' speech. He was shunned
and avoided not only by his own party but by Labour MPs. Foot was
appalled by such behaviour, whatever Mr Powell had said. This was no
way to treat a human being. Foot therefore approached Powell in a
crowded Commons library, slapped him on the back and asked how he
was getting on.

But he has a sharp side too. He never forgave Mr Cecil King for
ending his political, or polemical, column in the old *Daily Herald*
(which he had written for 20 years) when the *Mirror* Group acquired

the *Herald.* He encouraged acquaintances in Fleet Street to write articles denouncing Mr King for his general badness. Nor was Foot above being feline about the Gaitskellite revisionists, in particular the late Anthony Crosland.

'One trouble with Crosland,' Foot would say, 'is that he has a bogus Oxford accent.'

Again, he was once lunching with a friend at the Gay Hussar restaurant in Soho, one of his favourite resorts. (He is not a member of any gentlemen's clubs and does not greatly like being entertained in them. 'My club is Soho, just as it was Hazlitt's,' he says). On this occasion he had recently emerged from hospital after an operation for the removal of a cyst in an awkward spot. During his stay in hospital he had been attacked by a columnist who incorrectly alleged that, owing to his position, he was receiving favoured treatment. The columnist, happening to be lunching at the same restaurant, approached Foot with a hand outstretched and a 'Good to see you, Michael.'

'Fuck off,' said Foot.

His health is still a subject of speculation even among his friends, to Foot's irritation. Oddly enough, he was encouraged by his experience on holiday in Cyprus, when he nearly drowned. He proved to himself, however, that he was still a strong swimmer.

The real worry is his eyesight. Foot has never read his speeches. He prepares them in his head on his Hampstead Heath walks. When he was Employment Secretary, and accordingly from time to time required to read chunks of Civil Service prose concerning complicated negotiations, he would in effect say:

'I hope the House will bear with me while I read this boring stuff before I get on with my own speech.'

He now finds it even more difficult to read from a 'brief' or prepared text because of a bad attack of shingles, which left him with defective vision in one eye. This accounts for the sidepiece, on one side only, of his spectacles.

But he is both taller and stronger than the cartoonists suggest, wiry rather than frail (but then, cartoonists always get the sizes of politicians wrong). Until three years ago he turned out regularly for *Tribune* in the annual cricket match against the *New Statesman:* no very taxing athletic achievement, certainly, but nevertheless a feat for a man in his sixties who, 15 years previously, had suffered a car accident that almost killed him. In one of their matches the *NS* fielded a young bowler, the son of one of their contributors, who for his age was alarmingly fast.

'Take it easy, lad,' the *NS* captain instructed. 'Remember he is not only a very distinguished but a very old man.'

The bowler duly took it easy, and bowled a slow ball down the leg side. Foot promptly swept it for four. He swept the next ball for four.

The *NS* captain said:

'Right, if that's the way he wants to play it, you can let him have it.'

The bowler accordingly let him have it. Foot hit another four. He was then run out – running, either between the wickets or in the field, he treated with a Whiggish disdain. But good judges believe that, if he had applied himself and been properly taught, he would have made a nearly, though not quite, first-class batsman, despite his short sight, a disability, after all, shared by Geoff Boycott and Clive Lloyd.

Again and again, with Foot, one seems to come back to the car accident. His wife Jill was driving, and the accident happened just over the border on the way to London from Tredegar. He had then been MP for Ebbw Vale only a short time. The effect was curious. In the 1950s Foot had been pale, tense, a chain-smoker of old-fashioned Players cigarettes, his shoulders and collar covered with dandruff, owing not to personal uncleanliness but to his dreadful asthma (which endeared him to Beaverbrook, a fellow-sufferer) and its accompanying skin trouble.

This was the period of Foot the ranter ('Michael shouts,' his brother Dingle said dismissively); of Foot the Bevanite; of Foot, having lost his seat at Devonport in 1955, the editor of *Tribune,* saving the paper regularly in a financial sense and quarrelling with Bevan over the hydrogen bomb; and of Foot the acerbic panellist of the television programmes 'Free Speech' and 'In the News.' The Robespierre-like 'image' was wrong even then, but it had an element of truth to it: Foot could appear bitter, intolerant and humourless.

In the 1960s, after the accident, he changed. His cheeks became pinker, his asthma better, his manner more relaxed. He filled the Commons chamber not because of his passionate oratory but because he made jokes; for MPs, like most of us, will forgive almost anything for a good laugh, and why not? In 1964-70 he adversely criticised the Wilson Government but also sustained it, keeping the *Tribune* Group within bounds.

'Harold Wilson,' one Minister remarked at the time, 'will never realise the debt he owes Michael Foot.'

Sir Harold offered him a job, but Foot stayed outside. Foot's general view was that, though Sir Harold had let him down, was not the Left-wing figure he had imagined, he was better than any alternative then on display.

It would be wrong to see Foot's election to the National Executive Committee in 1971 as a first, conscious step towards political power. He stood, as he stood more recently for the leadership, because his friends asked him to do so. But we are none of us wholly aware of our real motives; and it may be that Foot, with his romantic disposition and tendency to hero-worship, is more than normally liable to self-deception.

He was brought into the 1974 Government with the clear task of making peace with the unions, following not only Mr Edward Heath's activities but also the 'In Place of Strife' fiasco of 1968-69. There are many who say that Foot made peace only too readily.

Certainly his (jettisoned) proposal that pickets should be given the legal right to stop persons or vehicles was shocking. And his refusal to allow non-religious conscientious objection to union membership was shameful, even if it had not come, as it did, from an agnostic who, as a young man, had been liberated, both sexually and in other respects, by reading Bertrand Russell. Moreover, friends of liberty, one of whom Foot constantly professes to be, may well feel disturbed by his exalt-ation of Britain in 1939-45, when, after all, we were in many aspects a totalitarian state.

But this is not the immediate point, which is that Foot did the job he was required to do with considerable skill. He displayed the same kind of skill when, in his later period as Leader of the House, he kept the Labour Government in being virtually single-handed, not only by courage under fire but by winning the trust of Mr David Steel. For Foot is trusted, and trust is the most important ingredient in politics.

Nothing in the past few weeks, indeed, has been more offensive – or more foolish – than the patronising way in which papers such as *The Times* and the *Daily Telegraph* have chosen to depict Foot: as some kind of amiable booby and bibliophile with the gift of the gab, lacking 'ability' and 'experience of government.' After all, the Department of Employment and the Leader of the House's department are at least as important as the Department of Education, the only previous experi-ence of Mrs Margaret Thatcher.

Nor does one become editor of the *Evening Standard* at 29, as Foot did, without having some administrative ability. Nor could anyone have produced the books Foot has done, one of them – on Swift and Marlborough – of unchallenged scholarship, without possessing appli-cation and industry well out of the ordinary.

We come back to the accident. Waking up in his hospital bed, Foot heard the melancholy strains of the English Methodist hymn:

> *I see the land across the sea*
> *Where mansions are prepared for me.*

Foot thought he was in heaven, or in some spot conveniently ad-jacent. In fact the sounds emanated from the Salvation Army band performing in the street below.. But they are lines that well express Foot's often cloudy political vision. And – who knows? – they may provide a guide to his own political future. *(16.11.80)*

Testament of Shirley Williams
Miriam Gross

MIRIAM GROSS: *When did you decide to go into politics?*
SHIRLEY WILLIAMS: I never decided, you know. It sort of fell out that way. I suppose that I just grew into politics because I was surrounded by it so early. My family talked a great deal about politics. They would get carried away with excitement talking about Spain or Germany or Auden's latest book or the PEN Club or whatever. And they would break off and explain things to my brother and myself. We would ask questions like, what's the Reichstag, why are you so excited about this fire? I was very young then, and I remember being confused, later on, when I heard about the Crystal Palace fire – for years I used to mix up the Reichstag fire and the Crystal Palace fire.

But my parents didn't just talk about politics, they were very much involved. My father went to Spain as a war correspondent for the Loyalists; he escaped at the last minute dressed as a Basque priest. My mother went to Germany and lectured against Hitler and had her books burned and all the rest of it. And a lot of political people came to the house. It was a time when socialism was bursting out all over in intellectual circles, but probably only in intellectual circles, really.

What did you feel about your mother's pacifism then? What do you feel about it now?
The first thing is that my mother was somebody of such absolutely uncompromising integrity that it was shaking to live with. I loved her very much, but how do you live with somebody with that much integrity? She would write to the tax authorities and say: 'I think you haven't remembered that I earned £500 for a second edition of "England's Hour".' She would worry herself stiff if she didn't pay bills within a week. She was just made like that.

They aren't made like that now because it was a special kind of Nonconformist high-mindedness, high thinking and plain living. A bottle of wine might appear if it was someone's birthday, but it was not a drinking household. She was keen on clothes, though – she wore a lot of smart and frilly clothes – and she liked literary parties, but only because she could sit down and talk seriously to other authors. She was pretty relentlessly serious, not much given to laughing.

So you see anything she believed in one had to take terribly seriously, and to this day I cannot dismiss pacifism. It still sits there and tells me that that's what I ought to be; but it simply conflicts with my belief that certain extreme political forces cannot be dealt with by non-violence.

Your father was a Catholic; when did you become a Catholic your-self?

Again, it was like politics, I just grew up with it around me. My father was a rather critical Catholic, not exactly lapsed but pretty fed up with the Church as it was then – don't forget it was the time of things like the Concordat with Franco and the Concordat with Mussolini. But in the end he was a religious man and he stuck with it more or less.

And then my parents had a kind of housekeeper-cum-nanny who lived with us – she was a very pious Catholic and she used to take me to church until I was about nine. When I came back to England from evacuation in Minnesota, at fourteen, I stopped wanting to go. After that I tried about every kind of religion, from the Quakers to Spiritualism, and I also tried doing without religion altogether. But after two or three years I decided that I probably belonged to the Catholic Church – like my father, in a pretty critical way – and that is where I ended up.

Has it helped you very much in your life?

Not entirely. It's a funny mixture, really. It is not a comfortable Church and people who think that it's rather cosy having religious belief haven't got a clue about it. Partly because it's full of inconvenient rules, not all of which I keep, but which from time to time I feel I ought to keep. It's a Church of sinners, which I like a lot, in the sense that the Quaker Church is a Church of saints.

I feel increasingly that if people lived rather more in accordance with the New Testament, they would probably be happier than they are.

I think that the great fault of the Catholic Church is that it has never really come to terms with women. What I object to, like a lot of other women in the Church, is being treated either as Madonnas or Mary Magdalens, instead of being treated as people.

What about the sacrifices that women have to make in order to have full-time careers? What kind of sacrifices have you had to make yourself?

The thing is that I was brought up – I now realise that this was much rarer than I thought it was at the time – in a family where the sexes were treated as entirely equal. My parents simply never thought that it was my job to do the washing-up just because I was the girl. And they never thought I shouldn't join in a political conversation in the same way as my brother did. So I assumed from the start that I would work; it never crossed my mind that I wouldn't.

It was only later that I discovered that women who work have to do two jobs, not one. And even for the luckiest women – and I was one of them because my then husband was good at helping – it still means that they have one and three-quarter jobs. In the end, the responsibility rests with you: if there's no food in the fridge then it's you who hasn't bought it; if the gas isn't paid then it's you. And it's you people assume will go out and buy so-and-so's birthday present.

It's very hard to find enough time for one's kids and spouse. Looking back on it, I probably didn't spend enough time with my husband, although we enjoyed the time we did spend together and our marriage didn't break up for that reason; it broke up because he met somebody else who I think was likely to be a more traditional kind of wife – which is not to say that she isn't a clever and attractive woman. I probably just didn't spend enough time with him, I wasn't around enough.

But I think that I've learned that lesson, and I've managed to spend about enough time with my daughter to make it okay. Time is the one commodity that I never have enough of and I think that most career women find that. They are desperate for time. Finally something goes. In my case it's taking enough care of my appearance.

I never look as good as I could. I'm not saying that there is any great potential, I know there isn't, but I could look better than I do and most women who spend time on themselves do look better than those of us who don't. But I just thought, to hell with it, I'm more interested in doing other things. I can look good occasionally if I really try but it takes so much time.

And I guess that there is an element in me that slightly resents it: the fact that if you're a woman you are supposed to look smart and well turned out and all those things, while for a man it doesn't matter. People don't judge a man on whether his suit has recently been pleated or pressed. The obsessive interest of the Press with my hair, for example – it's just gone on for years.

It doesn't have the effect of making me have my hair done, except very occasionally; it just makes me cross. Because I can't help thinking that they don't go on and on about Peter Shore's hair or Michael Foot's hair, or Keith Joseph's hair, and their hair is all as chaotic as mine. Mrs Thatcher's hair and my hair and Mrs Castle's hair – it's an endless subject. It's the endless trivialising of a woman in any kind of serious job.

What about the psychological aspect – working with men who are not comfortable with women as their equals, let alone their bosses?
It's something that hasn't really bothered me. But I think that's partly because I have a slightly chum-like approach – I'm always careful not to import sex into a work relationship. What I mean by that is that I don't import elements of flirtation or slightly come-on remarks – 'What are you going to be doing after we've finished this boring job?' – that kind of thing. I don't speak more suggestively or huskily to a man.

This is something I've particularly reacted against in America, where most professional women, I've noticed, immediately adopt what one could only describe as a bedroom voice when dealing with their male colleagues.

How do you think Mrs Thatcher does?
She doesn't import sex into it. But she does import a tremendous scolding-mother or headmistress thing. She seems to adopt all the stereotypes of the authoritarian woman, and it's impressive in a way – the Queen, the governess, the nanny, the headmistress, the matron, she strikes the lot, doesn't she?

Do you think that the concept of femininity means anything?
Yes. There are two things really. One is what you might call traditional femininity, which consists essentially in making men think of themselves as protectors. The other, more profound kind, is by no means a monopoly of women. I suppose it's a kind of instinct or empathy for other people, and perhaps most of all not being bound by unnecessary rules.

The House of Commons is a marvellous example of an almost totally male institution. It's absolutely riddled by rules that it has made for itself. Most of them are quite unnecessary, like those in a boy's school. And femininity is asking yourself all the time what human purpose is being served.

There has been a great deal of talk in the media about your niceness, but politicians often have to make decisions which will seem unkind to some people. How do you feel about making such decisions?
Well, I think there are three reasons why I've got the reputation for being nice. One is just by not looking very formidable; it's funny, but if you are not very well groomed, people will think you are quite nice.

Secondly, I think it is because I listen to people. I learn a lot from them, but let's be honest, people are flattered when you listen to them. And I think the third thing, which I've inherited from my mother, is a very strong feeling – I don't know what to do with it sometimes – of obligation when people turn to me for help. I feel that I am lucky and I'm quite well off and I have a nice job and my child and lots of friends, and here is some poor miserable character in trouble and I feel I have to do something. All that doesn't add up to being nice, actually, it's just what people call nice.

One of the doubts that some people have about the Social Democrats is that they seem to be mostly intellectuals. Do you think that intellectuals make good politicians?
I think that is a reaction to the Gang of Four, and it is changing as a wider range of people come on board. It's also fair to say that the Gang of Four and the other MPs who have joined them have done something that is rather uncharacteristic of intellectuals, which is that all of them have been through a kind of baptism of fire.

Generally I'm not a great admirer of intellectuals in politics – they can find lots of reasons for not doing what they ought to do. We need some of them, but a government of intellectuals would be disastrous. I don't think of myself as one.

Why do you think that the undemocratic Left have made such advances over the last few years in the Labour Party, and indeed in the country?

I think the real reason for the inroads made by the far Left in the Labour Party is that round about 1970 one small but extremely energetic section of the Trotskyite movement decided that they would never get anywhere except by working from inside a major party – what's called entryism. This was the decision made by the Militant Tendency when they abolished their membership lists and instead formed groups within the party.

It was a brilliantly effective move, partly because you get a very low attendance at most local party meetings, and it's easy to make that attendance fall even further by changing the nature of what you discuss; the more theological, abstract, unsocial meetings are, the more disagreeably lengthy and abusive, the fewer people will come.

What do you think it is that motivates these Trotskyites or militants?

Quite a lot of them were students who are now unemployed. They are often unemployed by choice: I say that advisedly, since I don't think many people are unemployed by choice. But some of these people have certainly chosen to devote themselves full-time to politics. A lot of them are the '68 generation, which was an extremely militant and highly politicised student generation everywhere – even in Britain.

Do you think what they want is simply power?

No, I think there is some genuine idealism there. It is a hard idealism, because ours is a harder time than ten or 15 years ago in terms of attitudes, of people being *macho* and tough.

It ranges from Mrs Thatcher to these young fellows, and they really have the same style – tough. They don't want to be sentimental or understanding or any of those dreary words. They really want to sock it to them between the eyes.

And then there's a nihilistic element, though I think it's much smaller in Britain than it is say in Germany: the feeling is, let's get the hell out of this suffocating bourgeois society and since we can't change it let's just destroy it. I think the third element is just a straight power thing, but they are all tangled together.

People often seem to be deeply attached to names and labels in politics. Do you object to the Social Democrats being called a party of the centre, for instance?

Yes, very much. I don't like Right, and I don't like Centre; I can live with Moderate. And Radical I like. I feel terribly strongly that I am not right-wing, and that a lot of the policies I believe in are very radical.

What do you feel about the fact that the leaders of two of our political parties may soon be women?
I find it fascinating. When I was in the States recently I kept thinking, why is it so inconceivable that women should become Presidents or even Vice-Presidents? And I finally came to the conclusion that the real reason for this, strangely enough, is that we are a monarchy. So that boys and girls alike have always had at the back of their heads the concept of a woman in authority – we've all grown up with Elizabeth I and Victoria and the present Queen. That's why, paradoxically, I'd have to say that I'm a monarchist, even though I dislike honours and I want to get rid of the House of Lords. Though I think we need a second chamber.

Who are your political heroes and heroines?
Well, in any old order: Julius Nyerere, though I was disappointed in his reaction about Zanzibar; but he's a remarkable man. Kenneth Kaunda, who was a student of mine, oddly enough, when I was a teacher in Ghana; a lovely man. Nehru, he was rather an English gentleman but there was a kind of blazing quality about him. Lincoln, if we go back far enough. Willy Brandt, very much.

It's funny, isn't it, that they all seem to come from abroad, maybe because I know more about the ones at home. . . . Attlee, though he was rather grey. Jim Callaghan – I found him a very good Prime Minister to work with. And Barbara Castle; although Barbara is a great old lefty, she has colossal guts, and the panache with which she marched into ministries which hadn't had women before was remarkable. She's much more sharply political than I am.

Do you read much, apart from books on politics?
I read a lot of poetry, in so far as I have time to read anything: Auden, Larkin, Frost, Seamus Heaney are the ones I'm reading at the moment. Not so much novels.

Finally, do you think the Social Democrats will be able to cure the ills of Britain?
I'm a bit frightened about that. But I think we would stand a considerable chance of dealing with what, to my mind, are the two besetting illnesses of Britain. First, the way in which politics have become totally polarised. Everything one government does is automatically undone by the next – it's an absurd way of governing.

And second, we must end parties based on class. We may look like intellectuals or any other damn thing, but the fact that we are going to have a party which is not affiliated to huge interest groups, whether it's middle-class and business or so-called blue collar and union, is in itself terribly important.

For the first time in my life I'm really scared that the country could seriously end up with a non-democratic structure, either right-wing or left-wing. It's to try and prevent that happening that, in the end, I left the Labour Party. *(22.3.81)*

The Politics of Spring
Editorial

Democratic politics is about choice: choosing a Member of Parliament, a set of policies, a government; and then – when they run out of energy, ideas or luck – having the right to choose the other lot. It is a system for the peaceful transfer of power of which this country has rightly been proud. It has given our society a rare stability and continuity in a period of national decline.

But over the past decade there have been unmistakable signs of dissatisfaction with the range of choices offered, as shown by protest votes, abstentions and weakening party allegiances. This process has been accelerated by economic failure, by the individual's growing sense of powerlessness over events, and by the apparent domination of the Labour Party by the unions and the Left. It has culminated – in a way that now seems inevitable – in last week's launch of the Social Democratic Party.

Whether the new party will succeed in changing the face of British politics depends on many unknowns, some of them outside its own control, such as Mrs Thatcher's luck with the economy, the coming debate on proportional representation, and the continuing fight for the soul of the Labour Party. To offer a warm welcome to the Social Democrats – as we do – is not to write off the moderate elements in the other parties, but to insure against their failure. The SDP restores the moderate option to British politics.

Given Mrs Thatcher and Mr Foot as opponents, this is a powerful short-term advantage for the new party. But it may become a longer-term problem for them if the other parties return to the centre ground they have normally occupied since the last war. The problem then will be one of identity, as the Liberals have found out to their cost.

After all, Macmillan, Heath, Wilson and Callaghan were moderates too – and only moderately successful in arresting Britain's economic decline. The new party will need to persuade people that, in their hands, similar policies, or a development of them, will produce better results. To ride the public mood is not enough, and it would not be honest politics.

Talking of honest politics, no kindly observer can withhold from the Liberals this week 'the meed of some melodious tear,' for they have fought a good fight in hard times and they deserve better than to be overtaken now by a wave they have been trying to ride since Jo Grimond's revival a quarter-century ago. The Liberals also deserve credit for pioneering some of the SDP's most popular ideas – the concern with local democracy, with the environment, profit-sharing, humanising institutions, making bureaucracy more responsive to people's needs.

But there is a difference: a matter of confidence. The Social Democrats offer greater credibility than the Liberals. This is because – as David Steel honestly admits – they have experience in government which modern Liberals lack. Their leaders' ministerial track record is known and broadly approved. They have been in where it hurts. They know what politics is about: hard choices, not easy answers (though their launching document, disappointingly, doesn't face all those hard choices). Having made a brave and agonising choice themselves, risking their own careers, they are entitled to ask others to question the assumptions of a lifetime.

At this stage, perhaps understandably, they offer principles rather than detailed policies. Mr Roy Jenkins is against 'manifestoitis' or 'enormous lists' and 'great catalogues' of promises. On the major issues of Europe, NATO and Third World development (causes supported by this newspaper over many years) they are commendably firm, but on incomes policy and related issues they are much too imprecise. On the economy they offer 'a consistent economic strategy, one that is not disrupted every few years by a political upheaval . . . positive support for a mixed economy without constant Conservative sniping at the public sector or repeated Labour threats to private enterprise.'

Some of these aims are as vague as support for motherhood and apple pie. Eventually – and well before the General Election – the party must decide what it wants done and then seek to convince the public that its policies will succeed where others have failed. A party elected on the basis of something for everyone would soon come unstuck, just as surely as one based on the dogmatism of Left or Right.

There are still confusing policy differences to be hammered out, as demonstrated by Dr David Owen's persistent use of the word 'socialism' and Mrs Shirley Williams's wish to end private education. There will be difficulties, to put it mildly, in persuading local Liberal parties to join an electoral pact at a time when their chances look good. This will need unusual tact and political skill.

With record unemployment and falling living standards, the new party will need more than generalised good will to convince working-class people to trust them when it comes to the crunch of facing the ballot box rather than an opinion pollster. Their decision not to provoke by-elections in their own seats, for reasons of tactical prudence, suggests that they know that.

These things having been said – and the new party must expect a continuing critique if and when its detailed policies emerge – Messrs Jenkins, Owen, Rodgers and Mrs Williams have brought an undeniable lift to the spirits of all those who feel excluded from the present system. As a party, they have no monopoly of conscience and reform, nor of personal freedom and social justice, but they have the advantage of being unhampered by ideological baggage and broken promises. Even if their great adventure should end in electoral failure it may catalyse reform in the other parties.

The SDP's arrival coincides with the daffodils and the first bright days of spring. Whether this tender plant has the resilience to survive a few hard winters remains to be seen. Reserving judgements is a matter of infinite hope. *(29.3.81)*

132. Labour's Split

10.
Various Arts

God, Literature and So Forth
Anthony Burgess

I don't know how many British novelists live on the Côte d'Azur these days, but I am certainly in the Condamine of Monaco and Graham Greene certainly, when he is not in Paris or Anacapri or on his remoter travels, lives on the Avenue Pasteur, Antibes. He is hospitable to fellow-novelists, and I see him less than, for the good of my soul, I should; I mean the sense of exaltation, or reassurance, or the sheer stimulation of communion with a superior artist.

To get to Antibes was like plotting a major campaign. I would have to get the dawn train. I limped up the hill to the station, sprayed by the hoses of the darkling street-cleaners, and started my pilgrimage.

Stations of the Cross: Cap d'Ail, Eze, Beaulieu-sur-Mer, Nice, St Laurent-du-Var, Cros-de-Cagnes, Cagnes-sur-Mer, Villeneuve-Loubet, Biot. Antibes is quiet at this season, though its harbour is full of small shipping. The sun is bright and mild, the air like chilled Pouilly Fumé. Greene's apartment is a hundred metres up the hill. I have, blast this left leg, to take a taxi.

Greene is on the fourth floor. His balcony overlooks the crammed shipping (like teeth so close set you couldn't twang dental floss between them). In summer the noise of motor traffic is as loud for him as for me. The days of authorial seclusion, Maugham and the Villa Mauresque, are long over. Writers live in small flats and hope to have a daily help. The best décor in the world, which you can't get in London or Paris, is marine sunlight. Greene looks well in it. Seventy-five years old, he is lean, straight, active. The blue eyes are startling, especially in all this light. We are to talk about his work, especially his new novella, 'Doctor Fischer of Geneva.'

ANTHONY BURGESS: Graham, you've practised all the literary forms – verse, drama, the novel, the short story, the essay, even biography. I wonder if you ever wanted to practise any other art.
GRAHAM GREENE: I'm tone-deaf. I can't draw or paint. I've worked in the cinema, of course – as critic, scriptwriter, even in the cutting-room – that was when I was a co-producer. All my novels have been filmed, with one exception – 'It's a Battlefield.' Ironically, that was the one book I wrote with the intention of adaptation to the screen.
A.B.: 'Doctor Fischer' cries out to be filmed, doesn't it? It's short, so no director is going to want to cut it. There's a fine scenic background – winter Switzerland – and a climax, an elaborate dinner-party in the snow with great bonfires, which you must have seen as film even while you were writing it.
G.G.: Well, yes, the preliminaries to filming it are already under way. I suppose you could say that, just as landscape painting was behind Sir Walter Scott, film is behind or before me. It's the great visual art of our day, and it's bound to influence the novelist.
A.B.: With all except one of your novels filmed, and several short stories, you're exemplary as the filmable novelist. How many of the films do you find satisfactory – I mean, as saying in dialogue and image directly what you've already said to the reader's imagination?
G.G.: 'The Third Man' certainly works, but of course I wrote that as a film – having first done a kind of literary treatment which reads well enough as a story in its own right. I saw 'The Third Man' again recently in Paris. There's a whole new generation discovering it. Yes, it still works. 'The Fallen Idol' too. I'm not happy about a good number of the others. Endings get changed. 'Travels With My Aunt' stops before the story I wrote really gets started.
When 'The Heart of the Matter' was filmed we weren't allowed to show a suicide on the screen. That ruined the whole point – self-elected damnation on the part of Scobie. Seeing a preview of 'The Human Factor' just recently, I was disappointed that so much of the book just couldn't find a correlative in cinematic images.
A.B.: Without having seen it, I'd say right away that it wasn't possible to deal with Buller, the boxer dog, who needs the devices of literary description to turn him into a character.
G.G.: Both Kim Philby and Harold Acton said that they liked Buller better than anyone.

A.B.: No wonder. Buller licks his testicles with the juicy noise of an alderman drinking soup. He leaves trails of spittle on the bed like a bonbon. You can't film the phraseology. I'd say also that you can't translate that bit about the alderman into another language. We make literature out of our own traditions as well as our own language. Which brings me to the Graham Greene style, which is wholly a matter of words. What is it that's peculiarly Greeneish in the way you use words?

G.G.: I started off with the desire to use language experimentally. Then I saw that the right way was the way of simplicity. Straight sentences, no involutions, no ambiguities. Not much description, description isn't my line. Get on with the story. Present the outside world economically and exactly.

A.B.: You're a strongly visual writer. I mean, I see things clearly when I read your work. The cinema images are redundant. It's all in the book.

G.G.: You think that? I think there are solidities – I mean I try to be accurate. Then someone comes along and says that boxers don't salivate like Buller. Or (it was you who said this) there are no carrots in Lancashire hotpot. Or there isn't an ABC on the Strand.

A.B.: I see you have a volume of Borges here, the man who kindly calls himself the Argentine Burgess. He seems to think a fiction writer ought to be able to make the external world out of his head and then, if he wishes, just make it collapse into nothing.

G.G.: Yet Borges is devoted to the very writers I admire so much. Chesterton, for instance, and Stevenson. I was walking on a crowded street with him in Buenos Aires. Totally blind, he was clinging to my arm. I mentioned Stevenson's best poem and he stopped, in all that roar of the traffic, and recited it from beginning to end.

A.B.: If Borges had written your new book, or Nabokov for that matter, the critics would start wondering why its hero has an artificial hand.

G.G.: The best answer would be because he lost his real hand in the London blitz, which he did. The artificial hand's there so that the ghastly Dr Fischer can insult him by referring to a 'deformity.' Also to stimulate the reader's imagination, make him wonder about the problems of making love with a false hand. But there's no deep symbolism – or if there is, it's not my job to find it. Critics and university professors rejoice in the *sous-texte* these days. The study of fiction has become less the study of the narrative art than a search for arcane meanings.

Take 'The Third Man.' One distinguished critic looked for arboreal significance in the names Harry Lime and Holly Martins. Now the original name of Martins was Rollo, which the actor Joseph Cotten wouldn't accept. If Lime has a connotation it's to do with quicklime, the disposal of bodies. No, it's dangerous to dig too deep. I try to be a straight writer.

A.B.: A highly readable one – not like Joyce or Faulkner. I approach your books in two ways. I swallow a new Greene novel whole, with great speed. Then I slow down for a second reading and taste it. Then three months later I go back to it for the various aftertastes I've missed.

G.G.: I'm happy to think that I'm read that way. The more I think of it, the more I worry about this division of literature into the great because hard to read, the not so great – or certainly the ignorable by scholars – because of the desire to divert, be readable, keep it plain. You don't find Conan Doyle dealt with at length in the literary histories. Yet he was a great writer. He created several characters –

A.B.: Eliot admired him but didn't think him worthy of a critical essay – not like Wilkie Collins. And yet Eliot lifted a whole chunk of 'The Musgrave Ritual' –

G.G.: Where?

A.B.: In 'Murder in the Cathedral.' You remember – 'Whose was it?' – 'His who is gone.' – 'Who shall have it?' – 'He who will come.' – 'What shall be the month?' And so on. In the Sherlock Holmes story we have 'Whose was it?' – 'His who is gone.' – 'Who shall have it?' – 'He who will come.' – 'What was the month?' Almost identical.

G.G.: Something ought to be done about this double standard. I admire writers like Stanley Weyman. Victor Pritchett had the nerve to write about Rider Haggard after reading only two of his books. Haggard has to be read entire. H. G. Wells too. I've been seeking out the novels of the so-called middle period in old bookshops and I find them remarkable. There's also Bulwer Lytton. His 'Pelham' deals with an illicit love affair in a thoroughly contemporary way.

A.B.: Why not write a book, or certainly an essay, on the literary snobbism which prefers symbols and ambiguities to the straight art of story-telling?

G.G.: I leave that to you.

A.B.: In the same way, Eliot admired 'My Fair Lady' but wouldn't take it with the right literary seriousness. Otherwise he wouldn't have accepted lines like "I'd be equally as willing for a dentist to be drilling than to ever let a woman in my life." Only Auden took Lorenz Hart seriously.

G.G.: He wrote songs with Richard Rodgers, didn't he? I met Rodgers and Hammerstein when they were doing a stage adaptation of 'The Heart of the Matter' –

A.B.: Not a musical, for God's sake.

G.G.: No, a very bad straight adaptation. I may not be musical but I've written popular songs. I like to put them in my novels, as you know. Now some of them have been set to music. They're broadcasting three of them on French radio.

A.B.: Write the book of a musical and I'll do the music.

G.G.: Oh, I had this idea of a musical in which a band of girls steal chasubles and croziers at an episcopal conference and then get themselves up as bishops before the Archbishop of Melbourne arrives. Melbourne falls in love with Canterbury. There's a good telephone song there – 'Cantuar calling Melbourne.'

A.B.: Do it, please. Auden, who took Hart seriously, was responsible for the lines:

> *Is this a milieu where I must*
> *How grahamgreeneish! How*
> *   infra dig!*
> *Snatch from the bottle in my*
> *   bag*
> *An analeptic swig?*

He's referring to a college where he's going to give a lecture, and there may be nothing to drink. Why should the analeptic swig be grahamgreeneish?

G.G.: I don't think he means my drinking habits. I can take alcohol – a couple of Scotches or dry martinis and a bottle of wine a day. My liver was vaccinated by my undergraduate thirst.

No, grahamgreeneish seems to refer to a particular kind of fictional character I've created – white men going to seed in outlandish places. Unshaven, guilt-ridden, on the bottle. One word I seem to be associated with is *seedy* – characters I mean, not myself. It's not a happy term, a bit vague. There are such people. But they seem to have become, in their transference to my fiction, symbols of something of mankind after the fall, perhaps.

A.B.: Would it be right to say that your novels were the first fiction in English to present evil as something palpable – not a theological abstraction but an entity symbolised in glass-rings on the brothel table, joyless sex, dental caries (Mexico in 'The Power and the Glory'), hopeless and empty men in exile?

G.G.: Evil's in Hitler, not in dental caries. I see we're getting on to myself as a Catholic novelist, I'm not that: I'm a novelist who happens to be Catholic. The theme of human beings lonely without God is a legitimate fictional subject. To want to deal with the theme doesn't make me a theologian. Superficial readers say that I'm fascinated by damnation. But nobody in my books is damned – not even Pinky in 'Brighton Rock.' Scobie in 'The Heart of the Matter' tries to damn himself, but the possibility of his salvation is left open. The priest's final words are that nobody, not even the Church, knows enough about divine love and judgement to be sure that anyone's in hell.

A.B.: I'm a cradle Catholic – and you're a convert. Do you see much difference between the two kinds of believers?

G.G.: Converts can be rigorous, of course. Evelyn Waugh showed great theological rigour when attacking some of my earlier work.

A.B.: I admired him greatly, but he scared me. I wanted to visit him but never dared. The daughter of his I met in America said he was approachable, no monster. If he had a son I suppose I'd be scared of him too.

G.G.: He has sons.

A.B.: I never knew that. What do you think of the present state of the novel in English?

G.G.: Beryl Bainbridge is very good. Muriel Spark too, of course. I used to read Frank Tuohy. And William Golding. R. K. Narayan I still love.

A.B.: Don't you find the British novel parochial?

G.G.: There was a time, in the nineteenth century of course, when it could be both parochial and universal. Not now perhaps. I don't read much American fiction. Bellow? I liked 'Henderson the Rain King' – a remarkable picture of Africa for a man who'd never been there. John Updike, no. The Southerners, no. Faulkner is very convoluted. Patrick White? I liked 'Voss.'

A.B.: Both Bellow and White got the Nobel Prize. When are you going to get it?

G.G.: Yes, I was asked that question by a Swedish journalist. How would you like the Nobel Prize? I said I look forward to getting a bigger prize than that.

A.B.: Which one?

G.G.: Death. Let's go and eat lunch. I miss English sausages. I don't like them all meat, on French lines. I like a bit of bread in them.

A.B.: I've been tempted to fly to Heathrow just to pick up sausages and then fly back again. Which reminds me – back again to Dr Fischer and his banger party. Here you have a man who loves to humiliate and finds his humiliands among the greedy, who will even eat cold porridge for dinner for the sake of the munificent presents they get afterwards. Who are prepared, at the end, to play a kind of Russian roulette with Christmas crackers. One contains a bomb which explodes on pulling. The others have cheques for two million Swiss francs. Fischer is misanthropic and cruel. Is he also evil?

G.G.: No, he's just a very sad man. The big Catholic verities like good and evil – you won't find these in my later work.

A.B.: I find compassion.

G.G.: Yes, I think you're meant to. We'd better leave. Can you walk as far as the station?

A.B.: With the help of my stick.

G.G. *(mischievously)*: That stick makes you look venerable. *(With glee)*.

A.B. *(sourly, in pain):* And you still have something of the look (Jesus Christ, my leg's going into spasm) of the (God help me) the (blast the bloody thing) juvenile delinquent.

G.G.: Yes, yes. Yes, something of that. If you miss your train, come back to the flat. We can talk more about God and literature and so forth.

A.B.: The horror, the horror.

G.G.: The juvenile delinquent, yet. *(16.3.80)*

The Good Companions
Gillian Widdicombe

Sir Peter Pears suggested that I meet him at his club, the Reform, in Pall Mall. When I approached its daunting portals he was standing outside on the pavement, wearing a warm tweed coat and a blue yachting cap. He had just discovered that the Reform does not admit women in the afternoon.

'So much for reform!' he said, and proposed tea at Fortnum & Mason. The waitress took one look at the silver-haired gentleman with gold-rimmed spectacles, and set the tea tray down beside him. After a small fuss because she had brought milk instead of lemon, Sir Peter turned to me with a genteel smile and said, 'Shall I be mum?'

When Pears and Britten met, in 1937, Britten was 23; a shy, struggling composer who had spent three unhappy years at the Royal College of Music, and was working for the GPO Film Unit, which had introduced him to the amazing influence of W. H. Auden. A weak chin disguised Britten's competitiveness and ambition; heavy eyelids seemed to shield his feelings. His mother had just died.

Pears was three years older, a handsome tenor earning £6 a week singing the morning services on the radio, as a member of the BBC Singers. Their companionship – more happy, stable and productive than many a real marriage – lasted nearly 40 years, until Britten died in Pears's arms in December 1976.

'Ben didn't find talking about music, or talking about himself, very easy,' Sir Peter said. I had asked him why, during Britten's lifetime, so little was written about the composer himself, or the circumstances which inspired him. We all knew that there was a dark side to Britten's music: lost innocence and the outsider's conflict with a bigoted society are recurrent themes in his operas; and clearly his last opera, 'Death in Venice,' was a very personal statement, a far more explicit and lyrical acknowledgement of homosexuality than its source, Thomas Mann's novella.

But even after the legal status of homosexuality changed in 1967, the taboo lasted because those in the Aldeburgh circle knew that Britten, had a strong puritan streak and an inescapable middle-class up-bringing. So had Pears, though he was probably more worldly than Britten. Now, however, three years after Britten's death, Pears has broken the taboo.

'It was established very early that we were passionately devoted and close,' Pears says. 'The word "gay" was not in his vocabulary. . . . Ben thought that decent behaviour, decent manners were part of a fine life. Gracious living, if you like. But "the gay life," he resented that. . . . He was more interested in the beauty, and therefore the danger, that existed in any relationship between human beings – man and woman, man and man; the sex didn't really matter.'

Britten's obsession with evil may have been exaggerated, Pears thinks. But he does agree that lost innocence – a lost child, lost childhood, innocence destroyed and the search for that innocence – were of fundamental importance to Britten. 'Ben had a marvellous childhood,' he says. 'And as he grew up, he became increasingly disappointed in the realities of adult life.' Britten was the youngest of four children in a comfortable house on the cliffs of Lowestoft, his father a dental surgeon, his mother a keen amateur singer. The atmosphere was like a party, centred round a nurse, a piano and an old rocking horse.

He started to compose at the age of five: piano sonatas, enormous symphonies, even a tone poem called 'Chaos and Cosmos.' The family did not publicise his precocity, but arranged for him to study with Frank Bridge while still at prep school. At 15 he was sent to Gresham's, where he enjoyed sports but not much else, burying himself in music and often surprising the other boys by reading scores in bed. By the time he was 17 there were boxes full of compositions, which he carefully preserved.

Towards the end of his life, in the difficult weeks after heart surgery, when he was physically unable to compose, he rather enjoyed looking through this juvenilia. Pears and Britten's publishers have recently been going through the boxes too. 'Ben never mentioned it,' says Pears, 'but some of it is awfully good.'

Perhaps Britten's mother spoiled him, but his father was always strict; and throughout his life Britten was grateful for this instillation of the work ethic and discipline. He enjoyed a regular routine, beginning the day with a cold bath and sitting down to work at his desk on a spartan wooden stool from 9 a.m. Before lunch he would play through on the piano what he had composed that morning. According to Pears, 'If he hadn't worked for three or four hours in the morning and another couple in the early evening, he'd have felt unused and miserable. Ben lived and breathed music. When we went for a walk he was always thinking about some project on which he was working. Even on holiday he was the same, unless we were actually playing tennis or skiing.'

The unhappy years at the Royal College left resentments. 'He objected very much to the sort of book on orchestration which students had to have a go at,' says Pears. 'He thought it unbelievably silly to say things like "Never double oboes and violins." I tried to persuade him to write this sort of thing down, but I knew he wouldn't because he distrusted talk about music. He thought music was the thing. He could compose what he meant.'

The other frustration at the College was that it failed to give Britten the thing he most needed: performance of his works. In three years only one piece, the 'Sinfonietta for 10 Instruments,' was played at the College, which explains why in later life Britten invited a number of younger composers such as Henze and Birtwistle to the Aldeburgh Festival. Neither he nor Pears could disguise the fact that some of these works gave them more pain than pleasure; but the important thing was not to repeat the narrow-mindedness that Britten had experienced at the College, where both Berg and Schönberg had been banned. 'Maybe he ought to have been more interested in the new noises,' says Pears. 'But electronics certainly didn't interest him at all.'

Britten was 21 when he met Auden. 'Cobwebs were blown away,' Pears says. 'Wystan had no respect for anybody. He just came out with things. He shocked Ben, but also released and freed him.' Auden's fixation with death was one of the many things that influenced Britten at this time, not least because Britten lost both his parents in the 1930s: his father died a year before he met Auden, his mother a few months before he met Pears. And the death fixation was probably increased by the fact that Britten's family had been extensively involved in the occult. Britten was often disturbed by premonitions, and even towards the end of his life casual Suffolk friends found that talking about strange happenings was a good way of drawing him into conversation.

The relationship with Pears started after another death, that of Pears's closest friend, a young writer and journalist called Peter Burra. By chance Britten had met Burra in Barcelona in 1936, when Britten had played his Violin Suite with Antonio Brosa; Burra was writing reviews for *The Times*. Burra and Pears were living together in Charlotte Street, Soho, and Britten visited them once or twice after his mother died. Then, in April 1937, Burra was killed in an air crash near Reading, and Britten went round to help Pears sort out Burra's papers. 'And that,' says Pears, 'was that.'

Pears came from a very similar middle-class background. 'Services, church and professional classes,' he explains. 'My father was a civil engineer in India. I was the youngest of seven children, and never met my father until I was 13, when he retired and came back to Sussex to live with "me and my mother," as I regarded it. But I was very happy at my prep school, and adored Lancing.

'I'd always been musical, and in adolescence music became the centre of my life. I went up to Oxford but was sent down for failing my first year exams and couldn't afford to go up again. So I went back to teach at my old prep school for four years. Played the organ, trained the choir. Sometimes deadly boring, sometimes quite fun. I remember there was one talented boy, a tiny pianist, who used to go round singing "I gotta woman crazy 'bout me".' At this point the ladies taking tea in Fortnum & Mason are treated to the distinguished tenor imitating a 12-year-old crooner.

'Then someone suggested I ought to sing,' Sir Peter continued. 'So I went up to London once a week to the Webber Douglas school and studied with a man I last saw as an usher at the Festival Hall. After a couple of dozen lessons I won an operatic exhibition to the Royal College, and found myself on stage at the end of the first term, singing the Duke of Mantua in the last act of "Rigoletto." But I only stayed there for two terms. Not a very distinguished academic career, I'm afraid.' Pears was also a composer of sorts when he met Britten. 'But I soon gave that up. One couldn't compete.'

Pears obviously finds it difficult to talk about the problems facing even so respectable a homosexual couple during those years. As for Britten, though he might joke about it with close and knowing friends, he never shared the promiscuity and outrageous delight of the Auden circle. According to Ronald Duncan, who wrote the libretto for 'The Rape of Lucretia' and knew Britten from the age of 21, Britten regarded sex as a very noble thing, and blinked with terror when he and Duncan shared an off-putting introduction to female nudity in a Paris brothel, a few months before Britten's mother died. In a forthcoming memoir Duncan proposes that Britten was 'a reluctant homosexual, a man in flight from himself, who often punished himself, who often punished others for the sin he felt he'd committed himself.'

Finding a companion who shared his musical tastes so exactly clearly improved Britten's confidence, for his next work was 'Variations on a Theme of Frank Bridge,' the first big success. Meanwhile, with his mother's legacy he was able to buy a converted millhouse at Snape, in Suffolk, which gave him the quietness and privacy he needed for composing.

But a *modus vivendi* was not born easily, so when Auden and Isherwood emigrated to the United States at the beginning of 1939, Britten and Pears decided to follow them. Until then Britten had not been too keen on going abroad (and he never became keen on foreign things such as strange food); but Pears had already toured the States twice, with the New English Singers, and convinced Britten that America could offer them a better life. In any case, there was a performance of the 'Frank Bridge Variations' coming up in New York, and Pears had friends with whom they could stay on Long Island.

When Auden set up his household on Middagh Street in Brooklyn, Pears and Britten attempted to partake of this communal living, sharing a large room on the same floor as Auden. Pears enjoyed it, but Britten's puritan streak began to rebel: it was far too bohemian for him; among other things, the house smelled. During those years Auden and Britten collaborated on various works, including the choral operetta 'Paul Bunyan.'

The friendship with Auden cooled. 'Bunyan' had been criticised for the over-cleverness of the libretto, and when they tried to collaborate on a Christmas work, Britten refused to set the immensely long poem that Auden produced, arguing that the very best fugues only needed 'Amen.' Britten had become more sure of himself, and was no longer inclined to be bullied by Auden.

Both later regretted the break, yet did nothing to bring about a reconciliation. Britten withdrew 'Bunyan' from publication, and Auden's name became a dangerous subject at Aldeburgh. It was only after Auden's death and Britten's heart operation, when his juvenilia began to amuse him, that he allowed 'Bunyan' to be brought out of the cupboard, revised and performed, shortly before he died.

'We were on the West Coast when we decided to come back to Britain,' Pears explains. 'We read an article in *The Listener* by E. M. Forster about Crabbe's poem 'The Borough,' the story of Peter Grimes. Ben suddenly got a yen for East Anglia. News of the war was pretty bad (not that we were proposing to do much about it, except to make music for those who were there), but we just said: "We've got to go back".' No doubt Britten regarded the luck of finding Forster's article a premonition, ending months of indecision. While waiting six more months for a boat, he met Koussevitsky, who commissioned the opera for $1,000 – another good omen.

'Coming back to Suffolk was like beginning again,' says Pears. What he doesn't say is that, in some ways, Britten began to withdraw from the real world. This part of Suffolk remains one of the most rural areas in Britain, and in the 1940s its inhabitants were virtually ignorant of minorities such as Jews, blacks, homosexuals. If local people thought Britten and Pears a queer couple, it was simply because they were musicians. Britten enjoyed a drink in the pub, or a chat with a local fisherman; and in this world of village communities, windswept beaches and unspoilt marshes he found peace and security. He hated having to leave Suffolk in the middle of a composition.

The retreat was not without drawbacks, however. For example, after 'Grimes' Britten lost touch with theatrical life, and his later works may have suffered as a result. It was hard to convince him that realistic props and sets were not necessary when it came to staging 'The Turn of the Screw' and 'Death in Venice.' And the later operas grew long prologues (a Wagnerian affliction), which some critics considered damaging to dramatic structure. When Britten wrote 'Owen Win-grave' for television he knew virtually nothing about television as a medium, because it had been banned from his part of the house. The housekeeper was allowed a set, but Britten only watched if Pears was appearing.

It was Pears who first suggested they should start their own festival; and though Britten was the more imaginative and decisive when it came to arranging programmes, he would never have started such an enterprise on his own. In turn, Aldeburgh gave Britten the ideal platform, and he felt secure when working with friends of his own choice, under his own direction. 'At first there was a certain amount of philistine opposition from the locals, who wanted to keep the golf course and the Alde estuary for themselves,' Pears recalls, with the nostalgia that affects everyone who was there in the early days. But the opening festival, in 1948, was so intimate and friendly that it seemed like 'a glorious lark. Ben regarded himself as chief purveyor of new works to Aldeburgh, and enjoyed feeling useful. I think those early years of the festival were the happiest of his life.'

Pears's musical influence on Britten, especially during the years 1940 to 1950, cannot be overstated. Britten began to tailor his vocal line specifically for Pears's voice, to the extent that even a singer so different, vocally, as Jon Vickers can feel himself pushed by the vocal line in 'Grimes' towards Pears's method of production – the most obvious example is the magnificent mad monologue, 'Now the Great Bear and Pleiades.' Vickers can also tell which were Pears's best notes – E was the favourite.

In a more general way Pears increased Britten's interest in opera, because he joined the Sadler's Wells Opera during the many months during which the libretto of 'Grimes' was being prepared, and Britten heard him sing a variety of roles, from Ferrando in 'Cosi fan tutte' to Alfredo in 'Traviata' and the Duke in 'Rigoletto.' They gave regular recitals together from the early 1940s.

Most important of all, the relationship led Britten to believe that interpreters were as necessary as creators, and to enjoy not only conducting his own works but actually belonging to a company. The English Opera Group was subsequently dominated by Britten: a strict, ruthless, inspiring colleague, never satisfied. Ironically, Auden had been the first to introduce Britten to the idea of stage unity stemming from the collaboration of author, designer, and composer, regardless of individual prestige and personality; but it never worked when Auden was around, whereas it did when Pears worked with Britten. In later years, Pears seemed deliberately to refrain from making suggestions while Britten was involved in composing or staging, which rather implied that the two had agreed it was better for Britten to work without interference. 'Ben loathed rows and disagreements,' Pears says.

Looking back over 40 years, Pears believes that the key to understanding Britten's music is this: 'Ben was a person of strong moral opinions.' Those who know his religious music have always assumed that he was a practising Christian, so convincing do the church works seem. This, Pears now says, was not the case. Britten rejected his Low Church background, and in no way followed the example of Auden, who became an eccentric Anglican in 1940. Shortly before his death he received Holy Communion from the Bishop of Ipswich: but it now transpires that this was to please his friend the Bishop, not because Britten believed himself on the threshold of Salvation.

His real feelings seem to be expressed in 'Grimes:' a complacent Anglican congregation sings hymns on Sunday morning while the victims of its persecution confess their anguish alone, outside.

Of all the roles and song cycles which Britten wrote for Pears, the first and last, Grimes and Aschenbach, are the most likely to remain identified with Pears's voice and personality. The actual characterisation of Grimes was determined by Britten and Pears together. In Crabbe's poem he is a savage fisherman, 'of brute feeling and more brute desires.' In the opera he is a poetic misfit, a rough but essentially romantic character.

But what of Aschenbach? No other Britten opera has raised so many unanswered questions as 'Death in Venice.' It appears to portray the man of strong moral opinions making his final admission of the triumph of sensuality over intellect, and to represent Britten's rejection of middle-class inhibitions.

Pears commits his own interpretation. 'For Ben the opera was, in some sort of way, a summing up of what he felt, inspired even by the memories of his own idyllic childhood. . . . At the end, Aschenbach asks what it is he has spent his life searching for. Knowledge? A lost innocence? And must the pursuit of beauty, of love, lead only to chaos? All questions Ben constantly asked himself.'

We should remember, however, that after the church parables Britten toyed with a variety of subjects, 'King Lear' and 'Anna Karenina' among them. He had probably known Mann's novella from the days of the Auden ménage, when Mann's son, Golo, lived on the floor above him and Pears. But he only got down to working on it after a decade of poor health, during which neither drink nor pills could help him.

He knew that he was unlikely to live long, though it was not until halfway through the opera's composition that his doctors decided on a heart valve operation, causing the second act to be written in white heat, with Britten often joking about 'laying down the pen.' The element of premonition no doubt appealed to him; but there is good reason to suppose that the principal reason for choosing 'Death in Venice' as his last opera was the very affectionate and practical desire to make Aschenbach into a marvellous last role for Peter Pears.

In spite of the shyness, the puritan streak and any other factors which provoked the long taboo, Britten himself was entirely realistic about the extent to which his private life and his friendship with Peter Pears influenced his composition for nearly 40 years. *(30.3.80)*

Supping Full of Horrors
Robert Cushman

Peter O'Toole has not acted a major Shakespearean role for 17 years. Bryan Forbes has not directed in the theatre before. *Macbeth* (Old Vic) is a very difficult play. So much for excuses.

The designer is new as well, though his set looks decidedly old: standard-issue rostra approached by what you might call the general run of steps, the only playful variant being the daunting height of the bottom rung, on which somebody is going to come to grief before the end of the season. Surveying this structure, and noting too the grubby William the Conqueror costumes, I settled down nostalgically to a one-foot-up, one-foot-down evening. Expectations were dashed, however, as Mr Forbes's production began to take on a quite untraditional identity of its own.

He stretches, for starters, one of Shakespeare's briefest plays to more than three hours' playing time. Built-up permanent sets are meant at least to permit unbroken transitions from scene to scene. Here there are constant blackouts, filled with optimistically spooky music, and lifting to reveal a stage on which, puzzlingly, almost nothing has changed. Occasionally a few dead bodies will have disentangled themselves from the picturesque poses in which they have been cluttering up the place; and the prospect may be altered by the loss or gain of a stool.

A cross is momentarily suspended, to show that someone has noticed the play's Christian imagery, though this perceptiviness does not extend to the English scene; Malcolm and Macduff conduct their heart searchings beneath a fully-manned gibbet. This is the single most curious stroke of the evening, though the presentation of the witches as one of the sexier sister acts on the blasted-heath circuit runs it close.

A more defensible idea, made risible by the shaky tone of the production generally, is the voluminous bloodiness of Macbeth's hands, and subsequently of Banquo's ghost. Either sight would be enough to send the protagonist into a coma. Unfortunately Mr O'Toole has been in this state from the outset, so he has nowhere to go. Chances are he loves the play, but his performance suggests that he is taking some kind of personal revenge on it, methodically draining it of sense and variety. His last line comes out as 'And *damned* be *him* that *first* cries *hold e-nough*'; and though the pounding beat may suit Macbeth *in extremis*, he has given much the same emphasis to all the words he has encountered on the way.

Eccentric rhythms reminiscent of Ralph Richardson are relayed to us in the fretful tones of Malcolm Muggeridge, with a few intimations of the self-disgust found in the role by Ian McKellen. Mr O'Toole's conception seems to be that of a man somnambulant with guilt from the first, waking only to occasional extremes of laughing sadism or cringing terror. These are effective but they are *very* occasional. They are belied too by his physical glamour, which is unchanging.

Nobody else in the cast seems able to get through to him. They try various methods. Frances Tomelty's Lady Macbeth – almost a Fourth Witch – goes for sex but elicits hardly a twitch in return. Brian Blessed's roaring Banquo slaps his noble partner's back a great deal. All, reacting to the rhetorical vacuum at the centre , try helplessly to be conversational; the only possible reply to poor Lennox's aggrieved 'Our chimneys were blown down' would be 'Well fancy that.'

Dudley Sutton's Macduff is a bit wild; when Macbeth's very convincing severed head was brought on at the end it looked so convincing one feared that, somewhere in the wings, Mr Sutton had lost control. Even as it was, Murphy's Law ran riot on the first night; lines were muffed and furniture bumped into. In the shambles John Tordoff's businesslike Third Murderer survived the best. *(7.9.80)*

Hiawatha at the National
Robert Cushman

On the bank of London's river
Stands a theatre built of concrete,
Built of louring, greying concrete;
Where, to greet the festive season,
Actors who appeared but lately
Dressed as Celts, undressed as Druids,
Now have changed their pigmentation,
Now assumed another warpaint.
(Body make-up by Max Factor?
Hard to tell; there is no credit.
Could this be the Hidden Factor?)
On they run in crouching posture,
Bending double, *at* the double;
(Which is quite a trick to master,
Guaranteed to put your back out);
Tell the tale of *Hiawatha,*
From the pen of Henry Wadsworth,
He the Fellow, he the Long One;
Though no longer than his poem,
Written in trochaic metre
With no rhyme but lots of rhythm,
As is known to every schoolboy
(Though it seems – I blush to say it –
Not to every theatre critic);
And no longer than this sentence.
(Can you hear me, Bernard Levin?)
Three the stages in this complex;
In this highly complex complex;
And the play of 'Hiawatha,'
Every afternoon and morning,
Currently adorns the largest:
The Olivier they named it,
Named it for our greatest actor,
He the baron, late of Brighton,
He the Moor *and* Jew of Venice,
Star of stage and magic lantern
Where he plays sadistic dentist
Or – I cannot wait to see it –
Ailing father of Al Jolson

In remake of early talkie.
Very big and grand this actor;
Very big and grand his theatre
And – despite a smallish cast-list –
And, I'd guess, a smallish cost-list –
This production big and grand too.
The adaptor and director –
First name Michael, last Bogdanov –
Specialises in such ventures:
Mystic poems, active poems,
Told for children but not childish.
Some reviewers brought their offspring;
Some brought other people's offspring.
Your reporter, Scrooge incarnate,
Sat without a young companion;
Noted, surly but approving,
How impeccable the silence,
How they watched and did not chatter,
How they listened without coughing.
Plot was not the main attraction;
For the tale was episodic.
Leaving you to muse and wonder
Why this tribe loved Hiawatha,
Just what made him so important.
Spectacle it was that held them,
From the faronade of kerchiefs –
Through the fingers of the West Wind
(He was Hiawatha's papa)
To the figure of the white man,
Posed against a fiery circle,
Gun in hand and set to use it.
(There's a thought to send you home with.)
So to Marty Flood, designer.
Commendations for the teepee
That enveloped all the action,
Gave a focus and a meaning.
Hail the Great Bear, Mishe Mokwa,
Black and huge and slain in combat
(Though if we were meant to triumph
In the death of one so furry,
They don't know the British public.)
There was joking, there was dancing,
And a pretty Minnehaha,
She the interest romantic;

Plus the odd interpolation –
Nothing though to vex the spirit.
'Hiya, Minnie.' 'Hiya, Watha.'
This variety of crassness
Was conspicuous by absence.
I'm surprised you raised the question.
Let me end with something joyful.
Merry Christmas. No, that's next week.
Hang this up outside the theatre:
I enjoyed it. Honest Injun. *(14.12.80)*

Bouquets of Barbed Wire
Clive James

A traditional feature of Wimbledon is the way the commentary box fills up with British players eliminated in the early rounds. Mark Cox was first aboard, but was almost instantly joined by Virginia Wade, keen to launch her new career as a commentator.

She didn't make a bad start, when you consider that Ann Jones was already in the box and well established, with an armchair and electric kettle. Ann had commented very politely during Virginia's only match. 'Ann Jones, how do you sum up the significance of this victory?' she was asked. The straight answer would have been that it was about to become very crowded in the commentary box, but she did not say so. Virginia was equally polite about Wendy Turnbull's match against Hannah Mandlikova. She told us what Wendy was doing wrong, without mentioning that it wouldn't have made much difference if she had done everything right. Virginia stressed the word Mandlikova on the second syllable. The umpire stressed it on the first. Dan Maskell stressed it on the third and eventually wore his opponents down.

Dan's all-court commentating technique has by now reached such perfection that you would expect he had run out of surprises, but this year he unveiled a new trick of saying the wrong name just before saying the right one. 'Ann Jones, Anne Hobbs rather . . .' The effect was to wrong-foot the listener. Down at the receiving end against Mandlikova, Ann Jones, Anne Hobbs rather, did her version of the baseline bossa nova, a dance performed by British female players when they are about to receive service. It is designed to waste as much energy as possible. Sue Barker remains the most spectacular exponent, often bouncing up and down more than 30 times before lunging sideways to intercept the service and hit it out.

Ann Jones, Anne Hobbs rather, bounced almost as much as Sue, but Mandlikova was not impressed. Anne Hobbs, Ann Jones rather, sympathised with her compatriot. 'When she was in trouble against Virginia Wade she pulled out some real big ones when it really mattered.' Mandlikova went up against Navratilova for an all-Czech semi-final, with Dan Maskell as the chief voiceova, although everybody else was in the commentary box with him, including Virginia. 'She's very relaxed,' piped Virginia, referring to Martina. 'She *knows* she's won the title twice. . . .' Martina went on to prove herself about as relaxed as it is possible to be when the new girl is wiping the court with you. Dan, meanwhile, was busily employing one of his favourite strokes, the one about cold balls from the refrigerator. 'When the balls come cold like this from the refrigerator they really do skid away.' Nobody had anything to counter that.

David Vine doomily interviewed the defeated Navvy. 'I've never seen you so disappointed.' 'You're gonna make me cry if you keep talking like that.' Meanwhile, almost unnoticed, Mandlikova's eventual conquerer marched steadily towards the final, peppered with some brilliantly disguised backhands from Dan. 'Mrs Evert . . . Mrs Lloyd, I beg your pardon.' But by now the men's competition was boiling up. It had gone into a lull while McEnroe carved his way through the unseeded players left in his half of the draw and Borg revealed that he had hit form early, no cliff-hangers. In the commentary box there was a lot of speculation about how long McEnroe could contain his feelings or even whether it was good for him to do so.

As McEnroe squared up to Rod Frawley, Mark Cox was in the box for a lot of man-talk about the alleged necessity for the bad boy to uncork the boiling lava of his personality, lest his genius suffer inhibition. Some of this sounded more like vulcanology than wisdom. 'He's obviously not content with his form, and he *has* to *find* a way of getting rid of that pent-up emotion.' 'Yes, he has all this pent-up emotion . . . that pent-up emotion . . . his biggest problem is going to be to find out how to release it.' Nobody counselled the advisability of keeping the emotion pent-up, although McEnroe had won his two previous matches with scarcely a murmur.

Frawley proving a tough nut to crack, there were early signs that the rift would soon spout lava. 'Wargh wharn whim glam heng,' whined McEnroe *sotto livello microfonico*, 'narf glahng shtum?' 'Will you please play on?' snapped the umpire. But something seismic was about to happen below that trembling crust. 'Ah cringh! Theeg ump glurg!

GLARGH!' 'It's all pouring out now,' said Box and Cox. 'Unsportsmanlike conduct,' said the umpire. 'Warning, Mr McEnroe.'

'He needs these outbursts to get the negative tension out of his system,' explained Mark Cox. What was never explained was why Frawley should sympathise, especially when the negative tension happened to explode at the precise moment when he might have expected to be winning a set. 'Advantage Frawley,' said the umpire. 'Waagh fahgn blahg!' shouted McEnroe, holding things up. In the third set Frawley was robbed of a crucial point by a clearly bad line-call. In a civilised tone he made his only protest of the day. Shortly afterwards McEnroe suffered a call no worse and did his complete Krakatoa number.

Whether he called himself or the umpire 'a disgrace to mankind' remains problematical, but since he delivered the accusation while pointing in the direction of the umpire, whom he had been arguing with for an hour, he could scarcely complain about being misconstrued. 'I wasn't talking to *you*, umpire. Do you *hear me*? What did I *say? Please* tell me!'

McEnroe shouted all this a few hundred times, as a child having a tantrum hopes to wear you down. The analogy is exact, since just as a child gets over the tantrum instantly but leaves the surrounding adults white-lipped, so McEnroe is all set to go within seconds of his latest eruption, while everybody else present, especially his opponent, feels like a participant in the last act of a Greek tragedy. 'Frawley bore up *so well* under the most difficult circumstances.' Yes, and he lost. Whether or not McEnroe plans it that way, that's the way it comes out.

The BBC has had a galloping case of Dallasitis. Dallasitis is a disease which afflicts British public service broadcasting companies who have fluked a hit with an imported American soap opera. The soap opera having become a cult, they spoil the fun by over-exploitation. In terminal cases they repeat the whole series from the top, so that everybody can get heartily sick of what had previously been rather fun.

Nevertheless I was poised before the screen night after night, eagerly researching arcane aspects of Texan speech patterns. 'I think we otter dance till Don' means 'I think we ought to dance till dawn.' Missed that one the first time round. It was remarkable how early and how firmly the makers of the series grasped the principle that everything depended on the girls.

All the prattle about JR is a side issue. What matters is for Pamela to get that sumptuous figure of hers into profile as often as possible, while Sue Ellen props herself unsteadily against the cocktail cabinet and Lucy, surprisingly agile for someone with no thorax, climbs a ladder into the hay-loft. Apart from the fact that Digger was played by David

Wayne instead of Keenan Wynn, the whole format was born full-blown, like Athena from the forehead of Zeus, or a big idea from the forehead of an executive.

The Beeb should realise, poor soft creature, that the 'Dallas' thing is only a gag if you play it straight. After all, that's what the actors are doing. With the possible exception of JR himself, everybody in the cast is working flat out to convey the full range of his or her, usually her, emotional commitment. Sue Ellen, in particular, was a study in passionate outrage when she realised the extent of her husband's perfidy. Her mouth practically took off. You will remember that JR swindled all the other big oilmen in Dallas by selling them his oil wells 'off the coast of South-East Asia' just before the wells were nationalised, presumably by the South-East Asian Government. This behaviour filled Sue Ellen with disgerst, and she reached for her gern.

Sue Ellen keeps her gern in a bottom drawer. Or perhaps it is JR's gern and on this occasion she was only borrowing it. Whatever the truth of that, you were left certain of one thing: that you could not be sure it was Sue Ellen who shot JR. Candidates for the honour were queueing up in the corridor. It is even possible that Miss Ellie shot him, since she has been showing increasing signs of madness, singing her dialogue instead of saying it. Don't be surprised if the sheriff turns up with a wornt for her arrest. There could be a tornt of wornts.

Andrea Newman's great strength as a writer is that she sees the drama and passion in the lives of ordinary people. Her housewives carry on like Maria Callas. Her builders are driven men. Mackenzie himself is the Lermontov of his profession. He might die in a duel. His sons might stab him. But there is nothing he can do to avert his fate, for his mistress has bewitched him. 'You've got magic hands,' she breathes, 'along with a few other magic bits and pieces.' You can see why Mackenzie has thrown caution to the winds – he has never heard a woman speak so poetically before.

Mackenzie's wife, a wan nurse known as Jean, appears to have no chance against this kind of competition. 'I'm an all-or-nothing kind of person,' she pipes, but there is no denying that the beauteous Diana has the breeding to go with the polish. 'Her mother,' someone explains, 'was Caroline Venables, the great society beauty.' But Diana is no layabout. She must work hard to keep up the payments on her hideous furniture. The furniture is distributed thinly around a dwelling which was created by Mackenzie. That, I have at last realised, was how they met. She was standing there in a pill-box hat with one foot in front of the other when along came Mackenzie and built a house around her.

Jean has a friend called Ruth. Married to a weed, Ruth finds solace in the arms of Diana's father, a wise old Hungarian whose name, if I have caught it accurately, is Applecrumb. Ruth would like to tell Jean all about that but can't. 'I feel we're all in terrible danger,' she tells Applecrumb when they are in bed together (not all of them at once, just her and Applecrumb). 'She's your daughter and my friend. He's my friend too.' Ruth is putting it mildly, since at one stage Mackenzie was more than her friend. She, too, has run her loving hands over the boiled-potato skin of the priapic builder's capable back.

'If Jean has it out with Diana,' muses Ruth, 'I'm so afraid that David might with me about you.' David is Ruth's feeble husband. He lacks Mackenzie's creative imagination. Mackenzie keeps on getting richer, but it has no effect on his manners or wallpaper. He goes on wearing his vest under his pyjamas as of old. By this time, however, the distraught Jean is beyond noticing her surroundings. She has called in the priest. To him she pours out her troubles, undeterred by the fact that he is wearing his hair long enough to invite instant defrocking. But if virtue is not rewarded, vice is certainly punished. Diana is bearing Mackenzie's child. Another little builder is on the way.

Diana's first instinct is to have an abortion, so as not to interrupt her career as a model, although the clothes she models are so badly cut that she could go on wearing them until she was in labour and nobody would ever know. Her mother has arranged abortions for her before. 'Is it that builder person?' But that builder person is outraged when he hears of the plot to kill his child. 'It's my child,' he brogues thickly. 'I want it.' Diana looks appalled. Her mother looks intrigued. Her father looks drunk. 'I could have eaten your Arp,' he smiles fondly, meaning that he could have eaten her up, not that he could have consumed some surrealist work of art in her possession.

That is as far as my critical analysis has reached, but the series is growing faster than one's ability to deal with it, like a home-grown yoghurt. Some general comments, however, might not be out of place at this point. That Andrea Newman's barbed wire entanglements should prove so popular is no great surprise. She has the energy of the true primitive. Her characters aren't even cardboard but you care what happens to them. My own prediction is that Mackenzie, while engaged in constructing some revolutionary block of purpose-built maisonettes, will fall off a ladder and be nursed back to health by Jean. Diana's affair with her own father will end in his death and her suicide or vice versa. Diana's mother will seduce the priest and the wimpy David will get off with Caroline Venables, leaving Ruth free to pursue her career as a dramatist. One day, as she is passing Mackenzie's abandoned building site, she will see a bouquet of barbed wire. . . .

Dallas and *Mackenzie* (both BBC1) are showing signs of convergence. The leading man in each series spent the latest episode in a wheelchair.

Some semioticist has probably already worked out a formula to explain this phenomenon. After a certain number of episodes of any given soap opera, the hero will be on wheels. Let f be the number of his love-affairs, n be the frequency with which he goes bankrupt, and p be the snapping-point of the viewer's credulity. When f times n equals p, the leading man will be rolling instead of walking.

JR was in a wheelchair because, as you may have gathered, somebody shot him. Fanned by the BBC news outlets in this country, and by similar organisations throughout the world, the whole planet was supposed to be on tenterhooks to find out who did it. Actually to anyone in possession of the appropriate semiotic formulae it was always transparently obvious who did it – Miss Ellie. The writers, however, worked a switch at the last minute. Having led absolutely nobody down the garden path by focusing suspicion on Sue Ellen for a few months, they finally sprang the news that the mysterious assailant had been Kristin all along.

The latest episode of 'Mackenzie' was also, alas, the last. Several instalments having already gone by since f times n equalled p, Mac was tardy in acquiring his vehicular sedentary device, but once tucked in he lost no time in setting about doing what he always did best – making large, emphatic gestures with his hands. Mac had crashed a car while driving with his eyes full of blood because his son Jamie had hit him. You could tell Mac was 20 years older than his son Jamie because Mac had a moustache and some white powder streaked into his hair.

Jamie was still obsessed with Mac's wife, who had once been his, Jamie's fiancée. 'There is something you can do for my father. Hold his hand when he finds out his new daughter is really his grandchild.' Diana, the classy mistress, suicided in order to get out of speaking any more dialogue. She took what Mac's wife described as a novadose. The whole series was a novadose, but millions of viewers will miss it.

The Letter
Andrew Motion

This poem won first prize in a competition sponsored by the Arvon Foundation in association with *The Observer* and London Weekend Television. The judges were Ted Hughes, Seamus Heaney and Philip Larkin. The poems that won second and third prizes are also reproduced below.

If I remember right, his first letter.
Found where? My side-plate, perhaps,
or propped on our heavy brown tea-pot?
One thing is clear – my brother leaning
across to ask *Who is he?* half angry
as always that summer before enlistment.

Then alone in the sunlit yard, mother
unlocking a door to call *Up so early?*
– waving her yellow duster good-bye
in a small sinking cloud. The gate creaks
shut and there in the lane I am running
uphill, vanishing where the woodland starts.

The Ashground. A solid contour swept
through ripening wheat, and a fringe
of stippled green shading the furrow.
Now I am hardly breathing, gripping
the thin paper and reading *Write to me.
Write to me please. I miss you. My angel.*

Almost shocked, but repeating him line
by line, and watching the words jitter
under the pale spidery shadow of leaves.
How else did I leave the plane unheard
so long? But suddenly there it was –
a Messerschmitt low at the wood's edge.

What I see today is the window open,
the pilot's unguarded face somehow
closer than possible. Goggles pushed up,
a stripe of ginger moustache, and his eyes
fixed on my own while I stand
with the letter held out, my frock blowing.

before I am lost in cover again,
heading for home. He must have banked
at once, climbing steeply until his jump
and watching our simple village below –
the Downs swelling and flattening, speckled
with farms and bushy chalk-pits. By lunch

they found where he lay, the parachute
tight in its pack, and both hands spread
as if they could break the fall. I still
imagine him there exactly. His face pressed
close to the sweet-smelling grass. His legs
splayed wide in a candid unshamable V.

Born in London, 1952. As a student, won the Newdigate Poetry Prize at Oxford, where he now lives. Lecturer in English at University of Hull since 1977. Publications include a collection of poems (1978) which won a Cholmondeley Award, and a critical study of Edward Thomas.

Out for the elements
Andrew Waterman

Starry tonight, and repetitious
sea harassing the empty strand,
as when it first cast adventitious
staggering life upon the land;
through sleights of wondrous generation
since to attain a consummation
in filaments of light I see
stacked on the Prom: humanity
with all its complex apparatus,
deep-freezers, televisions, cars
banks, supermarkets, churches, bars,
shows what once kindled to create us
subtilised now to a weird grace-
note shimmering on time and space.

The sand beneath my feet caressing
negligently each emptied shell,
dropped cans and condoms, spreads expressing
only conclusive flatness. Well
clear of its first-and-last mnemonic
and breakers issuing their sonic
premonitions, mankind who feigns
whole worlds dreamed to exalted planes,
within those intricate wired boxes
saying things like 'computer sales'
'topspin forehand,' 'don't tell tales,'
'I'm not contracepting' foxes
comprehension with monkey-tricks:
arts, avocations, politics.

Marvellous are the anthills, skuas,
acacias, zebras, whales, yet none
gone so tortuously askew as
man so inventively has done
from first imperatives. How did it
come about? How could nature bid it
we should attain such livings as
insurance, market-research, and jazz,
mining for coal, or crawling under
purring metal contraptions, or
inspecting wickets, or the law?
It all bends the mind; and no wonder
that some are put away, convinced
they're parrots or the Queen, brains minced.

That half-mile stretch of Epping Forest
around our first house, vaulting boughs
of oak, beech, hornbeam, where bird chorist-
ers thronged, sometimes a dozen cows
turned loose, and silver birches peeling
soft bark like paint, conferred a feeling
prelapsarian, pure and free.

Nine was the perfect age to be
I knew, just old enough for straying
without one's parents, not yet hit
by homework, tests. But then the writ
of adults intervened, conveying
me across London, stripped away
that whole first world, woods, friends and play.

So, Norwood; where, sent out for shopping,
I'd take a ball between my feet
and book in hand, and saunter, stopping
to trap a rebound. In our street
people considered thus combining
the two things odd; my mind was mining
the black depths of galactic space:
our island-earth, I read, a place
speck-like, lost, infinitesimal,
due to be swallowed by the sun;
life randomly from gas begun,
a sort of freak recurring decimal.
Perspective there on hacks who'd bore
at school of 'what you're cut out for.'

Also, the library held the ocean:
fascinated by frigate, barque,
galleon, longship, my emotion
hovered most round the Cutty Sark;
I travelled in imagination
all voyages of exploration,
Frobisher, Cook, Magellan, Drake;
and fought with Grenville, Nelson, Blake;
and in Marryat's books through pouring
suburban indoor afternoons
adventured tropic blue lagoons;
I clung to wind-tossed park trees roaring
'Eternal Father, strong to save,
Whose arm doth bind the mighty wave.'

No clues nor reason then for guessing
vagaries bringing me to stand
where waves are mightily depressing
this winter on Portstewart strand.
Our setting-forth's exhilaration
can never tell its destination;
nor can what's reached call back and warn
the younger self of not-yet-born
defeats and pains. That ghost still living,
a phosphorescence of the tide,
in me here as I walk beside
the North Atlantic's not forgiving
my failure to resolve distress.
Nor I him his ingenuousness. . . .

*Born in London, 1940. Senior lecturer in English at New University of Ulster
since 1968. Has published three collections of his work and is a Cholmondeley
Award winner.*
*'Out for the Elements' consists of 178 fourteen-line stanzas. Here we print a
selection from the first part of the poem.*

Rising Damp
U. A. Fanthorpe

*A river can sometimes be diverted, but it is a very hard thing to lose it
altogether.* (J. G. Head: paper read to the Auctioneers' Institute,
1907).

At our feet they lie low,
The little fervent underground
Rivers of London

(Effra, Graveney, Falcon, Quaggy,
Wandle, Walbrook, Tyburn, Fleet)

Whose names are disfigured,
Frayed, effaced.

These are the Magogs that chewed the clay
To the basin that London nestles in.
These are the currents that chiselled the city,
That washed the clothes and turned the mills,
Where children drank and salmon swam
And mills were holy.

They have gone under.
Boxed, like the magician's assistant.
Buried alive in earth.
Forgotten, like the dead.

They return spectrally after heavy rain,
Confounding suburban gardens. They infiltrate
Chronic bronchitis statistics. A silken

Slur haunts dwellings by shrouded
Watercourses, and is taken
For the footing of the dead.

Being of our world, they will return
(Westbourne, caged at Sloane Square,
Will jack from his box),
Will deluge cellars, detonate manholes,
Plant effluent on our faces,
Sink the city

(Effra, Graveney, Falcon, Quaggy,
Wandle, Walbrook, Tyburn, Fleet)

It is the other rivers that lie
Lower, that touch us only in dreams
That never surface. We feel their tug
As a dowser's rod bends to the source below

(Phlegethon, Acheron, Lethe, Styx).

Born in Kent, 1929. After St Anne's, Oxford, became a teacher; now a hospital receptionist in Bristol. Her first collection was published in 1978.

11.
Sport and
Other Exertions

Victim of his own Courage
Hugh McIlvanney

It can be no consolation to those in South Wales and in Los Angeles who are red-eyed about Johnny Owen to know that the extreme depth of his own courage did as much as anything else to take him to his death.

The calamitous experience could only have happened to an exceptionally brave fighter because Lupe Pintor, the powerful Mexican who was defending his World Boxing Council bantamweight championship against Owen, had landed enough brutal punches before the twelfth and devastatingly conclusive round to break the nerve and resistance of an ordinary challenger. The young Welshman was, sadly, too extraordinary for his own good in the Olympic Auditorium.

In the street, in a hotel lounge or even in his family's home on a Merthyr Tydfil housing estate, he was so reticent as to be almost unreachable, so desperately shy that he had turned 24 without ever having a genuine date with a girl. But in the ring he was transformed, possessed by a furious aggression that drove his alarmingly thin and unmuscular body through the heaviest fire and into the swarming, crowding attacks that gave him a record of 24 victories, one defeat (avenged) and one draw in 26 professional matches.

The record was built up in Europe and its reward was the European bantamweight championship and acceptance as a contender for the world title. Given the basic harshness of boxing as a way of earning a living, no one could blame Owen or his father or his manager, Dai Gardiner, for going after the biggest prize available to them, but some of us always felt that the right to challenge Pintor in Los Angeles was a questionable privilege.

Making some notes on the morning of fight, I found myself writing: 'Feel physical sickness at the thought of what might happen, the fear that this story might take us to a hospital room.' This scribble was not meant to imply any severe criticism of a match which, on the basis of the relevant statistics, could not be condemned as outrageous. Indeed, the apprehension might have been illogically excessive to anyone who set Pintor's career figures of 41 wins, seven losses and a draw against the fact that Owen's defeat had been a blatant case of larceny in Spain and the further, impressive fact that he had never been knocked off his feet as a professional boxer.

Yet it is the simple truth that for weeks a quiet terror had been gathering in me about this fight. Perhaps its principal basis was no more than a dread that the frailty that the boy's performances had hitherto dismissed as illusory would, some bad time in some bad place, prove to be terribly real. There was something about his pale face, with its large nose, jutting ears and uneven teeth, all set above that long, skeletal frame, that took hold of the heart and made unbearable the thought of him being badly hurt.

And, to my mind, there was an ominous possibility that he would be badly hurt against Pintor, a Mexican who had already stopped 33 opponents and would be going to work in front of a screaming mob of his countrymen, whose lust for blood gives the grubby Olympic Auditorium the atmosphere of a Guadalajara cockfight, multiplied a hundred times.

No fighters in the world are more dedicated to the raw violence of the business than Mexicans. Pintor comes out of a gym in Mexico City where more than a hundred boxers work out regularly and others queue for a chance to show that what they can do in the alleys they can do in the ring. A man who rises to the top of such a seething concentration of hostility is likely to have little interest in points-scoring as a means of winning verdicts.

So it was hard to share the noisy optimism of the hundred-odd Welsh supporters who made themselves conspicuous in the sweaty clamour of the hall and brought a few beer cups filled with urine down on their heads. But they seemed to be entitled to their high spirits in the early rounds as Owen carried the fight to Pintor, boring in on the shorter, dark-skinned champion, using his spidery arms to flail home light but aggravatingly persistent flurries of punches.

The first round was probably about even. Owen might have edged the second on a British scorecard and he certainly took the third, but already Pintor's right hooks and upper cuts were making occasional dramatic intervention, sending a nervous chill through the challenger's friends around the ring.

It was in the fourth round that Pintor's right hand first struck with a hint of the force that was to be so overwhelming subsequently, but this time it was thrown overarm and long and Owen weathered it readily enough. He was seen to be bleeding from the inside of his lower lip in the fifth (the injury may have been inflicted earlier) but since both Pintor's eyebrows were receiving attention from his second by then the bloodshed seemed to be reasonably shared.

In fact the laceration in the mouth was serious and soon the challenger was swallowing blood. He was being caught with more shots to the head, too, but refused to be discouraged and an American voice behind the Press seats said incredulously: 'I don't believe this guy.'

Pintor was heaving for breath at the end of the fifth but in the sixth he mounted a surge, punished Owen and began to take control of the contest. The official doctor, Bernhard Schwartz, checked the lip for the second time before the start of the seventh. Pintor dominated that one but Owen revived heroically in the eighth, which made the abrupt disaster of the ninth all the more painful.

Pintor smashed in damaging hooks early in the ninth but their threat appeared to have passed as the round moved to its close. Then, without a trace of warning, Pintor dropped an awesome right hook over Owen's left shoulder.

The blow hurled him to the floor and it was here that his courage began to be a double-edged virtue since he rose after a couple of seconds, although clearly in a bad condition. There was a mandatory eight count but even at the end of it he was hopelessly vulnerable to more hooks to the head and it took the bell to save him.

By the tenth there was unmistakable evidence that the unrelenting bombardment had damaged every part of Owen's body except his heart. He was too tired and weak now to stay really close to Pintor, skin against skin, denying the puncher leverage. As that weariness gradually created a space between them, Pintor filled it with cruel, stiff-armed hooks. Every time Owen was hit solidly in the eleventh, the thin body shuddered. We knew the end had to be near but could not foresee how awful it would be.

There were just 40 seconds of the twelfth round left when the horror story started to take shape. Owen was trying to press in on Pintor near the ropes, failed to prevent that deadly space from developing again and was dropped on his knees by a short right. After rising at three and taking another mandatory count, he was moved by the action to the other side of the ring and it was there that a ferocious right hook threw him on to his back. He was unconscious before he hit the canvas and his relaxed neck muscles allowed his head to thud against the boards.

Dai Gardiner and the boxer's father were in the ring long before the count could be completed and they were quickly joined by Dr Schwartz, who called for oxygen.

Perhaps the oxygen might have come rather more swiftly than it did but only if it had been on hand at the ringside. Obviously that would be a sensible precaution, just as it might be sensible to have a stretcher immediately available. It is no easy job to bring such equipment through the jostling mass of spectators at an arena like the Auditorium, where Pintor's supporters were mainly concerned about cheering its arrival as a symbol of how comprehensive their man's victory had been. The outward journey to the dressing-room, with poor Johnny Owen deep in a sinister unconsciousness, was no simpler and the indifference of many among the crowd was emphasised when one of the stretcher-bearers had his pocket picked.

There have been complaints in some quarters about the delay in providing an ambulance, but in the circumstances these may be difficult to justify. Dr Ferdie Pacheco, who was for years Muhammad Ali's doctor and is now a boxing consultant with NBC in the United States, insists that the company lay on an ambulance wherever they cover a fight, but no such arrangements exist at the Auditorium and the experienced paramedics of the Los Angeles Fire Department made good time once they received the emergency call.

Certainly it was grief and not blame that was occupying the sick boy's father as he stood weeping in the corridor of the Californian Hospital, a mile from the scene of the knockout. A few hours before, he had sat by the swimming pool at their motel in down-town Los Angeles and listened to them joke about the calls Johnny's mother had been making from Merthyr Tydfil on the telephone they had recently installed.

The call that was made to Mrs Owen from the waiting room of the Californian Hospital shortly before 7 am Merthyr time (11 pm in Los Angeles) had a painfully different tone. It was made by Byron Board, a publican and close friend of the family, and he found her already in tears because she had heard that Johnny had been knocked out. The nightmare that had been threatening her for years had become reality.

She can scarcely avoid being bitter against boxing now, and many who have suffered such personal agony because of the hardest of sports will be asking once again if the game is worth the candle. Quite a few of us who have been involved in it most of our lives share the doubts.

But reactions for us are bound to be complicated by the knowledge that it was boxing that gave Johnny Owen his one positive means of self-expression. Outside the ring he was an inaudible and almost invisible personality. Inside, he became astonishingly positive and self-assured. He seemed to be more at home there than anywhere else. It is his tragedy that he found himself articulate in such a dangerous language. *(21.9.80)*

The Name Game
Geoffrey Nicholson

If rugby players were selected because they sounded the right men for the job, would Slow have won his England cap in 1934 or Tardy found his way into the Paris University Club second-row? For that matter, who would want to be on the receiving end of a Dospital pass?

On the by-name-and-by-nature principle, it would equally be asking for trouble to pick Fowler and Lawless, Savage and Vile. You might take a chance on Roughley – after all, this is meant to be a man's game – but with the current wave of prejudice against stamping in the rucks, Treadwell's inclusion might seem tactless. Hammer, Wrench and Cosh would be better left in the dressing room along with the old England hooker, Mangles. And who but the Springboks would have dreamt, in the late Thirties, of playing W. E. Bastard of Natal?

So whom do we pick? Some are naturals: Tony Swift, the Swansea right-wing, for instance, and all those Sharps, Keens and Strongs. But others are obviously right names in the wrong positions, like A. Back who won his Oxford Blue in 1878 as A Forward. We can therefore feel free to move our players to wherever they sound most apt.

By that token Hare should be switched to left-wing to balance Swift on the right, so leaving a vacancy at full-back. Here we ought to go for reliability above all, and the French offer Constant, Loyal and Roques. But it would be even more reassuring to know that Dieu (in this case Dominique Dieu of La Rochelle) was on your side. He gets the vote and the captaincy.

We'll leave the centres until we have decided on the half-backs. There was a Harlequin called Bussell, but since I can't find a Hustle to play inside him, I think we'll have to settle for Wrigley and Trickey. They sound too clever by half, so we don't need any more fancy Duckham-and-Dodge stuff in the centre. What we want is an incisive runner – say a Carver or a Cleaver – playing alongside a crash-ball specialist like Bullock or Hefer.

Now the front row. The simple solution would be to have Woodhead and Roughead propping at tight and loose respectively with Hook in between. But the way things are going in the game these days it might be advisable to resurrect a Broughton Wasps player of the 1870s, a Burtonian of the Thirties and a more recent Rosslyn Park international. This would give us an all-action line-up of Sockett, Waggett and Wackett.

In the second-row, Yale and Chubb, of course, would have made ideal locks; however, I can't find any mention of them. So, a man-mountain for the lineout, the early New Zealander Everest and for their value in the maul, either Burrow or Mole. On the flanks: Hunter at open-side, and since he's a bit inclined to wander, a dogged tackler on the blind-side, say, Bloxham, Bagwell or Leech. At No. 8 Rücker selects himself despite the umlaut.

Replacements: Packer (all-purpose forward), Hacker (utility back).

As an ex-player referee, it's between Booker of Coventry (though perhaps he smacks a little too much of soccer), Baldy of Montelimar (to save the crowd the trouble of inventing an abusive nickname), and Sawyer of Broughton ('You think you got away with that, but I saw yer'). *(13.4.80)*

Prizes were offered for readers' own contributions to the Name Game. Here are some of their suggestions . . .

A.C. Toole of Bracknell and A. Mitchell of Binfield launched a High Fliers football team of Swift, Nightingale, Bird, Sparrow, Crowe, Heron, Robins, Starling, Woodcock, Partridge and Peacock. And from P. Marriott of Cambridge came a wet-weather team of Poole, (Paddy) Rice, Nelson, Webb, Waters, Mariner, Coates, Brolly, Marsh, Waddle and Drake.

To play football against the Metropolitan Police: Hood, Kopa, Robb, Steel, Sweeney, Law, Crooks, Coppell, Laidlaw, McNab and Dibble (from Andrew Browell, Newcastle-upon-Tyne). This was matched by P. Wynn Owen, Maidstone, with his Unsavoury cricket XI of Butcher, Humpage, Graves, Marsh, Knott, Lynch, Mallett, Hogg, Dye, Savage and Dredge. And redeemed by Dick Whitfield, Camberley, with the Goodies football side: Hope, Joy, Bliss, Light, Proudlove, Goodlass, Bonnyman, Goodfellow, Darling, Noble and Love.

Others got so carried away that they made things more difficult for themselves by composing specialist teams like David Pyatt's Festival of Light soccer XI: Priest, Paul, Saul, Daniel, Gabriel, Pray, Bishop, Cross, Christian (capt), St John, Isaac. 'There is, of course,' he added, 'no vice-captain.' (If you don't remember Pray, he played for Bury in 1900, while Christian was an Old Etonian of 1879).

A ladies' cricket team, the Heigh Ho's – Grace, Rose, Phebey, May,

Valentine, Belle, Shirley, Marie, Virgin and Hooker – was picked by Findlay Rea of Sevenoaks to meet a 'scratch side' of Catt, Kitcat, Lyon, Lamb, Roe, Roebuck, Fox (capt), Bullock, Dolphin, Eele and Human.

Arguing that Rugby Union is a particularly physical game, George Mackay, Manchester, makes the case for a team composed of Hare; Tongue, Tooth, Mandible, Neck; Hands, Fite (of Brive, which explains the pronunciation); Limb, Boddy, Hart, Back, Bone, Hipps, Knee and Legge.

Jack Bingham, Hove, offers a culinary cricket team of Beet, Root, Salmon and Hake, accompanied by draughts of Mead. Then Lamb, Partridge, Currie and Haggas. For afters, Eccles and Peach, and as twelfth man, a wide choice of Graces. Q.N. Ford of Camberley in fact listed not only an XI of Gentlemen – King (capt), Prince, Grace, Earle, Bishop, Barron, Knight, Noble, Lord, Freeman and Trueman – but a team of all the Graces including W. G. and Mrs H. M., all authenticated by Wisden.

A few clergymen took part, and we particularly commend the well-balanced soccer team entered by the Rev. Leslie Paxton, Derby – Leiper; Burley, Strong, Manley, Boot; Wylie, Brain, Weaver; Brawn, Nutt, Shoulder.

Cricket opening partnerships included Adam and Eve (A.J. Reilly, Derby), Holmes and Watson (Hugh Langford, Hull), and the dithering Cumming and Waite (Derek Woodhouse, Newcastle-upon-Tyne). Several suggested Bore to take first strike, but we preferred Mr Woodhouse's casting of Bore and Bored as the crowd. He also nominated Wild and Woolley as his fast bowlers; not as vicious a pair, perhaps, as Markham and Topham (Rob and Nick Davies, Leeds).

Mrs M. Bradley, Caerleon, fields Partridge at cover, Gunn at point and, for equally good reasons, Garlick at long-off. D. V. H. O'Shea, Bristol, apart from finding a promising spinner in Snary, suggests Fagg for carrying the lemonade at twelfth man. M.C. Jeanes, Daventry, gives that job to Jeeves, but R. E. Dowling, Tonbridge, should know better than to send on Bacchus with the drinks. His wicket-keeper, Howat, already sounds a bit slurred.

First Prize in the Name Game goes to brothers Chris and John Farrington whose Rugby League XIII was solely and ingeniously composed of former Wakefield Trinity players. The winning entry, with their comments, reads:–

Malpass (mais bon catcher!); Smart, Sweeney, Todd (a murderous duo at centre), Pearce; Caress (beautiful handler at stand-off), Rollin; Steel, Burrows, Sampson, Reynard, Fox (a cunning pair), Pickup.

The substitutes are Bullock and Wild; the reserves to travel, Bath,

Ball and Field; and Shepherd, Woolley, Lamming and Sheard make up the committee.

In the cricket section the prize goes to David Lowe of Birmingham, whose well-reasoned selection (slightly abbreviated) runs:–

'Discarding the doubtful claims of Bolus, Padmore and Hogg, my opening batsmen would be a 1930s Surrey and New Zealand partnership of Block and Blunt.

'I feel it would be tactful to ignore Leyland's striking record, and Hever and Kortright sound a little rustic, so my next three batsmen would be the more adventurous Pullar, Hooker and Cutmore.

'For all-round qualities at number six I would choose a South Australian of the 1920s, Stirling, at the expense of Smart, Reddy and Eagar. He would also captain the side.

'W. C. Hands must have made a marvellous wicket-keeper, and the spin bowling should be capably performed by Breakwell and Turner, although Suttle, Lobb, Rist and Tidy would make adequate alternatives.

'Rather than select the talents of Sharp and Quick as opening bowlers, I have chosen the more subtle skills of Seamer and Shuter, with A. Fielder as twelfth man.

'In view of the recent call for neutral umpires, I have selected West Indian and Indian ex-Test cricketers, Solomon and Ghorpade (Gawphard), with Judge (Middlesex) as standby.

'However, given the more violent nature of present-day cricket, perhaps a sort of Punk XI would be more effective: Savage, Gunn, Butcher, Mallett, Cosh, Gurr, Box, Burnup, Crush, Lynch and Warr. The last would be declared captain so that it could be announced that Warr's declared. Umpires Fiddling and Cheetham.

Our man on the football terraces is D. H. Holdstock (no doubt a club director) of St Leonards-on-Sea, who writes: 'Starting with the goalie, names like Armstrong, Divers, Palmer and Twist came to mind, but I finally decided on Denial (Oxford United, '62). Full-backs present numerous possibilities – Craggs, Burley, Lynch, Block – but for effectiveness I've settled for Fowler and Rough.

'The mind boggles at a half-back line where you've managed to squeeze your way past Boyle and Whitehead only to find your passage blocked by Pyle. But perhaps these are a little too painful, so we'll have Clinging, Clamp and, if you're past them, Carver. A snappy forward line of Quigley and Swift on the wings, strikers Flack and Pythian, with what better captain than Leadbetter. A possible substitute for games against Italian or Argentinian opposition would be Dick Le Flem.'

Mr Holdstock also nominates a no-hopers XI to play against: Leek, Pratt, Fell, Hasty, Pyle, Ricketts, Hampton, Willey, Dick, Trollope, Slack. Substitutes: Nimmo, Askey.

Life is not quite so raw in Rugby Union where D. Colin Morris, Worcester, nominates: Fielding; Hastie, Weaver, Speed, Stagg; Brain (capt), Bridge; Bendall, Batterham, Packer, Hands, Springman, Hunter, Peel, Biggar. As he explains: 'I considered playing Marques at full-back, but as he is now only effective inside his own 22 metres line, plumped for the safety of Fielding . . . Hunter, the only player I've included from your XV, is a must in case Stagg plays opposite a Rutter, and they become involved with each other.'

Mr Morris supported his entry with an Evil XV: Lawless; Rottenburgh, Roge, Hele, Roughley; Bent, Askew; Crabbie, Bastard, Vile, Bigot, Sulley, Mangles, Savage, Fowler. This would be opposed by an Ecclesiastical XV comprising Lord; Deacon, Priest, McVicar, Dean; Christian, Church; Abbot, Pope, Bishop, Cope, Challis, Creed, Hym, Sanctuary. He adds: 'I would combine these last XVs and with the addition of Maturin (a promising young player), Beer (essential), Buzy and Bonamy (the French representation) send them off on the Barbarians' Easter tour of South Wales.' *(11.5.80)*

Pinter on Cricket
Miriam Gross

MG: Why does cricket appeal to you so much?
HP: I tend to believe that cricket is the greatest thing that God ever created on earth.
Greater than sex, for example?
Certainly greater than sex, although sex isn't too bad either. But everyone knows which comes first when it's a question of cricket or sex – all discerning people recognise that. Anyway, don't forget one doesn't have to do two things at the same time. You can either have sex before cricket or after cricket – the fundamental fact is that cricket must be there at the centre of things. To put my cards on the table, I must also say that cricket means England to me.
In what particular way?
Well, the first thing is that you play cricket on grass, and I know there are grasses all over the world, but it's not like English grass, you know.
No, I want to correct this: it deosn't finally matter about the grass or the horses looking over the hedge or the white clouds in the summer

sky and all that. You can also play cricket in pouring rain, well not pouring rain but terrible drizzle, on an awful ground with a miserable bar (the bar of course is one of the points of cricket), with bloody awful beer and terrible sandwiches, and, as I say, pissing rain which you still have to play in because it isn't pissing quite enough – in other words, a context which is quite displeasing; but the fact remains that whatever the context the over-all activity is still a thing of beauty and the people taking part in it, believe it or not, are in a certain sense transformed by it.

Although it's often full of bad humour and irritations and selfishness, I do think – and this is a very nineteenth-century view of it all – that the game of cricket is good for the moral fibre and soul of the people who engage in it. *(5.10.80)*

I'm Beethoven, Fly Me
Anthony Sampson

It's common enough nowadays to go round the world in 30 days if you have a mind to do it. And it won't surprise anyone who has studied the crazy state of air fares to be told that it's cheaper to fly round the world than to many much closer destinations. Those planning to fly farther than Europe would be well advised to check with some professor of air travel (no ordinary expert can disentangle the intricacies of prices) whether it's not cheaper to fly by way of San Francisco, Honolulu and Tokyo.

But there are still psychological oddities about flying round the world. It's one thing to make the journey: it's another thing to really *believe* that you've done it.

They used to say that when you travel by air your mind still goes by sea – in the days when ocean liners still worked. (If that were still true, your mind would be stuck in the dock for months waiting for a passage.) But my mind certainly insists on taking a much later flight; and I suspect it's only people who have lost all sense of place, like politicians and bankers, who can take all their minds with them.

It may be reassuring to check up that the world is in fact round; but it's still hard to come to terms psychologically with the fact of the Pacific; and many more regular travellers, I discovered, have the same problem. The world still *seems* more like a kind of saucer which is curved from California through Europe as far as Japan, but then has a great void underneath. As Fred Astaire used to sing: 'The Atlantic wasn't romantic and the Pacific wasn't terrific.' The fact that the Pacific occupies half the world still isn't comprehensible.

Reality is further confused by the problem of time and the dateline. If you fly westwards, pursuing the sun – which most experts agree is the most sensible direction – the arrangement of time seems, in theory, ideal: to keep on adding extra hours to the day and then to miss out a day altogether. It would be a pleasant enough way to rearrange any normal week at home missing out, for instance, Monday. But across the Pacific, flying through a very long day or a very long night, the whole arrangement becomes much less credible, until, when a whole day suddenly disappears, it loses all touch with reality.

The Pacific is made still more unreal by the business of eating. Most doctors now insist that when you are flying you should eat or drink nothing except water – lots of water, to off-set the dehydration of the pressurised cabin. But planes have always been a kind of caricature of the consumer society; they want to cram in as many meals as possible, and the Pacific provides the captive customers they dream of: in one night I found myself offered three dinners. No doubt when supersonic planes eventually cross the Pacific, the airlines will be able to achieve their ultimate ambition of continuous dinner which – since the plane will land at a much earlier hour – can merge into lunch.

Airlines, airports and international hotels all conspire to make every place look like every other place, and they are greatly assisted by the spread of air conditioning, which provides the same atmosphere everywhere. Looking out at Hong Kong from an air-conditioned taxi I caught myself thinking: 'The climate's remarkably like Taiwan.' It was not until the quick walk from the taxi to the hotel that I was aware of the hot steamy air. It's only in the more old-fashioned hotels like Raffles at Singapore with its fans and verandas that you can have no doubt about where you really are.

Then there is the 'in-flight entertainment,' which means that if you travel by the same airline you can cover the whole world to the strains of Beethoven's Fifth Symphony. And once in the airport the same clickety-clickety indicators announce the flights to every other part of the world – which makes you feel even less certain where you actually *are*.

Halfway through my travels I began to succumb to the delusion which is familiar to globe-trotters: that the plane itself was *home*. An odd kind of home perhaps, always with that formal arrangement of chairs, the same little windows and unexpected guests: but still more credible and relaxed than transit lounges or hotel lobbies, and sometimes even quite cosy.

172. Sport and Other Exertions

There are only two kinds of plane: full ones and empty ones, which are as different as luxury and squalor (an empty economy cabin is a palace compared to a crowded first-class one). The most comfortable airline is likely to be the one that is least well known, where they are still quite glad to see passengers.

It is the confusion about home, no doubt, which accounts for a good deal of people's anxiety about travel. Freud suffered greatly from travel angst when going by train – he sometimes insisted on arriving at the station an hour beforehand – and eventually traced it to his own childhood fear of being taken away from home and his mother's breast.

And it may be significant that the greatest anxiety about air travel appears at the conveyor-belt, when the passengers' darting eyes betray their true fears about being separated from their property. In the democracy of the baggage-claim, there is no distinction between first and economy, between leather suitcases and tin boxes. They all seem to be carrying the same warning, as they say about rich men on their death beds: 'You can't take it with you.'

In my travels, I soon found myself separated from my heavy suitcase which had decided to go off to Columbus, Ohio, while I went to Washington. For a short time I felt furious and helpless. Then I realised that I could do without almost everything inside the suitcase. I could buy an extra shirt or suit in Taiwan at a quarter of the price. It was a marvellous moment of liberation – until soon afterwards the phone rang to tell me that the suitcase was on its way to meet me.

The only real aristocrats of the air are those who can walk straight out of the airport with a bag over their shoulder, carrying themselves with themselves. *(23.11.80)*

The Road to the Isles
Christopher Brasher

Porridge and kippers for breakfast in the Black Bull, Milngavie, which you pronounce Mullguy, and I knew it was going to be a good holiday.

I was off the London to Glasgow night sleeper at 6.30 that morning, and at the entrance to the Botanic Gardens by 7.00. The rain came down in stair rods and the loos were locked. So I sheltered under the eaves, changed into waterproofs and set off along the bank of the

Kelvin, a purist start to a cheating journey. I was walking out of Glasgow, the black city of the industrial revolution, in which reside most of the problems of our society, bound for the Highlands where live, so legend says, a hard and romantic people.

By Kelvinside I walked through dripping, purple rhododendrons. The birds sang in the rain, and my spirit was light. An hour later, I came out on to the Beardsden road, a dual carriageway of hurrying machinery. There was a bus stop and as I halted to look at the map, along came a bus with Milngavie on the front, so I boarded it and arrived in time for breakfast at the Black Bull.

With kippers in my teeth, I spent £8 on a deerstalker to protect my specs from the rain and thought of the hats I left behind when I believed the weather forecast. And then, still in the rain, I set off on the West Highland Way, Scotland's first long-distance footpath.

I rounded a corner and came to quiet Craigallian Loch which, said the Countryside Commission's guide, 'achieved its apotheosis in The Fire – a bonfire on the slopes above the loch where the unemployed made their rendezvous, ate, gossiped and sang. There are many splendid tales of the tough characters and rough living of those days: of men who, unable to afford sleeping bags, slept in brown paper or under the *Glasgow Herald;* of fights on wet dark nights for the restricted comforts of a telephone kiosk; of epic journeys by lorry or motorbike to tackle desperate climbs with primitive equipment. For these folk there will always be a certain magic in the Craigallian area, where later comers see only the spruce plantation above the loch.'

That was all I saw in the rain. But I thought about the man in whose footsteps I trod: Bob Grieve, who as a boy had walked this way in the Thirties when he was unemployed, long before the days when he became the great planner who thought longer and harder about the future of the Highlands than anybody in this century. His *via sacré* turned west here, to its panorama of Loch Lomond. But the mist hung low, and I went straight on, dipping under the steep wooded flanks of Dumgoyach, where I passed a huge silver pack-frame concealing a small, red-headed girl carrying what must have been her entire worldly possessions.

Age, I thought, has its compensations, for with age comes the knowledge that weight is the back-packer's enemy. Mao said a journey of 10,000 miles starts with a single step – and so it should be when packing a rucksack: a journey on foot starts with the saving of an ounce because ounces add up to purgatory.

All I had was a rucksack weighing 20 pounds, and that included tent, sleeping bag, and food for two days, all of which amounted to freedom to do and go as I pleased. I pleased to stride along an old, disused railway track heading for a spot on the map labelled 'Inn' where I downed a couple of pints and couple of butties and walked on in the rain to Drymen, passing an expatriate Scot from Hampshire and a bearded overweight Devonian who was having trouble with the Countryside Commission's stiles.

My walk had made that pure start in Glasgow but then cheated on the bus, so I decided 'to hell with purity – do as you want.' So I left out cloud-capped Conic Hill and the dripping rainforest, and hitched a lift to Balmaha with a man and his son who had walked the last four stages of the West Highland Way. I began to realise that the Countryside Commission had started something bigger than they knew when they opened this long-distance walk.

From then on, I seldom walked alone: first with Malcolm, the librarian from Paisley, whose feet I treated with Deer Tallow, which ancient remedy does wonders for your confidence even though I suspect it is no more effective than Vaseline; and then with Margaret, the evolutionary biologist who taught me about wild orchids; and then with Steve McCoy – the Real McCoy – a Post Office engineer from Belfast with heavy boots that took him five months to break in; then with a dentist from Yorkshire, in his shorts despite the wind and rain. Once, on the eastern shore of Loch Lomond where, thankfully, there is no road, I met four men sitting on the beach beside their camp fire, drinking tea out of beer cans with the tops cut off. They had come out of Glasgow that morning on their bicycles, 40 miles by hilly road, and then had carried their bikes along the lochside until the beach reminded them of lunch. They made a journey like this, they said, to somewhere in the mountains every Sunday and I knew then that the old traditions – the tradition of the weekend escape into the hills – which was part of Glasgow and of Manchester and of Sheffield in the Thirties, was still very much alive.

For me, it was a night in the Rowardennan Hotel, where I sank into a bath and 22 miles of effort washed into the hot water; a night camping on Loch Lomondside where ferocious gusts pulled the tent pegs out of the sand and collapsed the tent; and a night in Scotland's oldest inn, the Kingshouse on Rannoch Moor.

I had cheated to get there, accepting a lift from a McGregor and Minister of the Church of Scotland in order, so I told myself, to avoid the boring part of the Way. When I set off next day, after a night of too much fluid with Malcolm the Librarian and Real McCoy, the cheeky librarian asked: 'Where's your taxi?' So I left him at the bottom of the Devil's Staircase to catch his bus back to Glasgow, while I tackled the mountains to Fort William and there, at the highest point of the Way, I met this little old couple – she no more than 5 ft 2 in. and not far off the old-age pension.

They were brewing-up in the wind and the rain and she said that they did this every year for their holiday – the Cleveland Way two years ago, Offa's Dyke last year, and now the West Highland Way. They camped every night. Are you never tempted, I asked, by a bed and breakfast farmhouse? 'Sometimes,' she said, 'but we've always resisted it.'

What a heart, I thought; what a lucky man. And I went on to Kinlochleven and a pint and a study of the map. Not for me the long swing westward along the old Military Road, the product of the 1745 uprising. Instead I determined to stride up over the high peaks into the clouds, with a slight tremor of the heart at my audacity. But what a day it gave me, alone in the rain and the mist, and yet certain that with map and compass in my hand and rucksack containing tent, sleeping bag and food on my back, I could survive. Late in the evening, with 20 good miles of satisfaction behind me, I came down into Glen Nevis. A rescue helicopter lifted an exhausted soldier off Britain's highest and stormiest mountain that night, while I walked on and collapsed into a bath.

As I lay there, steaming in the water, I thought that if I laid a trail of honey all the Pooh Bears of the world would come sniffing and trampling along it. And so it is with long-distance footpaths. Once they are designated and laid, people many and diverse are attracted to the trail. I, who had set off alone, had never yet been alone, so I thought that tomorrow I would head north into the hills, in which resides one of the last great wildernesses of Europe. *(28.6.81)*

176. Sport and Other Exertions

12.
Darker Thoughts

Dug-out Britain
Paul Ferris

There are some people (I am one of them) who are neurotic or cautious enough to keep a small store of survival food. Now and then I remember to rotate my tinned pilchards, dried apricots and Bulgarian bottled water from Waitrose.

The nuclear survival game, in Britain of all places, looks a shade pathetic these days. The British Isles are packed with targets relevant to East-West conflict – air and naval bases, control centres, radar and radio sites, nuclear weapons plants and caches, ports and oil refineries. We probably have more targets per square mile than any other nation on earth.

Under the circumstances a shelf of tinned food may be laughable, but at least it's something.

To concentrate our minds on a future where we may all find ourselves doing bizarre things, officialdom has kindly supplied the nation with tentative predictions about nuclear attack. 'It is thought' that we 'might expect' about 200 megatons of nuclear bombs and missiles, aimed at some 80 targets.

One megaton (MT) equals a million tons of TNT. Nagasaki received a comparative pipsqueak, a bomb of about 20 kilotons (KT), or 20,000 tons of TNT (Hiroshima's was only 12.5KT).

The 200MT figure comes from the Home Office, who had it from the labyrinthine Ministry of Defence, but no details are available. It might be a meaningful prediction, a good guess or a desperate hope. As it stands, 200MT represents more than a thousand times the explosive power of all the bombs that the German Air Force claimed to have dropped on Britain, 1939-1945, not to mention the radiation effects.

No doubt it has the virtue for the Home Office of sounding realistically terrible while offering hope that all is not lost. Tens of millions of citizens, it is predicted (on the basis of secret studies), could survive, especially if they do what the Government tells them when the time comes.

Although none of the 80 targets is specified, many of them are fairly obvious: ports like Dover and Southampton that would service the British Army of the Rhine, east coast radar at Buchan and Boulmer, airfields like Lakenheath and Greenham Common, US weapons storage at Burtonwood and Ditton Priors, very low frequency radio stations at Criggion and Rugby which probably communicate with submarines.

Many cities would also be 'hit,' among them Glasgow, Sheffield, Birmingham and Swansea. But the principle behind the Home Office thinking is that the bulk of the attack would fall on military targets, most of them outside the great conurbations.

The truth about what could happen, if such a thing exists in this tangled subject, may not be as bad as Mountbatten's 'no survivors,' but it is bad enough. A Home Office scientist told me in passing that he used to have nightmares when he first worked on weapon effects.

Travel will not be forbidden, but major roads will be blocked by police, leaving minor roads to become jammed of their own accord if people are so foolish. Local authorities tend to think that many would take to the roads. These are not abstractions. Among the towns covered by Buckinghamshire's thorough war plan is High Wycombe. Two miles north-west of the town, near the village of Naphill, is the underground control centre of RAF Strike Command, where admission is strictly by special pass marked with a red 'H'.

The chalk in which it is buried would protect it from radiation, though not from the blast of a nearby weapon. Unless a shadow centre elsewhere is the real one, leaving High Wycombe as an expensive decoy, this is where air commanders will control Britain's attack and defence; it is also where the decision would be taken to sound the famous four-minute warning.

Strike Command is an obvious target. Accordingly Bucks County Council has arranged that if a war crisis develops, it will move excavating plant, vehicles and fire brigade out of the town to safer parts of the county.

The district control centre for Wycombe, where the town's chief executive and a chosen staff will hope to run what remains after air attack, is going to be in the basement of a solid eighteenth century house at Marlow, low down near the Thames, with six miles and some chalk ridges between it and Naphill.

All this is good thinking on somebody's part. But the populace can be expected to reach similar conclusions. The county planners, whose war rooms are in a basement at Aylesbury, think that up to three-quarters of High Wycombe's 67,000 inhabitants would flee northwards into rural Bucks, and there are plans to feed and shelter them.

The effects of nuclear attack is a subject in itself. Every kind of case can be made, from cautious optimism to a powerful desire to change the subject.

In its '200MT' scenario the Home Office has calculated that the 'probable attack pattern' would do damage, ranging from total to slight, to about 15 per cent of the land area of Britain. A pamphlet version for a wider public is slightly different, and says that 'about 80 per cent of the land area might suffer no blast effects at all.' This is supposed to be a comfort.

Half an hour with a calculator suggests that, in any case, both figures are optimistic. They seem to play down the likely effect of blast in the outer ring of the imaginary circles that scientists draw around a weapon's 'ground zero.'

Nothing like a national shelter policy is envisaged. Bunkers for all are variously costed by the Home Office at between £10 and £60 billion, and dismissed as a fantasy. The best that officials can do is to insist that millions are sure to survive by accident, as it were, and that millions more can save themselves. Ninety per cent of industry and installations might be destroyed, and only 15 million people left. Simple precautions could save as many again.

Primitive sheltering from fall-out would be better than nothing. Terraced houses with fewer walls exposed would give enhanced protection, making Coronation Street safer than a council estate. Both would be safer than retirement bungalows or my flat at the top of a tower block. But it is hard to believe that DIY on Armageddon minus one will save 15 million lives.

Enemies of civil defence (CND, left-wing radicals) denounce it as a confidence trick, even a cloak for sinister plans to subdue political unrest in time of crisis. These claims are often extravagant, laced with feverish predictions of martial law and military takeover. But it is clear that civil defence is not always what it seems.

Humanitarian at one level, it is at bottom concerned with protecting the State against collapse from within.

General Sir John Hackett, once a NATO commander, author of 'The Third World War,' has written elsewhere that in civil defence 'survival for those who can be saved and ultimate regeneration of the national stock must be the objective.' These are the realities behind the charade.

What matters to nuclear disarmers is to prevent the carnage of the next war. What matters to the State is to make sure that if its preventive policies fail, it will survive the carnage, bloody but unbowed.

The real point of civil defence is to ensure a network that will keep us, or what is left of us, going after the event. No one puts it in so many words, but it is there to be read, between the lines.

The network has its roots in a primitive system for containing revolution, had one broken out in the early 1920s. Regional 'commissioners' were set up to run decentralised government. The system was elaborated for the Second World War to cope with the national chaos, caused by bombing or invasion, that never came. It is still there, refined for the nuclear age.

The key to civilian government immediately after a major nuclear attack is a chain of 20 or so underground control centres, some purpose-built, some converted from old military sites. These are the 'sub-regional headquarters' (SRHQs), each controlling two or more counties.

The one I visited dates from the 1960s and is under government buildings in Hertford. It covers Hertfordshire, Bedfordshire and Essex. A 'D' notice asking the media not to publish the address is in force, for obscure reasons, since it has appeared in radical magazines.

The hundreds of civil servants who work in the building above are supposed not to know that under their feet are long vistas of concrete, brickwork and linoleum. A junior Minister will (if the plans work) be whisked here from London as the political crisis deepens, and appointed sub-regional commissioner.

His dictatorial powers will be 'unequalled since the Roman occupation,' in the words of one civil defence officer. They derive from emergency legislation, drafted years ago, to be passed by Parliament. If events move too fast for Parliament to act, the nebulous doctrine of the 'royal prerogative' can be invoked: in effect, power is taken as though the legislation had gone through.

Under the sub-regional commissioner will be a staff of about 170, ranging from senior civil servants, also from London, to local cooks and typists. Senior police and fire officers will be there; so will a BBC representative. A 20-strong military cell under a brigadier will 'advise.'

Steel doors secure them from Hertford and the world. Unless a weapon bursts over the town, they will live in discomfort but safety, radiation-proofed, generating their own electricity, breathing filtered air, provisioned by food and water sufficient for at least a month.

It is not certain that all would abandon wives and children to report for duty when the call came. To help persuade them, plans exist to take families to Hertford and lodge them at hotels or Government premises, presumably in basements: cold comfort for the inhabitants of SRHQ 42.

Days or weeks might pass before anyone ventured out, but in theory the attack would hardly be over before the controller and his miniature Whitehall would be starting to manage the affairs of their corner of Britain via telephone, teleprinter and radio links: the Emergency Communications Network. Private wires run between neighbouring SRHQs, and down to the next level in the chain of command, the county headquarters.

The county control centres, more than 60 of them throughout Britain, are like SRHQs scaled down. The controller will be the county's chief executive. Some of his staff will be local officials, some of them imported. Police, Fire and Army will be represented.

Basements under civic buildings, more or less radiation proof, are a common site for county controls. Hampshire's is under a car park in Winchester. West Glamorgan's is at a Territorial Army site on the foreshore at Swansea, and is merely a concrete building on the surface. Buckinghamshire's bunker is under the county buildings in Aylesbury. 'Bunker' is a rude word with many officials, conjuring up a safe place that the rest of us will envy. Some of them almost boast how vulnerable their basements are. Questions about the number of administrators who will be under cover are met defensively.

The totals are not small. The SRHQs, averaging about 200 apiece, account for 4,000. County controls have as many again. The lowest level, more than 400 district councils, each with its designated staff, might contain 16,000, though 'bunker' is hardly the word for the poor protection that many of them afford. Nor are their communication links up to much.

Somewhere in Britain, one assumes, a national seat of government exists. In time of crisis many Ministers will leave London, to be either sub-regional or regional commissioners. The latter are likely to be senior members of the Government.

One is told that regional commissioners, accompanied by small staffs, will not go underground at first, but will hide themselves away in lonely hotels or country houses, waiting to see which bunkers they should occupy as the system emerges from chaos. It sounds so improbable, it might even be true.

Hunting for hidden sites amid innocent English landscapes is an amusing pastime (no doubt Soviet surveillance satellites are better at it than journalists). Speculating about the bunkers as they would be in action, when they would be trying to pin together the torn fabric of the nation, is less entertaining.

A breath of nightmare attends even the paper exercises that the

Home Office runs at its home defence college at a country house near Easingwold, in Yorkshire, to teach the basics of nuclear-crisis management. Local government officials, senior policemen and high ranking Army officers play a two-month war game that lasts two working days of real time.

Populations die of blast or radiation, wander, scavenge, riot, starve, but ultimately survive in decent numbers. How else could the game be allowed to end?

I talked for two or three hours with a lieutenant-colonel on the staff of the UK Land Forces peacetime headquarters at Wilton. He argued, as officers do, that the Army was neither trained for civil power nor wanted it, and that most of it would have gone to Germany anyway. On balance I would believe him before the radicals.

This is not to say there is nothing to worry about. Sir Leslie Mavor, who ran the Easingwold college until January, when the Home Office gave him the job of co-ordinating civil defence volunteers, sees a period of 'real danger.' Mavor thinks there could be a 'nasty situation' which might 'last a long time while communications are assembled, in which the regional military commander might start disposing of his forces in the light of a purely military appreciation.' Some sort of 'local military takeover' was possible, but would 'surely be no more than a passing local aberration.'

How a shattered people might behave after an attack is too large and emotional a subject to write about here. An assistant chief constable on the course at Easingwold said to me that 'our difficulty, including the Army officers', is that we've got absolutely no idea what it would be like. I have a feeling that given the nuclear holocaust that is in the scenario, we may be back in the Dark Ages, a new society with new rules. Law and order will be what the country wants it to be.'

I said, ' "Holocaust" is a word that's anathema to the Home Office.' He said, 'I'm a policeman. I call a spade a spade.'

The situations that civil defence has to cope with are not easy or agreeable to grasp. The system is caught awkwardly between years of neglect and the present parlous state of East-West relations. There is a need to argue and explore a subject that most people would like to forget. More and more left-wing local authorities are saying a plague on it, anyway.

CND's argument is that to contemplate the unthinkable is to make it more likely. This makes no sense to me. I would rather contemplate it than ignore it. Still, CND are right to keep harping on the scale of the catastrophe. As Professor John Erickson, of Edinburgh, says, they have done us all a service by at least initiating a debate.

Sir Leslie Mavor, who refers to himself as 'Mr Home Defence,' is a retired air marshal: a lean Scotsman, upright, like a stalk. A return to normal after a nuclear war, says Mavor, should not be thought of as a return to a normality we would recognise in 1981. He wants 'straight thinking' now, the better to equip ourselves for the ultimate.

Is this madness or wisdom? It is a question we might all begin to take seriously. Mavor has no doubt that a Britain of some sort would survive, utterly changed. Would it be a democracy? Who could tell?

But 'if there is one thing that is as near as dammit certain, it is that after a nuclear war we will never pass this way again.'

I shall go and check my tinned pilchards. *(5.7.81)*

A Strategy of Love
E. P. Thompson

Arguments about European nuclear disarmament usually rest upon an essay in futurology. And so, in similar degree, do mine. We are probing the darkness a few historical yards ahead – to 1983 when the Cruise missiles are installed; to 1984 when the Russian 'answer' is in place; to 1985 when the MX missile system is constructed. . . . And, thence, to what?

In my argument we need not look much further ahead. Civilisation, in the northern hemisphere, may not reach the year 2000 at all. I don't argue this only from the manifest dangers of accident; nor because of the Pentagon's new targeting plans; nor because of the coming crunch for oil; nor because of the instability of regimes (Pakistan, Oman) which might turn the ignition-key.

I argue from the deep thrust towards collision; the militarisation of both opposed blocs and also of the Third World; the growing influence of the armourers, and of their security services, opinion-managers and ideologists.

Military planning, on both sides, proceeds according to worst-case hypotheses. It is never possible to refute such projections, since the worst always could happen. It often does. Strategists imagine the worst possible scenario of enemy action and then design weapons and counter-strategies accordingly. This summons forward exactly what it was designed to oppose, and opens the way to even worse cases beyond. This has landed us where we are today.

I can't refute the argument that if nuclear disarmament succeeded, but only in Western Europe, then the USSR might draw Western nations into its 'socialist family.' Yugoslavia argues a different case, and I don't think that present Soviet leaders have expansionist designs of this kind. They have enough troubles with Eastern Europe already. But more hawkish Russian leaders could arise.

Other worst cases could happen. I could suggest a worst case, with a Reagan USA, in which Euro-Communist or Socialist governments in Italy, Greece or Britain were sharply destabilised by NATO agencies. Or in which a Chancellor Franz Josef Strauss stirred up the distress of East Germany and Poland to the point of war.

There has been, for 30 years, a build-up not only of weaponry but of antagonistic ideologies. The division of Europe is now accepted as an irrevocable fact of nature.

The movement for European Nuclear Disarmament (END) challenges not only the weapons but this 30-year-old fact. The original sponsors of END's appeal, who included respected personalities from a dozen European countries (and some 70 British MPs from several parties) are not simpletons who suppose that the problems of Europe can be solved by a few moral gestures.

We stated in our appeal, 'We must resist any attempt by the statesmen of East or West to manipulate this movement to their own advantage.' No doubt geniuses in the Kremlin are watching the movement against Cruise missiles in the hope of extracting advantage, just as Whitehall, who do not care 2p about Polish culture or autonomy, are hoping to extract advantage for NATO from Poland's astonishing self-assertion today.

May I restate, in my own (perhaps extreme) terms, the position of supporters of END?

First, we are pessimists. We consider that the forces thrusting towards collision are now deeply enstructured within both opposed blocs, and it is probable that nuclear war in Europe will ensue.

Second, we mean to generate a counter-thrust, reversing the continent away from collision. The immediate objectives must be the halting of NATO weapons 'modernisation,' the withdrawal of Russian SS-20s from Europe, and the first steps towards the creation of a nuclear-weapons-free zone in Europe, as a space between the super-Powers, permitting nations on both sides to ease themselves away from their blocs.

Third, we envisage the development, over the next three years, of certain forms of common action towards these objectives of movements in both halves of Europe. We have never supposed that this would be easy, nor expected pressure in Russia to take the same forms as that in the West.

We propose only that there is an outside chance of breaking the thrust towards war at this point. A peace movement in the West might strengthen doves or latent Dubceks in the East. And we can reach out to the very extensive 'dissident' opinion in Eastern Europe, not in propaganda victories for the Western media, but in order to relate into a single cause pressures for peace, democracy, and national autonomy, East and West.

Our critics stand aside with sceptical smiles, and demand proof that we will succeed before they will allow us even to start. They want us to show them protest meetings in Budapest or marches upon Russian missile bases.

But we have no such proof. We say only that this may be the last chance we have; that it must be initiated by unofficial persons, where governments have repeatedly failed – that it must grow into a continental movement with a quite new kind of internationalist morale; and that END is winning attention (sometimes cautious or sceptical) in the East, through private exchanges which must, for the time being, remain confidential.

I am asking for patience. The work of 30 years cannot be reversed in a few months. But I am asking for more than that.

Civilisation is now so sick that we dare not look directly at ourselves. We threaten our fellow creatures daily with mass extermination. For decades we, in the advanced nations, have had our snouts deep in the trough of material goodies.

The twentieth-century is slouching to its end, gorged with goods and human blood. Its highest ingenuity now is all to do with death. It might be better if we got the last episode over quickly and the earth was done with us.

It has been fun, for some people, while it lasted. But now it is beginning to bore. It might even be amusing, for a change, to give our lives to some ideal or spiritual end. We, or some of us, could resolve to hand on this planet to the third millennium in a state which offers some hope to its inhabitants. To do even this will require the exercise of every skill and resource of our culture.

The R & D (research and development) for the weapons to kill children born in the third millennium is already under way. And what R & D is going ahead for survival?

One example. This year our Government has welcomed Cruise missiles; has exported arms eagerly to the Third World; has settled for Trident, that futile phallic symbol of a geriatric British imperialism; has overspent its 'defence' budget by £650 million in six months; and has *cut* the study of Russian languages and society in our universities.

Yet here, in Slav and Chinese languages, are some of the primary tools of survival. If we are to communicate – to argue – across that gap, then this small investment could scarcely have higher priority. This cut

Darker Thoughts. 185

symbolises the fact that our rulers have lost the will to survive.

The future is being costed, but we would search in vain, anywhere in our stinking State, for any penny of R & D devoted to preparing the least gesture of love.

But I am sorry that I mentioned the word. It has no place in any realist political vocabulary. Nor does END expect to carry all before it by flower-power. We are striking directly at the mutual and collusive strategies of the super-Powers, and we expect the going to be rough.

Nothing will be easy. Even an initial success – a step towards non-alignment by Poland today or by Greece tomorrow – could lead swiftly on to new emergencies. But we offer a possible strategy of love where nothing else is offered but delivery-systems and megatons.

Worst-case analysis *assumes* failure: failure is built into its projections. It has no other perspective. It is, already, a terminal ideology. What it does, by blocking all exits with hideous worst cases, is to pass on to the future nothing but more missiles. The solution is always deferred, yet what is passed on is always worse. Everything is pushed forward to some anonymous distant future, which future we are busy fouling up today.

We cannot shuffle off the present on the the back of the future for ever, giving to our inadequacy the fine name of 'deterrence.' Already that future has become only a best case hypothesis. If there is to be a future, then we must begin to make it happen now. *(24.8.80)*

Strangelove HQ under MAD Mountain
Ian Mather

A suspicious blip on a radar screen has General James V. Hartinger jumping into his car and racing to the mountain. He would have 30 minutes if missiles were fired from the Soviet mainland, just 15 minutes if they were launched from Russian submarines off the American coast.

Naturally, he is a bit edgy. 'I can get there before an intercontinental missile,' he says. 'I have a car with a red flashing light. All the cops know me. I test them out occasionally.'

General Hartinger heads the North American Air Defence Command, which uses satellites, radars and sensors to scan for incoming missiles or bombers. His office is in the centre of Colorado Springs on the edge of the Rocky Mountains. But at the first hint of an emergency he must drive quickly out of town, up a hill and into an underground headquarters designed to withstand a nuclear attack, built inside Cheyenne Mountain.

The journey took 20 minutes in normal traffic conditions. Should the general not make it, huge blast-proof doors, each a yard thick and weighing 25 tons, would be slammed in his face, and a deputy would take over. It is a job of unnerving tension and pressure. For the United States has no defence against nuclear attack. Its deterrent philosophy rests entirely on being able to detect approaching missiles and get its own missiles and bombers off the ground in time to retaliate.

Strategists call it MAD – Mutually Assured Destruction – the implication being that neither side will find it profitable to risk an attack.

The radars are ultra-sensitive and the computers complex. Three times in less than a year NORAD's computers have detected a nuclear attack on the United States which was not actually taking place. On each occasion the crews of B52 nuclear bombers raced to their aircraft for take-off, and the crews of intercontinental missiles began preliminary launch procedures.

The general is a restless competitive man, aged 55, sensitive about his cheek jowls. He was an Army sergeant in World War Two, and later became a fighter pilot, shot down twice in Korea. He is a lacrosse champion, and is proud of the fact that he once played baseball at Wembley.

The general is never parted from his walkie-talkie set, through which he keeps in touch with 'the mountain.' When we met in his office he had just returned from attending the annual rodeo show in town with his wife. He was holding her broad-rimmed hat in one hand and his walkie-talkie in the other.

Despite the false alarms, he has faith in the NORAD system. On the first occasion, before General Hartinger took over, someone fed data indicating a nuclear attack into a computer and failed to report that it was only an exercise. New procedures have been designed to prevent a repetition, he says. Then a faulty microchip produced some digits instead of noughts, again indicating a missile attack. Three days later, there was a 'deliberate' false alarm when the same procedures were repeated to locate the faulty chip.

The alarms lasted less than two minutes on each occasion. 'We can contact every one of our sensors in less than 60 seconds. Each time they showed nothing was coming our way. So I say No, No, No, No. There is no way a flock of geese could start a nuclear war.'

From the outside, Cheyenne Mountain looks like any other pine-covered ski resort peak. It starts at 11,000 feet. But inside, in caverns artificially blasted out of the solid granite, are 15 steel structures, each free standing on giant springs to enable them to withstand nuclear blast along a tunnel one-third of a mile long, at the end of which were the blast doors. They fit flush into the tunnel wall when closed, so that a nuclear blast would roar right through and out of another entrance, leaving the headquarters intact.

'If we have to button up we can survive here for 30 days,' says Major Bob Fore, one of a staff of 350 military personnel on round-the-clock duty inside the mountain. 'We have food, water reservoirs, and our air comes through biological, chemical and radiological filters.'

When I visited the centre an illuminated map of the United States and the Atlantic showed the whereabouts of Russian missile-carrying submarines (detected by sonars, satellites and US submarines) within firing range of the United States, each submarine represented by a cross. There were two far off the coast of California, one just inside the 12-mile limit off Washington, three in the area of the Greenland-Iceland-United Kingdom gap (the only route through which Russian submarines can reach the Atlantic from their northern base at Murmansk), and one a long way off the west coast of Ireland. The path of a Soviet aircraft travelling between Newfoundland and Cuba was also shown.

A second screen indicated what was described as the 'decay track' of a used Russian space defence satellite which was due to impact east of Moscow.

In addition to satellites, NORAD uses two sets of radar to detect incoming missiles. Missiles launched from the Soviet mainland would be picked up by the Ballistic Missile Early Warning Systems, which are three radars, each the size of a football field, at Fylingdales in Yorkshire, Thule in Greenland and Clear, Alaska. Missiles from submarines would be detected by radars in Florida, Massachusetts and California. NORAD satellites can pick up an object the size of a chair at up to 35,000 miles from the earth's surface.

Above the screens are digital clocks with ominous indicators such as 'Time of First Event' – that is, the time a Russian missile is fired; 'TTG,' meaning 'Time to Go'; 'NYI' – 'Not Yet Impacted'; and 'IMPD' – 'Impacted.'

NORAD does not launch any American missiles. It simply passes on information to 40 American agencies and to the President. Only the President can order a nuclear attack. This order would be transmitted to General Richard Ellis, Commander-in-Chief of Strategic Air Command which controls all US land-based missiles and nuclear bombers.

SAC headquarters at Omaha, Nebraska, are not protected against nuclear attack. So General Ellis would take to the air with his battle staff. When I visited SAC, the general's aircraft, a converted Boeing 707 crammed with communications equipment, stood on permanent alert, guarded by security police with M-16 machine guns. Around the aircraft were two circles of ropes and a notice which said: 'Use of Deadly Force Authorised.'

The President himself meanwhile would also take to the air in one of a fleet of converted Boeing 747 Jumbo jets. One is always ready at Washington. During my visit to SAC, another aircraft of this fleet, painted blue and white and with 'United States of America' on its sides, was practising take-offs and landings.

America's most modern land-based intercontinental missile is the Minuteman Three. It is 60 feet long, just over five feet in diameter, travels at 16,000 miles per hour, can hit an area smaller than a football field at a range of 6,000 miles, and carries a nuclear warhead with 27 times the explosive power of the bomb dropped on Hiroshima.

Despite the horrific implications of this, many of the crews regard missiles as 'fun,' and one of their greatest thrills is to launch a missile – without a warhead, of course – from a test range at Vandenberg, north of Los Angeles. As the missile streaks up to a height of 700 miles it can be seen from Las Vegas 600 miles away.

'Minutemen have more thrust!' said the sticker on a refrigerator door inside the underground capsule which I saw.

Each Minuteman Launch Control Facility is 25 feet long and five feet wide, is buried 70 feet underground and suspended by a chain to protect it from nuclear blast. It controls 10 missiles positioned in silos between three and 10 miles away from the LCF and from any other missile.

The land-based missile force consists of 1,000 Minutemen and 54 Titans, deployed in 'wings' of up to 200 missiles each, divided into 'squadrons' of 50. Even within each 'wing' the missiles are dispersed over a vast range. The base I visited, called Francis E. Warren after a former Governor of Wyoming, covers 15,000 square miles of rough unfenced pasture and ranch land. The crews work 24-hour shifts, and often have to travel 150 miles each way to reach their Launch Control Facility. In winter, in deep snow, this journey is often the most hazardous part of the job.

The missile crew members, known as 'key turners,' are young, mostly in their early to mid-twenties. They earn around $13,000 a year, and wear dark blue uniforms, with different colour cravats indicating their squadron.

None of those to whom I spoke had ever met a Russian. All thought in terms of military targets rather than people. All said they would 'turn keys' if they had to, but believed the existence of the deterrent had been a principal factor in preventing war.

Francis E. Warren, north of Denver and east of the Rockies, is in classic cowboy country. The original fort was built to protect the advancing Union Pacific railroad from marauding Indians in the second half of the nineteenth century. Today it is a favourite place for tourists to buy cowboy hats – and the home of 200 Minutemen.

The missiles are poised in randomly sited, vertical silos. The top of each silo is covered with a six-sided concrete lid weighing 100 tons which is blasted aside by a preliminary explosion when the missile is launched.

A six-foot high wire fence encloses an area the size of a small football field around each silo. There is no one there. But highly sensitive sensors announce the presence of any intruder. Sometimes the alarms are set off by rabbits, birds, cows – and even weeds.

The two-man missile crews are subject to elaborate security precautions (overseen by black-booted, blue beret-wearing security police). When crewmen arrive at their underground capsule they must identify themselves at three separate blast doors using individual codes before the crew will let them in.

The next two to four hours of the shift will be spent checking the systems, after which the crew members can spend their time in any way they choose, provided they do not leave the capsule and that the two of them do not sleep at the same time. (There is only one bunk per capsule, in any case.)

One of the attractions of being a missile crew member is the Minuteman Education Programme, under which crew members can study for advanced degrees. The courses are adapted to the crew's work schedules, and at Warren over half the personnel are studying for master's degrees, mostly in management and business administration, a few in psychology. For exercise they can jog round the computer; 88 times round is one mile.

After the Vietnam war a lot of redundant pilots became missile operators, but that phase is now over, and the vast majority of the missile crews are young college graduates – including four women. All have had their backgrounds investigated by the secret service. They have also taken a missile training course lasting between 12 and 17 weeks, after which they are qualified to become the junior member of a missile crew with the responsibility of actually turning the key to launch a missile if necessary.

During training there are weekly counselling sessions and regular mental health checks. Apparently only 1 to 2 per cent drop out on grounds of conscience. Between 6 and 7 per cent fail on academic grounds, and another 1 per cent on medical grounds, particularly through sinus trouble which requires treatment that makes the sufferer drowsy. At the end of the course the fledgling crew member undergoes a six-hour evaluation test, after which he is qualified to 'pull alert,' as the jargon has it.

190. Darker Thoughts

'We have no problems with people being afraid to turn keys,' said Colonel Bill Barnes, Deputy Commander of Operations at Warren. 'Such people are screened out before they get here. But we do have problems with people who can't stand the confined space. Once they are in the operational wing we keep an eye on them all the time. If they have a problem, such as marital trouble, we will temporarily remove them from the duty roster.'

The first warning of a nuclear attack would be a warbling sound over the loudspeaker system in their capsule. 'They are taught to salivate whenever they hear that sound,' said Captain Garry T. Edwards, a Protocol Officer at the base. 'They immediately isolate the capsule by closing all blast doors. They go on emergency air, so they are completely sealed off from the outside environment.'

If it is a real attack, the crew will hear these words over their loudspeaker: 'Gentlemen, you have received an authorised launch instruction from the National Command Authority in Washington.'

Immediately, a printed code consisting of letters and numbers is fed to the crew through a small Telex machine. The two crew members then go to a red box on the wall, open it with their keys, and check the coded message inside against the message they have received. If the codes match, the launch message is valid.

To launch a missile the crew members sit in chairs at right angles to each other. They have to turn keys in locks in front of them within two seconds of each other and hold the keys turned for two seconds. The chairs are 12 feet apart, so no single crew member can launch a missile. A second crew in another capsule have to go through an identical procedure before a small 'missile away' sign lights up yellow.

Contrary to common belief, there is no way to abort the missile or deflect it from its target once it has been fired. It was explained that to do so would need a communications system to the missile which an enemy might be able to use to destroy the missile or direct it back on to its own silo.

After talking to many of those involved in the American nuclear war machine, I have reached two simple conclusions.

First, the danger of accidental war is less than I had thought, because of the large number of checks and balances built into the system – though it is true that the system is probably vulnerable to a madman at the top.

My second conclusion is that, if the order to launch were given, the crews would obey it. Without hesitation. *(9.9.80)*

13.
Exits

Death of a Beatle
Maureen Cleave

When John Lennon was killed in New York it was the Americans, his adopted countrymen, who set the tone of the mourning. Not only grief-stricken but awe-struck, they mourned him as a prophet outside his own country in a way that he might not have been mourned had he stayed at home.

To railings entwined with flowers, they pinned pictures of this gaunt face with all-seeing eyes, and in it I could find no trace of Beatle John, the terror of the 1960s, with a Napoleonic sense of his own superiority and an Olympian disregard for the rest.

'The one thing I dread,' he said, dismissing a third of the human race, 'is growing old. People grow old and then they've missed it somehow.'

Age takes us all by surprise, but its effect on him seemed so perverse: how could he have grown *less* cynical, *less* confident with time? Why was he moving through life backwards? How could someone as clumsy as he, unable to switch on the light without knocking the lamp over, really be baking bread and running a household composed of five giant New York apartments?

It was all very well to give interviews inside paper bags and bare your bottom in the cause of peace, but surely there was a laugh somewhere? What had happened to my old friend? Friend, buddy and pal, as he used to say.

Was all this prompted by love of a good woman, viz Yoko, or even earlier by a drop of acid on a lump of sugar slipped into his coffee, he once said, by a dentist he knew? Or was he still being funny and had the American papers missed the point?

I knew him from early in 1963, when the Beatles' record 'Please Please Me' was top of the hit parade, until 1966, by which time they were the most famous people in the English-speaking world. He didn't change all that much in that time: far from being surprised, pleased and grateful to be rich and famous, he seemed nettled at not having been so earlier. 'I was always rather surprised,' he once said, 'that I wasn't a famous painter.'

If he hadn't liked me, I would never have dared to like him, but I had a nice pair of red boots that were considered rather *outre* at the time and he fancied those. All the Beatles were obsessed by physical appearances, particularly by their own hair. The dreaded moment in any performance was when their fringes stuck to their foreheads with sweat, making them look slightly like Hitler.

John Lennon never succeeded in looking like a pop singer: his face was against him, that long pointed nose, small narrowing eyes, long upper lip. It was a Holbein portrait, not a contemporary image. His supercilious state was due in equal parts to a natural arrogance and short-sightedness. He was too vain at first to wear spectacles, too disorganised for contact lenses.

Other pop singers bought their parents attractive bungalows in the suburbs; John Lennon showed his father Fred the door. 'I've only seen him once before in my life,' he said cheerfully without a qualm, 'and I'm not having *him* in the house.'

His clothes were all wrong. 'Look at these trousers,' he would say, mystified, 'must have sat in something.' He once ordered a gorilla suit. 'I thought I might pop it on in the summer and drive around in the Ferrari – actually it's the only suit that fits me.'

He always said whatever came into his head. Sir Joseph Lockwood, then chairman of EMI, presenting them with some golden disc, fumbled with the words of the song title. 'You're fired,' said John. Groucho Marx would have said that, but with a script.

People were rude to them too at the beginning. This is what Paul Johnson wrote in the *New Statesman* in 1964, about the television audience in 'Juke Box Jury': 'What a bottomless chasm of vacuity they reveal! The huge faces, bloated with cheap confectionery and smeared with chain-store make-up, the open, sagging mouths and glazed eyes, the hands mindlessly drumming in time to the music, the broken stiletto heels, the shoddy stereotyped "with it" clothes. Those who flock round the Beatles, who scream themselves into hysteria, whose vacant faces flicker over the TV screen, are the least fortunate of their generation, the dull, the idle, the failures.'

There is a touch of Hogarth in the description. They put up with this fairly good-humouredly much of the time. Ted Heath said they didn't speak the Queen's English. 'And I bet,' said John, 'that a lot of people that voted for him didn't speak the Queen's English either.'

His favourite childhood author was Richmal Crompton of the 'Just William' books, and I always thought he had a lot in common with William: the untidiness, the anti-social behaviour, the unself-consciousness. Like William he was always battling against the odds, yearning for the impossible. Like William he triumphed at the last.

He always found his own story, the Beatle story, romantic. He liked to talk about both the rags and the riches; indeed, by the time they reached the top, there wasn't much else to do but talk.

You can become a solicitor or a social worker without idolising other solicitors and social workers, but it is impossible to become a pop singer without first being a fan. Some of this early naivety survived their initial fame. 'I can remember what it was like,' John Lennon said, 'waiting for Gene Vincent, and thinking: He's coming! He's coming!'

They had years, uninterrupted by National Service, in which to be fans, in which to plot and plan for their turn which would surely come. 'I used to read the ads in *Reveille* for guitars and just *ache* for one. I used God like everybody else for this one thing I wanted: Please God, give me a guitar.'

'This boy at school had been to Holland. He said he'd got this record at home by somebody called Little Richard who was better than Elvis. Elvis was bigger than religion in my life. We used to go to this boy's house after school and listen to Elvis on 78s; we'd buy five Senior Service loose in this shop and some chips and go along. The new record was "Long Tall Sally". When I heard it, it was so great I couldn't speak. You know how you are torn. I didn't want to leave Elvis. We all looked at each other but I didn't want to say anything against Elvis, even in my mind.

'How could they be happening in my life, *both* of them? And then someone said: "It's a nigger singing." I didn't know Negroes sang. So Elvis was white and Little Richard was black. This was a great relief. "Thank you, God," I said. There is a difference between them.

'But I thought about it for days at school, of the labels on the records of Elvis and Little Richard. One was yellow and the other was blue, and I thought of the yellow against the blue.' (This story had a nice ending. Years later he met Little Richard in Hamburg. 'I's a star,' said Little Richard with his customary diffidence, 'you's a light bulb. One day you gonna be a star too.')

Children liked the Beatles because they looked like furry animals, puppies that you could pat and fondle, but they were of course grown men, and they had rakish habits. John, Paul, George and Stuart Sutcliffe (who later died) after 18 months in Hamburg, playing and eating and sleeping on the stage, knew each other better than most married couples, in sickness and in health, for better or for worse, and always for poorer. Everything was a group activity including, as John Lennon said later when he spilt the beans in *Rolling Stone*, sex. These Bacchanalian revels were called orgies to rhyme with Porgy and were part of any tour – indeed the tour of any group – away from home.

'I hope I grow out of it,' John Lennon said, 'being so sex mad. Sex is the only physical exercise I bother with.'

I once put forward a case for marital fidelity. He was interested in this, as he was in all new ideas. 'Do you mean to say,' he said, 'I might be missing something?'

Everything happened so fast. When Cynthia was first brought to London with their son, John Charles Julian, they were all installed in a not very nice flat beside the West London air terminal. There were always fans outside, just a few, day and night in all weathers. John always ignored them totally. He was frightened of them.

Then he, George and Ringo all moved to palatial mansions in Weybridge and Esher. They saw only each other, scarcely knowing day from night.

John's was, for him, preposterous: the sitting room had yellow tartan walls. 'What day is it?' John would ask with interest when you rang up. There were no regular meals, but there probably hadn't been those since they were 15.

They gave each other presents: George gave John a pair of crutches, John gave Ringo a small stuffed puppy in a glass case standing on a little carpet. They dropped in on each other in their Ferraris and Rolls-Royces.

They played Buccaneer and the dictionary game, watched television with the record player turned up high at the same time. They took each other's photographs, recorded each other's voices and late at night would set off for London and the clubs.

John would sleep almost indefinitely. Those who were nervous of him were reassured by this natural indolence; he usually co-operated because he was too lazy to argue.

He added daily to his possessions but they got the upper hand: a giant compendium of games from Asprey's that he could open but not shut, a suit of armour called Sidney, more telephones of which he did not know the number, the Rolls-Royce with television set, refrigerator, writing desk and yet another telephone. He only got through once to somebody on this telephone, and they were out.

He was a young man waiting for something to happen. 'This won't do at all,' he said. 'I'm just stopping here like at a bus stop. I think of it every day, me in my Hansel and Gretel house, and it won't do. I'll get my real house when I know what I want. I'll take my time.'

There wasn't much time left and he went on wasting it. He loved money but he was disappointed in fame; it hampered him. 'Here I am, famous and loaded and I can't go anywhere.'

It is difficult to cope with such fame, unless, like the Royal Family, you have a training and a supporting set-up. Others in his position take up eating and paranoia and hypochondria; all the Americans have psychoanalysis as a matter of course. He tried pills, drink, pot and dope, not – I think – to satisfy a self-destructive urge but rather from boredom.

John's disposition was basically cheerful; he was delighted to see anybody who got in from the outside, to know what you had read, what you had seen. I cannot think that his life was blighted by the loss of his mother – though he was made very angry by it – or that he resented being working class, or that a noble mind was overthrown by evil capitalist pressure. He was bored. He had too many choices, too little to do. He had never done a conventional day's work in his life and he had no self-discipline. The rot set in when there was no reason to get up in the morning.

His bad and unpredictable behaviour prevented his meeting more interesting people and his laziness inhibited him from learning anything new. But there were a few more creative years left, and he wrote some of his best songs.

How he composed songs was a mystery. He did say he thought of the words and the music together. He once arrived at the recording studio with the tune for 'A Hard Day's Night,' the theme song for their new film, in his head, and the words written on the back of a birthday card sent to his son Julian. 'To Baby Julian,' it said, 'from Jackie, a morning regular.'

'But when I get home to you,' the song ran,

'I find my tiredness is through

And I feel all right.'

I said I thought that 'my tiredness is through' was a weak line. 'OK,' he said obligingly, getting out his pen, and crossing it out, he wrote:

'I find the things that you do

They make me feel all right.'

The last time I saw him he was off to the doctor to have a piece of sea urchin removed from his toe.

'Don't want to be like Dorothy Dandridge,' he said, 'dying of a splinter when I'm 50.'

Poor John. As it turned out, he could have done with those extra 10 years. *(4.1.81)*

The Dream of Graham Sutherland
Nigel Gosling

A few weeks after the Nazis retreated from Paris in 1944 I drove up from Normandy to visit Picasso in his house in the Rue des Grands Augustins.

Patriotically I took him what I held to be evidence that art was alive and well and living in Britain: two illustrated books, one about Henry Moore, and the other about Graham Sutherland. There was no doubt in my mind that, as Moore incarnated the birth of British sculpture, Sutherland represented the rebirth of British painting. The great man expressed interest, but not surprise; he seemed familiar with the work already.

Between that date and his death at the age of 76 Sutherland produced many impressive pictures, but nothing has altered the image I had of him then. He already represented in a wonderfully vivid way a particular phase of art in this country – the re-emergence of romanticism. He was not the only painter of his generation to work in this style: but he was so outstandingly the most gifted that he became the symbol of it.

When, later, the national mood changed and art interest (I hate to use the facile word 'fashion') moved on, he became artistically marooned on his temporal island; indeed he deliberately removed himself from possible infection by later trends, living first in Kent and then, more and more, in the South of France or, latterly, Wales. He preserved a powerful continuity in his work, the strength of an artist who dreamed a dream in his youth and never let go of it.

It was by no means a peaceful, comfortable vision, though at the start it appeared so. Born into a civilised middle-class family in 1903, he spent his childhood in Surrey, was sent to Epsom which had a bias towards science, and passed an unhappy year as an apprentice in a railway works in Derby. But at 16 his father yielded to his real interests and he entered the Goldsmith's School of Art in London.

Almost immediately he began to produce work which was both original, talented and, from the point of view of his career, seminal. A shy, inward-turned character, he became interested in Samuel Palmer, the friend of Blake; and he did a whole series of etchings inspired by the mysterious work of that artist. The medium suited him exactly – fine-drawn, meticulous, close-focused; all his life the tangled style which emerges naturally on a copper plate was to re-appear in his paintings.

Like most British artists, his style was predominantly linear, the complexities of the forms he liked to invent often seeming to arise from the movement of his wrist. When he did come to use colour, it was used purely emotionally; he preferred acid greens and pinks, burnt oranges and reds, which carry the feelings of the etcher's sharp tools and caustic juices.

What was most significant, though, was the twist which he gave to Palmer's pastoral elegies. The glimmering calm gave way to uneasiness. Sutherland became obsessed with nature, but not as a healing balm against industry as Palmer had seen it. Romantic agony found its way back into the undergrowth; branches split or withered, nature rotted, insects crawled. For Sutherland nature was an intense affair between heaven and hell. It was a relationship marvellously expressed in a set of small landscapes done when chance took him to Pembrokeshire in the early Thirties. The mixture of wild coastline and orderly cultivation, rendered in sulphurous black and orange and brown, became vivid paraphrases of nature – visions based on a perception as much emotional as visual.

The Neo-Gothic revival was very much in the air and Sutherland became an ardent Gothic obsessed with death and detail, with confusion, distortion and ambiguity – from which elements he created a strange new harmony. Lean and ascetic in appearance, quiet and scholarly in manner, he would have seemed at home in one of Dürer's engravings, pouring over an insect's wing or a twig or a skeleton. Spikes and curves and pinnacles permeated his painting; he used thorns as a metaphor for suffering. Meditative and religious by nature (he was a Roman Catholic convert), he was manifestly more concerned – at least artistically – with the Crucifixion than the Transfiguration.

The romanticism which runs like an underground stream beneath all British art joined the other great source of our native inspiration, landscape, and Sutherland emerged as a latterday maestro of the blasted oak and rotting skull. He contrived his menacing images out of details of real, closely observed objects, turning them into sinister shapes which often seemed both traps and victims, tight-strung skeins of vegetable arteries, bunches of unanalysable forms like post-nuclear monstrosities, all seen with an unflinching eye that found a kind of beauty in them.

Such expressionist twisting of nature is not new in art – Arthur Rackham's illustrations were a recent British example – but Sutherland practised it in a highly sophisticated way which exploited a wide and intelligent knowledge of modern European painting, an acute aesthetic and moral awareness and a scrupulous personal morality which was demonstrated when, in 1954, he resigned on a matter of principle from the board of Trustees of the Tate Gallery. He withdrew to the privacy of Provence. His paintings changed somewhat. He widened his range, heightened his colours. English undergrowth turned into vines, ferns into cacti, birds into cicadas – but his Englishness clung. And, in these days of faceless inter-city art, that is something to be glad of.

By chance his series of portraits became better-known in Britain than the imaginative work on which his reputation will rest. A streak of dandyism lurked inside the recluse (he was a natty dresser and liked a cultured background to live and work in) and his sitters were mostly celebrities. He lacked the artistic brutality to decompose and recompose them as he did the subjects in his best paintings, and they begin today to look like salutes to Augustus John.

I doubt if the portraits cut much ice in the international art scene; but his real work does and always did. His translation of the special *angst* of his generation into pigment was done in a very English idiom. He speaks for a place and a time; but it is in a language that will surely be understood for many years to come. *(24.2.80)*

The Rage of Kenneth Tynan
Gore Vidal

New Year 1977. Hollywood. The house of a director who had had three important, as they say, successes in a row, swiftly followed by a triad of failures which meant that soon he would have to leave town or start all over again or both. *Almost* everyone was at the party. Kenneth Tynan and I stood at the far end of the flagstoned ('fag stoned,' I hear Ken whispering in my ear) drawing-room. Since I thought that Ken was rather hurt at being made so little of, I said, to be consoling: 'Have you noticed how, no matter what you say, no one ever listens?' Ken nodded. 'They don't even,' he said, 'way-way-huh *wait* for me to stop stammering.'

We met a quarter-century ago in London. Ken was the country's leading drama critic. I was writing a film in England. Ken wore a plum-coloured suit. Held that fatal cigarette between middle and ring fingers. Talked Marxism with passion at the Mirabelle, where we drank Musigny Comte de Vogüé, courtesy MGM, my studio. 'Money ought not to breed money,' he declaimed as the dawn broke over Curzon Street.

We went back to his flat in Mount Street. One wall was covered with a more that life-size reproduction of Hieronymus Bosch's 'Garden of Earthly Delights' triptych. In one corner lived, upside down, a deeply discouraging sloth. That night the sloth, in very slow motion, crawled down the arm of a demented American novelist and, with slow deliberate speed, as the US Supreme Court might say, sank its teeth into the novelist's plump wrist. Screams in Mount Street.

I have never much enjoyed the theatre, and I dislike bull-fighting almost as much as I hate those Anglos who delight in the kitsch of blood and sand. Ken seriously disliked the novel ('Nothing but padded stage directions') while his knowledge of politics was more theatrical than profound. We were opposites – who, somehow, sometimes, got on.

In the Fifties, Ken surfaced in New York. Broadway was made for him; he for it. He even made an occasional sortie into the intellectual world. With awful fervour, he would preach Marxism to battle-scarred former Stalinist-Trotskyite-Henry Wallace-ite Republicans. Finally, an editor of *Partisan Review* turned to him and said: 'Mr Tynan, your arguments are so old that I've forgotten what the answers are.' Ken had the good grace not to join in the merry laughter.

In the Sixties, Ken, Elaine Dundy and I went on an eating tour of France. I drove. Ken did not. But he read the map marvellously well. 'Just the place to write a novel,' he murmured, as we arrived at the Hotel de la Poste in Avallon, where whatever money that had been bred was taken from us. At Annecy we rowed on the lake. Ken's long tubular white body (are they grown anywhere but in England? like the marrow?) grew very pink in the sun. We recalled passages from E. Nesbit. Later, the Marquis de Sade.

As is well known, England's youthful prodigy insisted that he would be dead by 30. But 30, then 40, came and went. When 50 came, health went. Even so, Ken was quite ready to soldier on. Yet once he had created, launched and left the National Theatre, I'm not sure that he quite knew what it was that he ought to do. I suggested politics but he said, no – wrong temperament.

Shortly after Ken invented sex in the Sixties, he thought that he should do a magisterial book on Reich and get, as it were, the whole thing together. But the book did not write itself, the only way that sort of work could have been done. He did not have the theoretical mind. What sort of mind was it? The tense that I just used I do not believe: I still expect him to ring up with an elaborate accusation: why did you tell Elaine that I said that Kathleen told Tracey that I had . . . Oh, he was difficult in private relations!

But he was made for public occasions. Performance was everything to him. Like Hazlitt and Leigh Hunt, the only two describers of theatre in his class, he could make one feel the excitement of an audience on a certain night; show us the sweat bubbling beneath the make-up of an actor who has managed to make bright the air within the proscenium arch.

Ken left England in order to live longer. He left New York City for Hollywood for the same reason. But there are not many people in Hollywood for someone like Ken to share his enthusiasms with. Hollywood is a company town, and if one lacks power within the company there is no audience for even the most brilliant of stammerers. Yet he got a good deal of work done. He wrote some of his best pieces about – inevitably – performers who excited him. The portrait of Ralph Richardson is a marvellous comic reconstruction of a persona that, as Ken so beautifully demonstrated, was not shaped in haunts of coot and hern but *is* both coot and hern.

I saw a good deal of Ken in Hollywood. He would be in splendid if rather fragile form for an hour or two; then he would lose his breath. If he was in my house, he would go, shakily, to his car where he would inhale oxygen from a cylinder that he was obliged to travel with. At night, he slept with tubes in his nostrils, feeding oxygen to a pair of lungs that did not work at all except for a quarter-inch which, finally, last week, shrank to nothing. But he could be jaunty about his curtailed life. 'I live like the sloth,' he said. 'I move very slowly. And it suits me. I never liked running about. I prefer,' he lied, 'life in slow motion.'

Some time ago, Ken was given a good deal of money to write a biography of Laurence Olivier. Although Ken delighted in Olivier the performer, he was less than thrilled by Olivier the manager: 'He'd have revived all of Ivor Novello if we'd let him.' Then the Press made trouble, and the life-lord withdrew his complaisance. I told Ken he was well out of it. 'Write,' I said, 'about yourself. You're more interesting than Olivier – which isn't saying much. You've spent 30 years in a world that fascinates others. . . .' And so on.

The last time I saw Ken he was working on his autobiography. He was enjoying himself. But he wondered if he would be in good enough health to get the book done this year. Death was not mentioned. As he talked, I studied his face. He looked very thin and curiously young, the way people often do in the last lap. I noticed that when he mentioned his illness, there was a sudden gelid glare in those gooseberry eyes: rage, pure rage. He will live to finish it, I decided. That was last winter. I have a hunch that fury saw him through to the end. *(3.8.80)*

The Man who Made our Flesh Creep
Philip French

Alfred Hitchcock was a neat, carefully composed man who always wore a dark suit, plain tie, white shirt and brightly polished shoes, whether in the studio or receiving the Press.

Despite his bulk – his weight varied between 14 and 20 stone – he seemed compact, even delicate. Except when making visual points, his hands were folded over his ample belly, and his expressions were limited to movements of his eyes and the inverted triangle of his lower face, like a ventriloquist's dummy. Talking in a level, slightly monotonous London accent, he met every question with a polite, amusing and colourfully informative answer.

He never sighed, he never mocked his interviewers for their ignorance or their pretentiousness. Indeed, since the 1920s he assiduously cultivated stern cinéastes and Fleet Street columnists alike, a habit that was later to lead to the slightly embarrassing situation whereby he regularly assured old British friends that his 1930s films were his personal favourites while leading his new-found French admirers to believe that the philosophically more profound post-war American movies were the ones he set greatest store by.

Always he seemed in as total control of himself as his professional collaborators attest he was of his movies, which with the sole exception of that 1963 masterpiece 'The Birds' (for technical reasons) and the 1969 disaster 'Topaz' (for dramatic ones), were worked out to the last detail before they went on the studio floor.

One felt that Hitch had paid a considerable price in spontaneity to acquire this intimidating poise, and that it related to the very centre of his art. This resided in exposing the complacent, the safe, the seemingly invulnerable to the horrendous chaos that lay all around them.

This is the essence of the Hitchcock touch, the characteristic setpiece that turns the most mundane event into an occasion of terror by a slight twist or visual conceit – a fugitive criminal caught up in a game of blind-man's buff at a children's party, a couple on a dance floor who know they'll be killed if they try to sit it out, a windmill with sails turning in the wrong direction, a man whose life depends on overbidding at an auction, and so on. The list of such Hitchcockian scenes is endless. Like Dickens's Fat Boy in 'Pickwick Papers,' he delighted in making our flesh creep. By playing on his audience's paranoia and social insecurity, he was exorcising similar fears of his own.

In the 80-year history of the cinema only two directors, Chaplin and Hitchcock, have been immediately recognisable to audiences the world over. Both were lower middle-class London boys shaped by the Edwardian era who had to cross the Atlantic to realise their talent fully and to wait until old age to receive that accolade each craved as the ultimate sign that his native country recognised his true worth.

Chaplin (born 1889 in Walworth, knighted in 1975) was universally identified with his tramp persona. Hitchcock (born 1899 in Leyton-stone, knighted 1980) was known for the personal appearances with which he signed his films and those deadpan trailers he made and the pawkily comic introductions he recorded for his TV series.

The rear view of him in his first important movie, 'The Lodger' in 1926, was apparently a chance walk-on; in his fifty-third and last movie, 'Family Plot,' the prominent glimpse of that familiar plump profile, silhouetted behind an office door, was carefully calculated to elicit ripples of happy laughter everywhere.

More than anyone else, Hitch made the general public aware of the film director's key role as ringmaster and manipulator, by advertising his own presence and by sharing the secrets of his trade through endless interviews in the Press and on radio and TV. In this way he linked himself to that major tendency in twentieth-century art that sees artists seeking to share the mystique of their craft with audiences and to make the technical process of creation the subject-matter of their work.

Not all Hitchcock's movies are thrillers (he filmed plays by Galsworthy and O'Casey, and the admirable 'Rich and Strange' is a tragi-comedy about bourgeois marriage), and not everything that is best about the thrillers is connected with their shock value. But once he had accepted that title of 'Master of Suspense' he became obsessed with the posing and solution of tricky technical problems (shooting a whole film in a lifeboat, unbroken 10-minute takes) and playing elaborate games with audience expectations by providing the solution to the mystery halfway through ('Vertigo') or killing off the major star in the first half-hour ('Psycho').

Hitchcock's life was as quiet as Chaplin's was wild and wilful, and his role as dutiful son and devoted husband is the sort of thing that gives stability a good name. He was the least autobiographical of artists, though his origins as the son of an East End greengrocer and his education by Jesuits are things one needs to know to understand a coherent body of work that was inevitably shaped by his times and cultural circumstances.

In view of the close relationship that homicide and religion were to have in his films, it is wonderfully appropriate that he should have been a classmate of the future Cardinal Heenan and that his ballroom-dancing teacher should have been the father of the future murderess Edith Thompson.

Exits. 203

There is little chance that his best films, and several of his bad ones too, will ever want for audiences. His influence and example are likely to remain potent, even if, as pastiches and outright re-makes have shown, he is essentially inimitable. But there will never be another career quite like his – growing up with a new art, learning its every aspect as a young man, then living through the transition to sound, the arrival of TV and the wide screen, the relaxation of censorship, and staying at the top for 50 years, changing with the times, catering to new tastes, but remaining his own man. *(4.5.80)*

Steve McQueen: Death of a Loner
Philip French

Hollywood's loner heroes have generally come in threes – Cagney, Robinson and Bogart in the Thirties; Mitchum, Lancaster and Douglas after World War II; Newman, McQueen and Redford in the late Fifties and early Sixties. And with each wave they have become sadder, more vulnerable yet inwardly more resilient.

Steve McQueen came to the screen after a disturbed childhood and adolescence in the Mid-West, his father having left home for good shortly after the child's birth in 1930. He drifted from town to town, job to job, did a stretch in reform school, went to sea with the merchant navy, spent three years with the United States Marines.

But then, in search of a role, or roles, he drifted into the New York theatre, and he studied with some of America's best acting teachers and worked on Broadway before hitting Hollywood. His first featured role at the age of 28 was as a somewhat elderly teenage rebel who turns up trumps defeating a menace from outer space in the low-budget SF movie 'The Blob.'

He first made his mark in 1960 as second-in-command of 'The Magnificent Seven' and most of his characteristic effects were on display there – the crinkled forehead, the slight tightening of the skin around those watery blue eyes, the twitch in the corner of the lips, the broad horizontal grin. He was a taciturn man, his customary posture that of bunched shoulders, hands thrust in pockets, head down, walking the windy streets of a grimy American city, a national type writ large.

Although he played in action movies, and took pride in doing his own stunt work with the motor-bikes and fast cars he loved in 'The Great Escape,' 'Bullitt' and 'Le Mans,' McQueen's usual roles were those of apparently simple men coping with immense inner struggles of conscience which cut them off from their fellows. And this was as true of the Western, 'Nevada Smith,' where he played an orphan revenging his parents' murder, as of the underrated Vietnam allegory 'The Sand Pebbles' (1967), which contains possibly his finest performance.

His notion of himself and his relationship to society was indicated by his choice of Ibsen's 'The Enemy of the People' in 1978 as the personal production with which to return to the screen after five years of virtual seclusion following a revaluation of his career. He carried with him a cloud of melancholy that was perhaps tinged with a tragic sense of life. In his penultimate picture, 'Tom Horn,' he etched an outstanding portrait of a Western gunman whose time had passed. It had about it the same valedictory quality John Wayne brought to 'The Shootist' while he too was dying of cancer.

Three weeks ago in America I heard a statement McQueen taped at his Mexican sanatorium. They were brave words thanking his Mexican hosts and the people who had written to him, but the choked delivery was that of a man *in extremis*. When these words were accompanied on the TV screen by the rugged sensitive face we'd seen for the last time in 'Tom Horn,' a film that had as its subject the dignity of dying, the effect was unbearably moving. *(9.11.80)*

Sartre's Funeral
Patrick O'Donovan

Jean-Paul Sartre was buried without ceremony in the Paris cemetery of Montparnasse. The funeral procession which came from the hospital where he died at the age of 74 was like one of those huge, silent and shapeless demonstrations in which he had so often taken a leading part.

Utterly non-conformist, even to Communism, with no party of his own, he had refused all State and international honours all his life. But a quiet and formidable crowd waited to see his coffin go by. They spoke quietly. They were dressed in the height of informality. The afternoon was dreary and grey, and the crowd grew and waited patiently. Among the mourners was writer Simone de Beauvoir, his companion for half a century.

The procession came down the Boulevard Edgar Quinet like the overflowing of some great event. The road was filled from side to side. There were no leaders, no shouting, no flags, no symbols. The lorry carried a tall hillock of fresh flowers, mostly red. Then came a motor-hearse of conventional respectability and then a coachload of close mourners. They stared out dully. One young woman in the back seat was deeply distressed.

This little cortège was surrounded by a ring of young men holding hands to keep back the crowd that spilled off the pavements and blocked the roadway. There were few police, and the youths had to heave away at the vast crowd that now blocked the entrance to the cemetery.

It was curiously quiet, even as they pushed their way down towards the waiting grave. Behind the cortège the crowd continued to walk slowly, in numbers that would choke a large football stadium.

I cannot imagine Sartre would have liked the cemetery itself. It is a walled city of the dead, crowded with miniature chapels and temples, housing the heaped-up coffins of the rich and middle-class for whom he never had a good word.

Most of the cemetery seems almost habitable, but the old atheist of Protestant antecedents is buried among a forest of crosses, a crowd of angels, deep crypts kept for the use of religious orders, pious Latin inscriptions, family vaults, all guarded by mad old men in uniform who practise a macabre sense of humour that one thought was exclusively English and had gone out with the Tudors. Many of the iron doors to the tombs have been broken open, but relations still bring flowers and there is no sign of the sort of desecration found in England.

Sartre's body was lowered into a temporary grave. He will be cremated in a private ceremony at Père Lachaise cemetery and the ashes returned to Montparnasse. There are a number of these temporary graves about the cemetery, each labelled with the name of an undertaker whose discreet parlours line the streets outside the wall.

The body was lowered into a concrete pit of the utmost practicality. Here death, for all its decoration, seems invested with a peculiar and ugly horror. His grave contained no other coffins, but he went down and down past empty shelves at the side.

They had paraded the coffin by a roundabout route through Paris. It took them an hour and a half to walk it to the grave. It is hard to imagine any man of letters in Britain who would now draw such a crowd in death. But then to the French and to the world Sartre was a furiously honest politician who also wrote.

Everyone seemed to know who was being buried. It was an intellectual rather than a working-class crowd. It was young or middle-aged. It showed no grief but an intense interest and respect. It wore no mourning and indeed there was a feeling of strength and confidence about it. For this really was a demonstration.

Sartre in his time had denounced almost everyone but the students, and it was clearly from that class, now and of years ago, that his crowd came. It was too great and impersonal an event to be solemn, but it was clear that something that was considered great and worthy was being bid farewell. *(20.4.80)*

Tito and Jovanka
Lajos Lederer

I first met Tito in 1950, two years after I had forecast in *The Observer* Yugoslavia's break with the Soviet Union.

I was invited to Belgrade and was met at the airport by Tito's private secretary. He told me that Tito was curious to know on what evidence *The Observer* had based its exclusive story of the break with Moscow, widely denied at the time.

I met Tito at his villa in Uzice Street. He was then 58, but looked no more than 40, a bronzed and poised figure in well-cut Western-style clothes, a dazzling silk tie and white shoes. He told me about the Russians' penetration of Yugoslavia and their unpublished threats. 'There are 30 Red Army divisions on or near our borders,' he said, 'and there's much more than that happening. We know every Russian and Soviet sympathiser in our country. We even know how many shoelaces they have.'

I was unable to check these claims, but it was abundantly clear that Tito was deeply suspicious of the Soviet Union and had an intense dislike for Stalin. At a party at his villa in Bled, to which my wife and I were invited in 1951, Tito moved among his guests with his Alsatian dog Tiger at his heels. He told me: 'I not only love Tiger, I admire him. He has more perspicacity than I have. He smelt the Russian danger before I did. Until 1947 he never attacked anybody, but that year he bit the Soviet ambassador, Lavrentiev.'

As we parted, Tito said he hoped he would see me again, adding: 'Don't go through official channels if you want to talk to me. Just phone my office and they will fix a date.'

I knew, of course, there was a risk here. Tito could conceivably try to muzzle me. He could attempt to use me. He did.

In 1953, he invited me to see him in Belgrade again. 'Lederer,' he said, 'I have a gift for you.' A box of cigars? A bottle of Slivovitz? No. He said: 'I would like you to know that my chargé d'affaires in Moscow has had a meeting with Molotov, and Molotov has told him that the Soviet Union is now ready and willing to restore full diplomatic relations with Yugoslavia.'

My front page report of the rapprochement created a minor sensation. But, to my astonishment, the story was immediately and emphatically denied by Tito's own ambassadors in London and Washington. I went back to Tito on the Tuesday after my report was published to ask what the game was. Tito smiled and said: 'Can you stay on for a couple of days – then I'll explain.'

Two days later Tito, in a speech at the Air Force Club in Belgrade, confirmed every word of my report. He explained afterwards that when his chargé d'affaires had first reported the meeting with Molotov and the Russian offer, he had suspected a trick. 'Molotov hates me,' he said. 'I had a feeling – and my senior colleagues shared it – Moscow was up to something unpleasant. We thought a likely explanation was that Molotov had acted on his own initiative, and that if we openly rejoiced over it the Kremlin then would deny it. We would be humiliated – I would be humiliated. But by Thursday there was no denial, so I knew the offer Molotov had made was genuine and was backed by the Soviet Presidium.'

The personal relationship I established with Tito lasted 30 years, and at one point I asked whether his wife Jovanka would allow me to write a series of frank articles about her life with Tito. She agreed at once, but said she must first have the President's consent. Tito reacted with a burst of laughter. 'Go ahead, Lederer,' he said. 'I'd love to know what she really thinks about me!'

The series was never written, for soon afterwards their marriage began to fail, not through love turning to dislike, but out of love grown too possessive.

They first met towards the end of the Second World War, when Tito was almost 50 and Jovanka Budisavljevik only 18. But she had already won some local renown for her exploits as a Serbian partisan. On one occasion she had mined a bridge singlehanded to hold up a German advance. Like Tito, she came from peasant stock. After the war, with the rank of major, she served on his military staff. They married in 1952 after Tito, then Prime Minister of Yugoslavia, had divorced his second wife. For the next 25 years their marriage appeared perfect.

By then Tito was in his eighties and liked to doze after seven in the evening, when his private secretary left the villa. But his rest was often interrupted by telephone calls from one or other of the party hierarchy. Jovanka began a routine response of: 'Can't it wait till morning?' In time, this became more strident and commanding: 'I don't care how important you think it is, I will not have the President disturbed tonight.' And she would hang up.

Tito was unaware of the problems this was creating, until one of his trusted lieutenants raised the matter with him. He told Jovanka: 'You will in future allow me to decide what requires immediate action and what can wait till the next morning.' When Jovanka protested, Tito warned her that if she continued to insulate him from the Party leadership on her own judgement, he would have to leave the villa.

But Jovanka would not now give up her self-appointed task of protectress. And the breaking-point came when a Party high-up told Tito he'd been unable to advise the President on a matter of extreme importance because Jovanka had forbidden it. Tito did not hesitate. He had his personal belongings packed, and left. Feeling that he was forced to choose between Jovanka and Yugoslavia, he put his country first.

The break could not be kept secret, for Jovanka was soon noticeably absent from functions she would normally have attended. This led to rumours of all kinds – that Tito had taken a mistress and Jovanka had left him; that Jovanka had been banished; even that she was conspiring against Tito with a Serbian general. No evidence was ever produced in support of such stories, but Jovanka had enemies. It was well known in the Party that she frequently influenced Tito's attitude towards individual officials and that heads sometimes rolled as a result.

Tito tried to bring about a reconciliation, but each time he attached conditions which Jovanka rejected.

Towards the end of 1978 Tito planned a New Year's Eve party on his Adriatic island retreat of Brioni and sent Jovanka an invitation. To his chagrin she turned it down. 'Even I never realised how tough she could be,' Tito remarked to his colleagues. The party was cancelled.

Late last year Tito held his annual reception for foreign diplomats at his hunting lodge about an hour's drive from Belgrade. Hotel managers summoned to provide a feast found Tito, at 87, in spectacular form, greeting each guest with effusive warmth. He let it be known that he was again planning a New Year's Eve gathering at Brioni and that this time Jovanka would be at his side.

Within a fortnight, Tito was stricken. A blood clot was diagnosed that led to the amputation of a leg, and, after a long struggle in the Ljubljana hospital, to death. The New Year party never took place, and Tito did not return to the villa in Uzice Street until last week when he was buried in its grounds, and Jovanka led the mourning. *(11.5.80)*

Britain's Failed Dictator
A. J. P. Taylor

Oswald Mosley was a man of promise unfulfilled, a man who long outlived his fame. His brief period of prominence lay 40 or even 50 years ago. Yet men still remember him vaguely, either as a political thinker who might have inspired the Labour Party, or as the potential British Dictator, the man who brought Fascism to Britain and might have been Hitler's gauleiter here.

The Mosleys were Staffordshire gentry whose seventeenth-century ancestor acquired the manorial rights of Manchester as an investment. From this they grew rich. They became hard livers and hard fighters. Mosley, looking back, said: My father fought his father and knocked him down. I fought with my father and knocked him down. Such was my family.' Mosley was educated at Winchester, which gave him intellectual arrogance. He was also a fencer, which gave him the figure of a fighter. During the First World War he served in the Royal Flying Corps. He ended the war with a reputation for courage and a slight limp from an air crash.

In 1918 Mosley became a Conservative MP with no pronounced ideas about politics. He sooned learned politics in action. He was not afraid to challenge the giants of the day, such as Churchill. He did not spare even Curzon, the Foreign Secretary, who subsequently became his father-in-law. In 1921 he denounced Lloyd George's policy of repression in Ireland. In protest, he renounced his Conservative allegiance and within a short time joined the Labour Party.

Like so much else he did, he went in at the top, being personally sponsored by Ramsay MacDonald. Mosley and his wife, Lady Cynthia, became MacDonald's companions on foreign tours. With the second Labour Government came his great chance. He was commissioned to act with J. H. Thomas in producing an economic plan against unemployment and the Great Depression. Thomas had no ideas and no will. Lansbury, who succeeded Thomas, had will but few ideas.

Mosley provided both. Assisted by a small group of young economists, he produced a set of projects which might have transformed Britain and which in some ways are too daring even for today. Here was the planned economy in embryo, a British New Deal. There was to be planned investment, economic cooperation between Great Britain and the Dominions, and the direction of labour. The Mosley programme was rejected by the Labour Cabinet. Mosley took it to the Parliamentary Party. It was rejected again. He took it to the Labour annual conference. It was rejected for a third time.

In those dark days of 1931 there was much talk of a government which would contain all the men of constructive spirit – Lloyd George, Churchill, and by now Mosley, who had come to rank with the great. But Mosley lost patience, always his besetting sin. He resigned abruptly from the Labour Party and set up a short-lived New Party, which fought one by-election and was then swept away by the General Election of 1931.

The New Party had won support from men of the Left, including for a short time John Strachey and Harold Nicolson. Aneurin Bevan at first gave it his unofficial blessing. But now Mosley turned away from the Labour Party and all its works, turned indeed away from the parliamentary system and the British Constitution.

Where some of those on the Left drew their example from Stalin's Russia, Mosley found his in Mussolini's Italy. What impressed him was the display: Black Shirts, mass marches, slogans instead of ideas, and the silencing of opponents. Mosley was always a Romantic, dreaming of Napoleonic triumphs. Dictatorship was in his blood. Now he began to act the part of an English Fascist dictator.

He duly dressed himself and his followers in Black Shirts and marched them through the streets. He set up Black Shirt barracks in London and other cities, where the unemployed were drilled into becoming Storm Troopers, or so Mosley imagined. Mosley was not alone in this enterprise, though he was the sole Leader. Wealthy men, including Lord Nuffield and the first Lord Rothermere, contributed large funds to the British Union of Fascists.

Mosley's speeches took on a new character. Previously they had advocated economic reform in a rational, even if forceful, way. Now they advocated Action, the slogan of the BUF, Action for its own sake, sensational and violent. There was much denunciation of 'the old gang,' and a call to sweep away the encumbrances of the past.

There was another new element; brutal violence in its naked form against those who dared to challenge Fascism or its Leader. The violence was not all on one side. Communists and their allies organised resistance to the Fascists. But it was Mosley who had provoked it. Violence made both Fascism and Mosley unpopular.

Mosley tried other themes. Though he later claimed not to have been anti-semitic, he denounced the Jews for advocating war against Hitler, which came to much the same thing. Mosley now looked to Hitler as his example. When the war came he tried to stand aloof. Events caught up with him. As the Battle of Britain drew near, Mosley and his wife were interned as possible collaborators with Hitler if the Battle went the wrong way.

Mosley always protested his patriotism, but he had given too many hostages to fortune in his speeches. The continued internment of the

Mosleys after the danger had passed, however, was totally unjustified; internment is a precaution, not a punishment.

After the war was over, Mosley lived at first in Ireland and then principally near Paris. He occasionally attempted a return to British politics, picking up racialism where he had dropped anti-semitism. Nothing came of this. But Mosley was still fertile in ideas. He was an early champion of the European Community, and often talked as though he had created it. Like John Gabriel Borkman, he waited for the call that never came.

What went wrong with Mosley that caused his wasted life? He was arrogant. He overrated his own cleverness and despised the stupidity of others. He was violent first in thought, then in action. He believed in sudden attacks, not in prolonged campaigns, and soon became bored even with his own. At critical moments in the fortunes of British Fascism, he was often away with a party of smart friends in Venice.

Mosley was, in fact, a highly gifted playboy. From the moment he modelled himself on Mussolini, he resembled nothing so much as an actor touring the provinces in a play which someone else had made a success of in London. Watching newsreels of Mosley on the march through the East End recalls the memory of another Londoner. Oswald Mosley aspired to be The Great Dictator. Sir Charles Chaplin played the role better. *(7.12.80)*

The Great Auk
Colin Legum

Although Churchill described Sir Claude Auchinleck as 'an officer of the greatest distinction, and a character of singular elevation,' the two war leaders never really got on together. Perhaps the fault was more on the Auk's side, since his make-up did not allow him to put up with what his very close friend, Field-Marshal Lord Ismay, described as Churchill's moods of 'a child of nature, as variable as an April's Day.'

But the real barrier between them was profoundly psychological: Churchill, ingrainedly prejudiced against India and Indians; and Auchinleck, with a love of the country and its people greater even than for his own.

He never again felt really at home in this country after leaving it to serve as a subaltern in India in 1903, where his father had served before him. Orphaned at a young age, he was too poor (as he confessed) to be able to afford the life of an officer in the British Army in those days.

Indeed, he grew so far away from his own roots that he could write about his countrymen like a colonial in this diary note on 1 July 1942, on the eve of the wars that turned the tide in North Africa:

'These damned British have been taught for too long to be good losers. I've never been a good loser, I am going to win.'

He went on to win the first Battle of Alamein which paved the way for the North African breakthrough.

Why, then, did Churchill relieve him of his command in favour of Montgomery only a year later? In private conversations, the Auk traced his disagreement with Churchill back to a stormy meeting of the Defence Committee on 1 August 1941. Churchill had been pressing him hard not to delay attacking Rommel since there was no possibility of getting more reinforcements and weapons to North Africa, while the German commander had time to build up his own forces.

The Auk disagreed. He could, he said, in six weeks raise a whole armoured division of trained and seasoned soldiers, unemployed because they had no equipment of their own.

'And where,' growled Churchill, 'are these men to be found?'

'From India,' Auchinleck replied.

'And how, General, do you know they wouldn't turn their guns and fire in the wrong way?' Churchill shot back at him.

To the Auk, with his knowledge of the fierce loyalty of his Indian troops, this was outrageous. He was denied the additional forces the Allies so badly needed only because of Churchill's prejudices, formed during his own wholly unsuccessful career as a young subaltern in India.

But though he was to be denied the fruits of victory in North Africa, he was to make one last important contribution – as Commander-in-Chief of the Indian Forces during the transfer of power. For him the most difficult decision of his entire life was how to deal with the officers of the Indian National Army, who had opted to fight for their country's independence by joining with Japan.

It was a time of great emotion. If he were to allow the traitorous officers to be executed, he would arouse much of India against the British; not to punish them would be a betrayal of the vast majority of Indian soldiers who had remained loyal. He decided on clemency and explained his decision in a long memorandum sent to all his officers in February 1946. It must rank as one of the great chronicles of Imperial history. He wrote:

'It is no use shutting one's eyes to the fact that any Indian officer worth his salt is a Nationalist, though it does not mean that he is necessarily anti-British. If he is anti-British this is as often as not due to faulty handling and treatment by his British officer comrades.'

As a young officer he had been outraged both by the way British officers treated their Indian colleagues, and the perpetuation of the Indian caste system in the Army. He patiently but firmly eradicated both.

After the independence of India and Pakistan he returned to England reluctantly, feeling it would be embarrassing for him to remain in the sub-continent. He refused a peerage. His only explanation was that 'there are already too many peers.' But the real reason was his strong dislike of the English establishment – beyond whose pale he always felt himself to be. He preferred it that way.

Still only 63 and vigorous, he had no future. For the rest of his life he suffered the deep humiliation of his dismissal by Churchill, and the private sorrow of his wife having left him during the war.

He returned to a life of loneliness – a gnarled, formidable oak with a broken heart. But, living by his own old-fashioned code of private conduct, he steadfastly refused to defend himself against the diminishing of his role by those two great war heroes – and no less great self-publicists – Churchill and Montgomery. Only once did he allow himself to write a letter correcting one of Montgomery's searing untruths, which he kindly attributed to a false memory.

With Oriental fatalism he left his career to be judged by history.

Living alone at 3 Downes Street, Mayfair, he found solace in music and painting, spending his weekends in Norfolk with his painting friends, the Edward Seagos. But his modest flat became a place of pilgrimage for Indian and Pakistani friends alike.

He would stride alone around London looking for new Indian restaurants. 'I think I've found something really good this time,' he would write at regular intervals. After lunch, we would go and choose snuff at Fribourg & Treyer in the Haymarket.

There were those moments of reward when, on entering restaurants or while out strolling, he would be greeted by men who had known him in the Army: 'Good God, the Auk!' – invariably followed by a stiffening of the arms at the side and a corrective 'Sir!'

Then the Auk's eyes – narrowly slit by decades in the hot sun – would brighten, and he would allow himself that infrequent, hardly perceptible, vulnerable smile which showed his real kindness and innate gentleness.

Finally, he could stand England no longer, and he took his music and painting off to Marrakesh, where he spent his last years alone with a faithful Muslim servant who loved to surprise his master and guests by putting on hideous false noses.

He expressed to me and other friends the wish that he would be buried in Pakistan. His heart belonged to the East. *(29.3.81)*

Brother Philip's Progress
Philip Toynbee

The novelist and literary critic, Philip Toynbee, died in June 1981, after 30 years with *The Observer.* **These extracts from his 1977-79 diaries, published two months before his death, were his last major contribution to the newspaper.**

1 August 1977

More than two months have passed since I finished a course of ECT (electroconvulsive therapy) at Bristol, and for the past six weeks I have been almost entirely free from depression. No exorbitant elation, thank God, but the dazed incredulity of a prisoner suddenly let out into ordinary daylight after three years in a dungeon.

But I must beware of such extravagant images as this; for whatever purposes this diary is meant to serve, it certainly won't serve any at all unless I keep it as simple and as truthful as I can.

13 August

But nothing is more repulsive than a false simplicity; which means, in my case, any simplicity which hasn't been arduously and painfully worked out. I know a few country people from our own neighbourhood whose Christian faith is still untouched by Darwin; whose biblical trust has been inherited from generations of unquestioning believers. But this, for most of us, is a state of lost innocence which we may genuinely respect but can imitate ourselves only by a kind of mental bluster that cows the active mind and heart.

18 August

'All must know first the voice crying in the wilderness of their hearts.' (George Fox). I heard that voice again last night, though as if from quite a long way off. I prayed that it won't come any nearer.

17 September

'Phenomena of psychological transference and combinations. If people were told: What makes carnal desire imperious in you is not its carnal element. It is the fact that you put into it the essential part of yourselves – the need for unity, the need for God. . . . To make the Christian faith palpable, it must be shown to be implicitly present, in a degraded form, even in the basest passions. What we are talking to you about is the very thing you are longing for with your whole soul, at this moment, in your present state. But you give it a false name.' (Simone Weil).

There is a crude answer to this: and crude answers aren't always the worst ones – 'You can't fob off a randy man with Holy Communion.' Nor, perhaps, ought you to try.

For Simone W, this passage is fairly tolerant about lust; but she still calls such desires 'base' and 'degraded.' So I'd say that she's writing about the sexual urge in its purest and least discriminating form. And though I use 'pure' here in the sense of 'unmixed', 'undiluted,' I mean to give it a positive moral sense as well. Two strangers meet; please each other both as persons and bodies; sleep together with friendly joy; part forever in the morning. To me this is a genuinely pure and delightful encounter; a marvellous reciprocity of giving and receiving. Therefore *holy*, to those of pure heart and mind unpolluted by prurient guilt.

24 September

Time to take stock. I've been making serious efforts to pray and meditate for about 18 months. With what results, if any?

Loved ones – my wife Sally and the children – all agree I'm less impatient than I used to be. And that was no minor failing. An intolerant, and intolerable, demand that things happen, people act, just when I wanted them to happen and act. I never really thought that the whole line of traffic in the jam ahead should immediately get on to the verge and let us pass; but I spoke and behaved as if I did think this. Possessed by a noxious demon of furious impatience. The rampant tumescent self.

Not that I'm now a model of saintly patience; far from that. I doubt if I've reached the average level. But now, when held up on the road, I get out my rosary and repeat my mantra – 'The Peace of God' – and nearly always manage at least to keep my mouth shut – instead of taking it out on poor Sally. (Though at bad times the beads get rough treatment and the unspoken mantra sounds more like a curse than a blessing.)

Ah, but should I take any pleasure from this improvement? Well, the self-congratulation is wry enough, surely, and scarcely involves me in the sin of pride. Relief at not behaving like an insufferable lunatic is hardly the fault by which the angels fell.

. . . And then the banana skin!

I got roaringly-boringly drunk on an evening out; felt, next morning, that I'd been set back months and months. And this was followed by several days of pain and fear.

But today I begin to wonder whether that cropper – or any other – need be a setback. Not that such mishaps teach lessons of future abstinence, or I'd have learned *this* lesson 40 years ago. But that break-out, that foolery, and all the fearful days that followed – surely they should somehow be *incorporated*. Perhaps it's part of *my* dance to fall flat on my face from time to time.

Days of doubt too, of course. Always lurking in the mind this mocking suspicion that the whole religious to-do is simply an old man's hobby. A warding-off of senile apathy.

7 November

To Tymawr [an Anglican contemplative convent] for mass yesterday. Calmed and strengthened.

It's not, I confess, the sacred moment itself which greatly affects me, but the whole process. Alarm at 6.45; morning dusk; quick shave and coffee. The swoop into the valley from St Briavels, on to the empty valley road and over Bigsweir bridge (sun just rising yesterday as I crossed the river). Up the misty Whitebrook valley; stopping to open the white convent gate; up the drive between cows and the little unmarked cemetery under the chestnut tree.

Coming into the chapel, and taking the place where 'Brother Philip' has been written on a slip by Sister Mary Jean. My growing familiarity with the strict order of the Mass. 'We are all partners of the one bread.' *That* being the heart of it for me.

Being an Associate of this holy place gives me immense satisfaction; the sisterhood of the nuns I know; even a growing sense that the Reverend Mother is indeed a true mother to me – though she must be 10 years younger.

They have their problems, of course, but how strong the sense of stability I get there!

3 December

The absurd but painful struggle against smoking. I first 'gave up' about 20 years ago, and once achieved an unbroken abstinence of nearly six months. What is so strange is that I deeply hate the wretched little poisonous tubes, and positively look forward, on smoking days, to the day I've set myself for renouncing them again.

9 December

I have resolved to give up booze entirely

10 December

An exception will be made, of course, on Christmas Day. At Christmas *time*.

Well, this first Monmouth Thursday, dreaded so much, passed off a little more smoothly than I'd feared. Much amazement all round at my Coke and bitter lemons. And I certainly found it desperately hard to *talk;* diving at one fell swoop from one extreme to another, as is my habit; swooping from garrulity to near-taciturnity. Was I a spectre at their feast of pints? Not quite that, perhaps, but when we left them, half an hour earlier than usual, I felt an immense release of tension.

14 December
O for a tankard full of the true, the swarthy Guinness!

26 January 1978
How harshly uncompromising they've all been about money, the great saints and gurus. We must give *all* to the poor; if we remain *the least bit* attached to physical possessions we shall never come to the Kingdom; to Enlightenment.

As for me, a self-inflicted poverty would impoverish not only my body but also my heart and mind. I wouldn't be a holy beggar but a whining, angry and resentful one.

So perhaps there is a certain humility in recognising that we are like the rich young man in the gospel, incapable of the heroism needed for true discipleship.

But was Jesus right in that case? He also said, after all, that in his father's house are many mansions; and surely there was a humble mansion even for that young man. Perhaps he was destroyed by having too great a demand made on him. Whereas a less stringent demand might have led him at least *towards* the light of the Kingdom.

12 February
There are messy days – days of fluster and bluster; and there are grinding days – days of gritted teeth. Sometimes, but not very often now, there are days of cheerful indifference to all deep and weighty matters, when pleasure wipes the mind clean of God and all his wiles.

For the flustered state the best cure is to go to Tymawr for Evensong and Compline: coolness and loving calm. For the grinding days there is no alleviation except in the knowledge that they have to come: they also serve. As for the days of careless pleasure, I take them gladly, and without apology. (Perhaps I should thank God for those genial hours when he has allowed me to forget all about him.)

9 March
A black morning – but this should be seen as an opportunity for exercising unfamiliar virtues: courage and calm. I need the courage to be calm: and then the calm will remove the need for courage.

Neither, of course, is a primal virtue, for calm could be the deadly serenity of perfect arrogance or total despair; and courage is often used in the service of the worst evil. Yet without those two what hope of practising the great virtues – the faith to be reborn; hope of the Kingdom; that love of God which always includes the love of man?

14 March
Had some wine with our neighbours Jeffrey and Nasi Hammond in

spite of resolution. The relief was instantaneous: the rest of the evening positively pleasurable. No excess, but the heart lifted, the tongue loosened, the company enjoyed.

20 March

St Teresa's four mystical stages: Recollection; Meditation; Contemplation; Union. I think I may have made some advance across the vast expanse of the first stage; even caught a rare glimpse of the second. At least I now settle down on the floor each evening with real pleasure; the expectation of a calming procedure ahead; even, with luck, an enlivening one as well.

3 April

If it were irrefutably demonstrated to me that there is no God, and no reality above or distinct from the material world, then I would consider that human life is too terrible to be endured. Fear, and some regard for the feelings of others, might prevent me from killing myself; but I would live out my life as a prisoner lives out his sentence.

But the fact is that I can no more conceive of such a demonstration being possible than Freddie [the philosopher A.J. Ayer], for example, can conceive of having a personal experience of God.

8 April

Yes. But even if the faith really is unshakable at some deep level of the heart and mind, the upper levels can be terribly lacerated by doubt, and worse.

In bed two nights ago I was beset by the suspicion that there may simply be nothing really true and serious in me at all. And next day, when Sally and I went to the convent for Evensong and a special healing service afterwards, I had to conceal a nagging self-disgust which swelled into a gloomy rejection of everything I saw and heard. 'What the hell am I doing in this *galère*!' I wondered, as the rich, over-ripe, all-too-familiar, *meaningless* words came rolling out. And what the hell do they all think they're doing, these ladies dressed up so absurdly and going through their absurd motions for the ten thousandth time?

I knew that this is what many Christians would call an assault by the devil. I also knew that it was a mood which would certainly pass before long. But this knowledge took the unpleasant form of making me conclude that even the mood itself was not to be taken seriously: something to be toyed with; relished for its interesting taste. 'He can't even seriously persevere in his inability to seriously persevere.' An infinite recession of frivolity.

9 April

But I woke after a good night in a much more pleasant state. I've reminded myself this morning that I was always an earnest self-improver: even at the worst periods of my ostensibly clownish degradation. Tumbling and tumbling I aspired to heaven.

21 April

Sally was attacked by some bug last week; stomach pains, headaches, exhaustion. I showed frequent 'sympathy'; often remembered to ask how she was feeling; brought coffee up to her bedroom. . . .

A day or two later I began to suffer the same affliction; and *God*, the difference in the attention I paid to it!

27 April

If you *must* lapse into smoking a cigarette try to choose a strong one, and *smoke it with the utmost relish.*

4 May

At Tymawr yesterday I felt that I was indeed in a rare state of joyful truthfulness. And it seemed to me that I could never have reached – never have been given – this blessed state unless I'd gone through that painful afternoon of revulsion, when even the smiles of the sisters seemed false and silly.

29 December

Suddenly yesterday morning I observed that there was bright blood in my pee. Cancer of the bladder, naturally! But I was amazed to find that this assumption hardly seemed to bother me – though I've suffered so cravenly from Timor Mortis all my born days.

But when Sally consulted one of her medical books it became quite obvious that the culprit was the beetroot we'd had for supper the night before. So my heroic composure was wasted, in a sense, but it's nice to know that I felt it, however briefly.

14 January 1979

The desert again last night. But now there is always a sort of knowledge that there is hope at the heart of the darkness. (It seems like a completely dead knowledge: a dry, remembered fact to which, in spite of its apparent lifelessness, I must cling with all my might.)

3 June

Records and tapes put carefully in order. The great satisfaction, always, of making these little inroads on confusion.

30 June

People become more difficult to meet and books become more difficult to read. As if I were being slowly forced into becoming a solitary and a contemplative. But this fills me with panic and rejection; for I know that I'm not ready for this, and I strongly doubt that I ever shall be. *(19.4.81)*

220. *Exits*

Sayings of 1980

NO ONE would remember the Good Samaritan if he'd only had good intentions. He had money as well. – *Mrs Thatcher. 13.1.80*

AS FAR as I am concerned, each year that passes makes me better at my job. – *Lord Denning. 21.1.80*

I DON'T mind how much my Ministers talk, as long as they do what I say. – *Mrs Thatcher. 27.1.80*

EUROPEAN Community institutions have produced European beets, butter, cheese, wine, veal and even pigs. But they have not produced Europeans. – *Mme Louise Weiss, MEP. 21.1.80*

COMMUNISM stops only when it encounters a wall. – *Alexander Solzhenitsyn. 17.2.80*

THE International Olympic Committee cannot solve the problems of the world. – *Lord Killanin. 17.2.80*

I'VE always felt reading romantic novels was a bit like eating a whole box of chocolates or going to bed with a rotter. You can't stop because it's so nice, but afterwards you wish you hadn't. – *Jilly Cooper. 17.2.80*

THEY may, in the fullness of time, even canonise me and make me a saint. – *Derek (Red Robbo) Robinson. 24.2.80*

IT IS difficult to strike if there is no work in the first place. – *Lord George-Brown. 24.2.80*

JESUS said love one another. He didn't say love the whole world. – *Mother Teresa. 2.3.80*

THE thing I notice is that I tend to look at things much more logically than my colleagues. – *Mrs Thatcher. 16.3.80*

THE attitude of all honest Afghans to Soviet troops is that of sincere hospitality and profound gratitude. – *Tass. 16.3.80*

GOVERNMENTS never learn. Only people learn. – *Milton Friedman. 30.3.80*

PUNK monetarism is a monetary policy based on half-baked understanding of half-baked dogmas. – *Denis Healey. 30.3.80*

THE Marxist analysis has got nothing to do with what happened in Stalin's Russia; it's like blaming Jesus Christ for the Inquisition in Spain. – *Tony Benn. 27.4.80*

I BELIEVE that God created man. I object to teachers saying that we come from monkeys. – *Rev. Ian Paisley. 27.4.80*

I HAVEN'T got the figure for jeans. – *Mrs Thatcher. 4.5.80*

I AM not interested in a third party. I do not believe it has any future. – *Shirley Williams. 25.5.80*

FRANCE, eldest daughter of the Church, are you faithful to the promises of your baptism? – *The Pope. 8.6.80*

I SURVIVED the Russians and the Gestapo, so I am ready to do battle with the Inland Revenue. – *Lord Kagan. 15.6.80*

I AM now convinced that the lads will have no horses to back unless they own them themselves. – *Joe Gormley. 15.6.80*

OF THE four wars in my life-time, none came about because the US was too strong. – *Ronald Reagan. 29.6.80*

A LEARNED man who is not cleansed is more dangerous than an ignorant man. – *Ayatollah Khomeini. 6.7.80*

JUST as people can price themselves out of jobs, they can price themselves into jobs. – *Sir Keith Joseph. 6.7.80*

I THINK Mr Carter has created Ronald Reagan. – *Senator Edward Kennedy. 20.7.80*

WHOEVER tries to climb over our fence, we shall climb over his roof. – *President Saddam Hussein of Iraq. 27.7.80*

THE thing I might do best is to be a long-distance lorry driver. – *Princess Anne. 24.8.80*

THE cliché 'charity begins at home' has done more damage than any other in the English language. – *Bishop Trevor Huddleston. 14.9.80*

I LIKE everything my beloved wife likes. If she wants to buy the top brick of St Paul's then I would buy it. – *Denis Thatcher. 14.9.80*

IT'S very dangerous if you keep love letters from someone who is not now your husband. – *Diana Dors. 14.9.80*

I DON'T think dogs have much fun these days without things like rats to chase. – *Barbara Woodhouse. 21.9.80*

WHEN a new set of Labour Ministers enter Number 10, as I trust they soon will, are they all to keep diaries? It will add a new terror to political life. – *Michael Foot. 28.9.80*

I FIRST became an adulteress to the sound of Mozart. – *Jacquetta Hawkes. 5.10.80*

ADULTERY in your heart is committed not only when you look with excessive sexual desire at a woman who is not your wife, but also if you look in the same manner at your wife. – *The Pope. 12.10.80*

222. Sayings of 1980

YOU turn if you want; the lady's not for turning. – *Mrs Thatcher. 12.10.80*

MANY of our institutions are under threat. *The Times* fights for them, and now *The Times* is going to fight for itself. – *William Rees-Mogg. 26.10.80*

WE have got to take the gloves off and have a bare-knuckle fight. – *Sir Terence Beckett,* Director-General, CBI. *16.11.80*

I LOVE entertaining. I have someone else to do the cooking, that's why. – *Joan Plowright. 23.11.80*

IT is quite clear to me that the Tory Party will get rid of Mrs Thatcher in about three years' time. – *Sir Harold Wilson. 23.11.80*

UNEMPLOYMENT is of vital importance, particularly to the unemployed. – *Edward Heath. 30.11.80*

EVERYTHING happens to the Royal Family in November. – *Lady Diana Spencer. 30.11.80*

IT seems to me quite impossible for any court to find that the refusal of a wife to have sex more often than once a week is unreasonable. – *Lord Justice Ormrod. 7.12.80*

Index of Authors